WE HAVE HEARD WITH OUR EARS, O GOD
Sources of the Communal Laments in the Psalms

SOCIETY
OF BIBLICAL
LITERATURE

DISSERTATION SERIES
Michael V. Fox, Old Testament Editor
E. Elizabeth Johnson, New Testament Editor

Number 159

WE HAVE HEARD WITH OUR EARS, O GOD
Sources of the Communal Laments in the Psalms

by
Walter C. Bouzard, Jr.

Walter C. Bouzard, Jr.

WE HAVE HEARD WITH OUR EARS, O GOD
Sources of the Communal Laments in the Psalms

Society of Biblical Literature

Dissertation Series

Scholars Press
Atlanta, Georgia

WE HAVE HEARD WITH OUR EARS, O GOD
Sources of the Communal Laments in the Psalms

by
Walter C. Bouzard, Jr.

© 1997
The Society of Biblical Literature

Library of Congress Cataloging in Publication Data
Bouzard, Walter C., 1954–
    We have heard with our ears, O God : sources of the communal
laments in the Psalms / Walter C. Bouzard, Jr.
        p.   cm. — (Dissertation series / Society of Biblical
Literature ; no. 159)
    Originally presented as the author's thesis—Princeton Theological
Seminary, 1996.
    Includes bibliographical references.
    ISBN 0-7885-0354-5 (cloth : alk. paper)
    1. Bible. O.T. Psalms—Criticism, interpretation, etc.
2. Laments in the Bible.   3. Laments—Middle East.   4. Bible. O.T.
Psalms—Extra-canonical parallels.   5. Middle Eastern literature—
Relation to the Old Testament.   I. Title.   II. Series:
Dissertation series (Society of Biblical Literature) ; no. 159.
BS1445.L3B68   1997
223'.2066—dc21   97-7383
                                                                    CIP

Printed in the United States of America
on acid-free paper

To the residents of the West Bank,
that their cities might find a just peace.

CONTENTS

ACKNOWLEDGMENTS

Martin Luther remarked in his *Large Catechism*, *"Deo, parentibus, et magistris non potest satis gratiae rependi"* (God, parents, and teachers can never be fully thanked or repaid). While Luther's comment enjoys a certain universal validity, it seems a particularly apt summary of my own sentiments upon the completion of the following project and my doctoral studies.

I am grateful, first, to the God who fashioned me and gifted me with whatever abilities I have been able to employ in this undertaking. I am thankful, too, for the opportunities afforded me to develop those gifts, especially during my years of study at two splendid seminaries of the Church.

My debt to my parents is likewise enormous. Throughout my life they have encouraged me to be the best I could be at whatever path I chose to follow. While I certainly hope that my own scholarship in future years will exceed what is represented in this dissertation, it is, for today, my best effort.

The third group mentioned by Luther, *"magistris"* (teachers), are people elevated to a place of honor just after God and parents in terms of their formative influence. I am profoundly grateful for my many teachers who have shaped my thinking throughout the years, including the faculty of Luther Seminary, St. Paul, who not only equipped me with the requisite primary skills for an earlier career in parish ministry but who, more than they knew, inspired me to pursue further academic study. Even more influential, however, have been the professors of Princeton Theological Seminary's Old Testament faculty from whom I have been honored to learn in recent years. I will ever be thankful for the instruction, counsel, encouragement, and friendship that they have shared with me. I am mindful of a debt of gratitude owed to Professors James F.

Armstrong, C.L. Seow, Katharine Doob Sakenfeld, and Richard E. Whitaker who instructed me both inside and outside of their seminars. Most of all I thank the members of my reading committee, Professors Dennis T. Olson, J.J.M. Roberts, and the Chair, Patrick D. Miller, whose patience and suggestions in earlier drafts of this work assisted me greatly. Any remaining flaws in the following pages occur in spite of their best efforts to the contrary.

Luther's triad lacks one further group of people who must be acknowledged with thanks, namely *familiari* (family). The days of graduate study and Princeton and the intervening years of dissertation work would have been impossible were it not for the constant and unstinting support and encouragement of my wife, Ramona. Not once in those years did she complain about the many burdens my studies necessarily placed on her and our family, even when she had every right to raise an objecting voice. I am thankful as well for the patience of my children and their willingness to accept as normal the too often absence of their father. My daughter, Green, was born just two weeks before we moved to Princeton and my son, Gabriel, came into this world just two days after my last comprehensive examination. Their lives have been measured by progress on "daddy's dissertation." Through all of that, as much as any, they have shown me a glimpse of what it means to be loved gracefully and without condition.

CHAPTER 1

THE SOURCES OF COMMUNAL LAMENTS IN THE PSALMS: INTRODUCTORY CONSIDERATIONS

GUNKEL'S FOUNDATIONAL WORK AND SUBSEQUENT DEVELOPMENTS

The central issue of the following investigation concerns the influences and possible Mesopotamian sources of a small collection of prayers within the Hebrew Psalter that, since H. Gunkel, have been understood to represent a distinctive psalm type known as the *Klagelieder des Volkes*, or the communal lament.[1] According to Gunkel these community laments found use on occasions of public calamity such as crop failure, pestilence, and danger from some enemy. When disaster fell, Israel tried by means of expiatory rituals to persuade Yahweh to act on behalf of the community[2] either through a confession of sin and concomitant plea for forgiveness or through a

---

[1] See especially Hermann Gunkel and Joachim Begrich, *Einleitung in die Psalmen: Die Gattungen der religiösen Lyrik Israels* (Göttingen: Vandenhoeck und Ruprecht, 1993), pp. 117–119 and Gunkel's "Psalmen," in *Die Religion in Geschichte und Gegenwart*, ed. by Hermann Gunkel and O. Scheel (Tübingen: J.C.B. Mohr, 1913), vol. iv, cols. 1934–1935. An English translation of the latter appears in *The Psalms: A Form Critical Introduction*, trans. by Thomas M. Horner (Philadelphia: Fortress, 1967), pp. 13–15.

[2] Hermann Gunkel, "The Poetry of the Psalms: Its Literary History and Its Application to the Dating of the Psalms," in *Old Testament Essays: Papers Read before the Society for Old Testament Study at Its Eighteenth Meeting, Held at Keble College, Oxford, September 27th to 30th, 1927*, ed. by D.C. Simpson (London: Charles Griffin, 1927), p. 126; *Einleitung*, p. 118.

1

protest of corporate innocence.[3] Gunkel distinguished between two sub-classes of the communal laments based on whether the psalm included confessional elements and therefore was a "Penitential Prayer of the Community," or whether the given text proclaimed the people's innocence and therefore was a "Confession of Innocence of the Community." Nevertheless both types were regarded by him as parts of the larger communal lament genre since both were understood to have been constituted by a) a passionate appeal and b) the divine response.[4] Of the latter element Gunkel notes:

> In the Book of Psalms the counterpart to the second element is the poet's "certainty of a hearing," which is an expression of his confidence that his prayer will be heard. Its appearance in the psalm is often quite sudden and unmotivated. Accordingly it may perhaps be supposed that on the days of lamentation in the earliest period the prayer was first uttered, whereupon the answer was proclaimed by the priest in God's name.[5]

In the Psalter Gunkel found the communal lament form in Psalms 44, 60:3–7, 74, 79, 80, 89:39ff., and 94.[6]

Aspects of Gunkel's larger form critical treatment of the psalms have been reevaluated and refined since his day, not excluding disputes over which features constitute the genre as well as disagreements over which psalms should be included in the form critical class known as communal laments. In spite of these differences, however, virtually all critical commentaries on the Psalms published since Gunkel have assumed his basic premises relative to the form critical classification of the psalms,[7] and few have dared to challenge the consensus that quickly surrounded the form critical approach. The position taken in the following pages likewise assumes the existence of distinctive poetic types, including the communal laments,

---

[3] Gunkel, *The Psalms*, p. 14.

[4] *Ibid.*

[5] *Ibid.*, pp. 14–15

[6] *Ibid.*, p. 14. Gunkel provides a slightly different list in his *Einleitung*, p. 117, where he mentions Psalms 44, (58), 74, 79, 80, 83, (106), (125). In addition, he notes a number of other psalms that represents mixed types.

[7] An exception is the recently published contribution by James Luther Mays, *Psalms*, (Louisville: John Knox, 1994). Mays acknowledges, but little employs, Gunkel's form critical evaluation in a self-conscious decision to avoid any confusion between form critical analysis and exegetical exposition. On Mays' method and approach see Chapter 4, n. 3, of the present work.

within the Psalter. This is not to say that all of Gunkel's suppositions about the communal laments are hereby adopted, especially since it will be shown, contrary to Gunkel's assertion quoted above, that the "certainty of a hearing" is in fact absent from precisely those psalms he identifies as communal laments. Moreover, penitential statements as well as statements concerning the sins of the people are likewise all but absent in this collection of prayers.[8] The absence of these putatively distinctive elements of the communal laments calls into question Gunkel's assumption about the expiatory character of the cultic *Sitz im Leben* of these materials even as it demands a reconsideration of those characteristics which may be said to constitute the communal lament genre.[9]

On the other hand, another of Gunkel's observations is embraced with less reservation. Gunkel, who regarded the discovery of texts originating in nearby ancient Near Eastern cultures such as Egypt and Babylon as vitally important to biblical research, expressed surprise in his early writings that more had not been done with those materials to aid in the exposition of Hebrew compositions.[10] The present investigation begins to answer that challenge by investigating the *balag* and *eršemma* compositions of ancient Mesopotamia and by comparing those materials with the communal lamentations of Israel.

Gunkel's assertion about the significance of the influences of other ancient Near Eastern cultures and their writings on the psalmody of Israel was quite correct as developments in subsequent decades proved. Even within Gunkel's lifetime scholars began to investigate more thoroughly the relevance of such materials for biblical research and especially their significance for the Psalms. Academic interest and imagination were further fueled by the discovery of the Ras Shamra materials in 1929. Besides finding connections with Egyptian and Mesopotamian compositions, Psalms scholars began to identify similarities and points of correspondence with the Ugaritic materials as well.[11]

---

[8] Joseph Murray Haar, "The God-Israel Relationship in the Community Lament Psalms" (Ph.D. dissertation, Union Theological Seminary, Richmond, 1985), p. 2.

[9] This discussion appears in Chapter 4 below.

[10] Gunkel, "Psalmen," in D*ie Religion in Geschichte und Gegenwart,* (Tübingen: J.C.B. Mohr, 1913), vol. iv, col. 1929; *Ausgewählte Psalmen* (4th ed.; Göttingen: Vandenhoeck und Ruprecht, 1917), p. vii.

[11] The following sketch of significant contributions to the question of influence between the psalmody of other ancient Near Eastern cultures and that of Israel is

Even before the uncovering of the Ugaritic materials, however, F.M.Th. Böhl discovered a Canaanite connection with the Hebrew psalms. Böhl suggested that the often extravagant language used to address the Pharaoh by the various petty kings of Canaan in the Tell el-Amarna period originated in Canaanite hymnology. If so, he reasoned, the existence of such language may point to Canaanite prototypes for Hebrew psalms.[12] Confirmation of this hypothesis would await the discoveries at Ras Shamra some two decades later. In the meanwhile Friedrich Stummer, in his investigation of Sumerian and Akkadian hymns, concluded that these materials, though not identical with the Hebrew compositions, nevertheless could be fairly said to have influenced them either directly or through the culture of Canaan.[13] Likewise Hugo Gressmann adduced data from the writings of Egypt and Babylon in an attempt to show that Hebrew psalmody, and in particular the "Psalter of David," affords evidence to show that it was connected with and had its roots in the psalmody and other literature of the ancient Near East.[14] Gressmann summarized his investigation thus:

> There was then, as all these examples indicate, a common basis underlying all the Psalmody of the Nearer East. The extent to which the Hebrew psalms have their roots in those of Babylonia or Egypt is a matter for research in the future. There is no reason for doubting that the psalms of the Old Testament have been influenced by the psalms of other nations, and it would be exceedingly interesting to state some of the conditions which led to this influence.[15]

Stummer and Gressmann's enthusiasm for seeing literary connections between Hebrew psalms and the literature of Israel's neigh-

---

conveniently summarized by A.R. Johnson, "The Psalms," in *The Old Testament and Modern Study*, ed. by H.H. Rowley (Oxford: Clarendon, 1951), pp. 186–189.

[12] F. M. Th. de Liagre Böhl, "Hymnisches und Rhythmisches in den Amarnabriefen aus Kanaan," *Theologisches Lituraturblatt, Leipzig,* 35 (1914), cols. 337ff.; *De Psalmen: tekst en uitleg* (Nijkerk: G.F. Callenbach, 1969), p. 25ff.; cf. also Anton Jirku, "Kana'anäische Psalemnfragmente in der vorisraelitischen Zeit Palästinas und Syrians," *JBL* 52 (1993), 108–120.

[13] Friedrich Stummer, *Sumerisch-akkadische Parallelen zum Aufbau alttestamentlicher Psalmen,* Studien zur Geschichte und Kultur des Altertums, Vol. 11, no. 1 & 2 (Paderborn: Ferdinand Schoringh, 1922), pp. 177–180.

[14] Hugo Gressmann, "The Development of Hebrew Psalmody," in *The Psalmists,* ed. by D.C. Simpson (London: Oxford University, 1926), pp. 1–21, esp. pp. 15–21.

[15] *Ibid.,* p. 20.

bors was not shared by G.R. Driver. In an influential essay published in the same volume as Gressmann's more optimistic contribution, Driver argued that analogies such as those identified by Gressmann did not constitute proof of literary borrowing.[16] Rather, Driver, convinced that Israel's monotheistic psalms remained distinct from the polytheistic Babylonian compositions[17] as well as ethically and spiritually superior to them,[18] argued that kindred phraseology, metaphors, and images indicated nothing more than that these were "ideas common to many people"[19] and especially those who shared a common Semitic ancestry.[20] Thus, Driver commented:

> These passages, I submit, shew that the Babylonian went through the same religious experience as the Hebrew—for he was ultimately of the same stock as the Hebrew—and came to express that experience in hymns and psalms of a similar kind, and sometimes even in words philologically the same; for both spoke languages derived from the same parent speech. Yet not only does this not prove that the one side borrowed from the other, but the fact also that the Babylonian failed to exhibit the same capacity for religious development as the Hebrew did makes it very unlikely that the Hebrews, who were spiritually far more advanced than the Babylonians, should have borrowed any of the external setting from their less gifted neighbours. Since the religious sense innate in the two peoples would in any case have had to seek means for its expressions, what could have been more natural than that both races, closely akin and speaking closely related languages, should have found expression for their ideas along similar lines?[21]

At most, Driver concluded, one may concede the possibility of slight and indirect Babylonian influence on certain legendary motifs in Hebrew compositions. As early as the Sargonic period, such legends, "which were not of native Semitic origin but of Sumerian or other origin, could have reached the Hebrews . . . and need not have been borrowed directly from Babylon in historical times."[22]

---

[16] G.R. Driver, "The Psalms in the Light of Babylonian Research," in *The Psalmists*, ed. by D.C. Simpson (London: Oxford University, 1926), pp. 109–176.

[17] *Ibid.*, p. 162.

[18] *Ibid.*, pp. 136–137, 172, *et passim*.

[19] *Ibid.*, pp. 124, 128, 130, 172f., *et passim*.

[20] *Ibid.*, pp. 125, 130, 172.

[21] *Ibid.*, pp. 136–137.

[22] *Ibid.*, p. 174.

The articles by Gressmann and Driver clearly defined the battle lines between those arguing for and against the possibility of literary influence by the cultic texts of other ancient Near Eastern cultures on the psalms of Israel. On the one hand, Gressmann discerned more or less specific points of correspondence between Israel's psalms and those demonstrably older writings of nations beyond Israel's borders and asserted the literary influence of the latter upon the Hebrew writings. Driver, on the other hand, denied the evidence offered by Gressmann, maintaining instead that similarities indicated no more than a common prehistoric cultural perspective shared by all nations of the ancient Near East, while the differences between the respective writings pointed decisively to the absence of foreign influences on Israel's sacred texts. Obviously, the scholarly discussion to that point lacked an arbitrating methodology that might serve to sort out what did and did not constitute literary influence.

As it was, Driver's cautionary comments on the matter seemed to have brought the discussion to a stalemate, in spite of a number of significant monographs on the subject that appeared in the wake of his essay. For example, in his study *The Assyrian and Hebrew Hymns of Praise*, Charles Gorden Cumming concluded that "the Hebrews were inevitably directly and indirectly influenced by Assyrian culture and religion,"[23] but implied that this influence was, after all, no more than indirect, as it was mediated by the Canaanite culture that had already been influenced for millennia by the civilizations of the Tigris Euphrates valley.[24] Three years after the appearance of Cumming's book, Geo Widengren published a comprehensive comparative investigation of the psalms of individual lament from Assyria and Israel[25] wherein he took up the specific arguments of Driver and his conclusion that "we cannot therefore believe that Babylonian hymns and psalms exercised any real influence on the work of the Hebrew psalmists."[26] To the contrary, Widengren asserted, similarities between the structure, phraseology, and religious contents of the individual Akkadian and Israelite psalms of lamentation point to the opposite conclusion, namely, that Israelite

---

[23] Charles Gordon Cumming, *The Assyrian and Hebrew Hymns of Praise*, Columbia University Oriental Studies, Vol. 12 (New York: Columbia University, 1934), p. 154.

[24] *Ibid.*

[25] Geo Widengren, *The Accadian and Hebrew Psalms of Lamentations as Religious Documents* (Stockholm: Bokförlags Aktiebolaget Thule, 1937).

[26] Driver, "The Psalmists," p. 172.

lament literature developed under Akkadian influences. In the end, however, Widengren was compelled to admit that the differences between the two cultures' literature more likely indicated that the influence of the older Akkadian traditions on the Israelite writings came "not directly, but by way of a Canaanitic cult-literature whose existence we are compelled to assume."[27] Similarly, R.G. Castellino reconsidered the individual laments of Babylon and Israel and concluded that while there *may* have been indirect influence of the Akkadian psalms on those of the Hebrews by way of Canaan, evidence of direct influence was lacking.[28]

Interest in any specific Akkadian influences on the Hebrew psalms waned with the increasing excitement over the discoveries of Ras Shamra. Böhl's earlier hypothesis positing Canaanite prototypes to the Hebrew psalms seemed to find confirmation in the many Ugaritic cultic texts that provided obvious and significant parallels to the mythological language, phraseology, and poetic forms of the Hebrew Psalter. Given the revelation of innumerable "Canaanitisms" within the Hebrew compositions, it is little wonder that interest in discerning more direct literary connections from the direction of Mesopotamia was, for a time, diverted, as scholars such as J.H. Patton,[29] W.F. Albright,[30] and, pre-eminently, Mitchell Dahood[31] focused on the Ugaritic texts. Indeed, Dahood's influential three-volume commentary on the Psalms was written, according to that author's own introduction, less as a commentary in the traditional sense and more as a translation and philological commentary utilizing the linguistic information offered by the Ras Shamra tablets.[32] Consequently, his treatment of the psalms found little allowance for literary influences from a direction other than Ras Shamra.

---

[27] Widengren, *Accadian and Hebrew Psalms*, p. 315.

[28] R.G. Castellino, *Le Lamentazione Individuali e gli Inni in Babilonia e in Israele* (Torino: Societe Editrice Internazionale, 1940), p. 255.

[29] J.H. Patton, *Canaanite Parallels in the Book of Psalms* (Baltimore: Johns Hopkins, 1944).

[30] W.F. Albright, *Archaeology and the Religion of Israel* (2nd ed.; Baltimore: Johns Hopkins Press, 1946), pp. 128–129 and *idem*, "The Psalms of Habakkuk," in *Studies in Old Testament Prophecy*, ed. by H.H. Rowley, (Edinburgh: T. & T. Clark, 1950), pp. 6–7, discovers Canaanite influence in Psalms 18, 29, 45, 68, 88, 89, and 92–96.

[31] Mitchel Dahood, *Psalms I: 1–50*, AB, Vol. 16 (Garden City: Doubleday, 1966; *Psalms II: 51–100*, AB, Vol. 17 (Garden City: Doubleday, 1968; *Psalms III: 101–150*, AB, Vol. 18 (Garden City: Doubleday, 1970).

[32] Mitchel Dahood, *Psalms I: 1–50*, p. xvii.

While the intrigue of the literary and cultural influences of Ugarit and thus of Canaanite culture accounts for much of the scholarly inattention to the question of Mesopotamian influence on the Hebrew psalms in recent decades, the larger cause was doubtless that previously mentioned methodological impasse reached already in the 1920's by Gressmann and Driver. There appeared to be no satisfactory means to resolve the rival claims of those who argued for and against literary influences originating from cultures outside of Canaan. In the absence of such a methodology, Driver's solution appeared quite reasonable: similarities stretching across cultural boundaries are attributable to a prehistoric common literary culture. This assumption obviated the need to identify specific literary influences from one culture to another, a task which Sigmund Mowinckel pronounced "often impossible to decide in any particular case."[33] Mowinckel followed that judgment with a description of the common literary culture of the ancient Near East which clearly echoed the point of view put forward by Driver:

> What matters is that we have here a great community of culture, which also embraces the style forms, the modes of expression and the cultic framework and situations to which this poetry belongs. And when compared with Israel, the whole of this common literary culture is prehistoric. It existed throughout the orient, even before Israel entered Canaan and participated in the Canaanite or—as we might in many cases term it—the common oriental culture. A natural consequence of this is that the psalmography presents in a great many examples kinship of style as well as of expressions and ideas both with Sumerian, Babylono-Assyrian and Egyptian psalmography, and likewise Israel is seen to be the one to learn from an earlier literary tradition. This need not mean dependence on any definite model, for instance on some particular Egyptian poem or other, as some people have thought; it means participation in a common literary culture.[34]

---

[33] Sigmund Mowinckel, *The Psalms in Israel's Worship,* trans. by D.R. Ap-Thomas (Oxford: Basil Blackwell, 1962), vol. 2, p. 178. Mowinckel clearly sides with Driver and attributes similarities between Israelite compositions and writings of other nations as a consequence of "participation in a common literary culture."

[34] *Ibid.* Mowinckel did, however, allow for the slight possibility of direct literary influence: "But of course this does not put out of the court the possibility that there may have been direct influences, for instance from the sun hymn of Pharaoh Akhnaton, or that some Israelite psalms may be remodelings of earlier Canaanite ones."

Thus defined, the assumption of a common literary culture seemingly relieved scholars from the task of investigating potentially legitimate instances of literary influence and, in a profound way, from answering the challenge put forth by Gunkel to employ non-Israelite materials in a serious effort to illuminate the Hebrew compositions. Since similarities in the cultic texts of various ancient Near Eastern peoples originated in the impenetrable common literary culture of prehistory, vestiges of that common origin, when observed, serve little more than to provide a basis for contrasting the religion of Mesopotamia with that of Israel. Even Mowinckel, whose treatment of communal laments included an acknowledgement of similarities in form and content between those prayers of Israel and Mesopotamia[35] as well as a historical connection between the two cultures' lamentations,[36] finds these facts significant only insofar as they serve to illustrate Israel's relative ethical and religious superiority.[37]

That little progress has been made in bridging the methodological impasse reached by Gressmann and Driver finds illustration in the only full volume of recent decades which attempts to compare the communal lament psalmody of ancient Israel with that of Mesopotamia, namely the recent investigation by Paul Wayne Ferris.[38] A critical analysis of Ferris's approach will be delayed until the fourth chapter of the present work. For now, it suffices to note that although Ferris's study includes a more detailed treatment of diverse Sumerian and Akkadian materials than Mowinckel's, his conclusion echoes Mowinckel's conviction, and that of Driver before him, that similarities between the respective cultures originated in a literary culture shared throughout the ancient world.[39]

That more progress in the matter of comparative methodology could and should be made, however, was indicated already by Geo Widengren in his discussion of Driver's essay.[40] First, and against Driver's explanation that a common, prehistoric original Semitic culture accounted for both the similarity of *parallelismus membrorum* and rhythm between Akkadian and Hebrew poems, Widengren pointed

---

[35] *Ibid.*, p. 182.

[36] *Ibid.*, p. 184.

[37] *Ibid.*, pp. 183–185.

[38] Paul Wayne Ferris, Jr., *The Genre of Communal Lament in the Bible and the Ancient Near East*, SBLDS, No. 127 (Atlanta: Scholars Press, 1992).

[39] *Ibid.*, pp. 174–175.

[40] For the following see Widengren, *Accadian and Hebrew Psalms*, pp. 2–12.

out that while virtually nothing is known of the "original Semites" nor of racial conditions in ancient Mesopotamia, the certain fact of these cultures' intermingling is more easily explained the similarities in their cultic writings.[41] Second, where Driver assumed that the "original Semite culture" from which both the Akkadian and Hebrew civilizations were derived occurred not very far back in time and, further, that such an original culture must have disappeared prior to the segregation of the Akkadian and Israelite cultures, Widengren noted that the chronology inherent in Driver's twin assertion collapses under further scrutiny. Since the Psalter dates, at the earliest, from 1000 BCE and since segregation from Akkadian influences must, by Driver's reckoning, antedate 2000 BCE, one must account for a thousand years between the segregation of the two cultures and that time when Israel's poetry reached its full development. Yet, Widengren noted, "In spite of this exceedingly long period, Israelite poetry is thus said to have developed on exactly the same lines as the Accadian—but without having been influenced by it."[42] Third, Widengren argued, Driver's supposition of a common Semitic origin cannot account for the points of literary correspondence between the racially and linguistically distinct Sumerians and Akkadians. For if the literature of Sumer influenced that of the Akkadian nations, as indeed it irrefutably did, then Akkadian lyrics would have been deflected from their original Semitic character. But if that was so, Widengren reasoned, similarities in Hebraic and Akkadian poetry cannot then be explained by any reference to any linguistic or racial community of origin. To the contrary, correspondences between Hebrew and Akkadian psalmody can only be explained by influence.[43] The Tell el-Amarna texts provided Widengren with further proof: not only did those texts prove that "Religious lyrics, modelled on the Accadian, obviously existed in Palestine as early as about 1,400 B.C.,"[44] but the fact that these texts were written in cuneiform rather than in hieroglyphs showed the extent of Babylonian influence on the land of Canaan.[45]

Widengren's case against Driver seems to have received little subsequent hearing, perhaps because he appears to have been

---

[41] *Ibid.*, pp. 2–3.
[42] *Ibid.*, p. 3.
[43] *Ibid.*, pp. 3–4.
[44] *Ibid.*, p. 5.
[45] *Ibid.*, p. 12.

unable to match his critique of Driver's notion of an original Semitic culture with the construction of a more persuasive comparative methodology of his own. In any event, it remains a curious fact that, in spite of Widengren's objections, the hypothesis of a general Semitic literary culture persists as an explanation for points of correspondence between the biblical psalms and those of Mesopotamia, including the communal laments.

This last point finds further illustration in the recent important study by F.W. Dobbs-Allsopp.[46] Dobbs-Allsopp investigates the city lament genre in the Bible and questions whether or not a literary connection between those materials and the Sumerian city laments existed. His method involves the development of a generic typology for Mesopotamian city-laments that he then uses to identify a kindred genre in the Hebrew scriptures. Both similarities and differences between the two types are emphasized throughout his thorough study. At the end of his examination, Dobbs-Allsopp concludes that "the existence of a native city-lament genre in Israel, generically related to the Mesopotamian genre, best accounts for the nature of the biblical data."[47] He thus denies any literary influence from the Mesopotamian city-lament tradition on that of Israel, even though he marshals a good deal of evidence to the contrary and in spite of his willingness to concede that "several features make it likely that the two genres had some type of closer past connection."[48] Of this past relationship he further comments:

> The nature of this connection, when it occurred, how it came about, etc., unfortunately, is difficult (if not impossible) to determine. It seems probable that the direction of the influence is from Mesopotamian to Israel, but even this is not certain.[49]

The majority of Dobbs-Allsopp's attention is given to an examination of prophetic oracles and to elements of the city-lament genre he sees present in them; he devotes only two pages of his study to comments on the communal lament psalms and the affinities these texts may have with lament literature of Mesopotamia. Dobbs-Allsopp explains his inattention to the psalms:

---

[46] F.W. Dobbs-Allsopp, *Weep, O Daughter of Zion: A Study of the City-Lament Genre in the Hebrew Bible* (Rome: Editrice Pontificio Istituto Biblico, 1993).

[47] *Ibid.*, p. 157.

[48] *Ibid.*, p. 158.

[49] *Ibid.*

While these psalms contain much imagery that is compatible with
the city-lament genre, they usually lack any of the genre's diagnos-
tic features. Therefore, the communal laments included for review
here are only those which explicitly complain about the destruction of the Temple, city, or country. Moreover, the writer has done
little more than sketch how these communal laments relate form
critically to the *balags*. A final evaluation of the *balags'* significance
for understanding biblical communal laments must await a more
detailed investigation.[50]

THE SCOPE AND STRUCTURE OF THE PRESENT STUDY

The present study intends to build upon the work of Dobbs-
Allsopp by investigating the Mesopotamian *balag* and the related
eršemma compositions. The purpose is to determine if and how these
communal lamentations of ancient Mesopotamia might illumine
what appear to be similar materials in the biblical psalms, the *Klagelieder des Volkes* and, specifically, whether the older Mesopotamian
lamentations might have influenced the lament tradition of Israel. In
that respect the work also intends to be faithful to the call issued
long ago by Gunkel for scholars to investigate the texts of those cultures surrounding ancient Israel in an effort to discover what light
they may shed on the biblical writings. By comparing and contrasting a clearly identified and related type of Mesopotamian genre,
in this instance the *balag/eršemma* compositions and the communal
laments of the Bible, the present writer brings a new understanding
of the origins and uses of the Hebrew materials. Thus, the following
investigation finds itself standing in a continuum with the earlier investigations of Cumming, Widengren, and Castellino, as well as the
more recent contribution of Ferris, albeit with a much narrowed
focus.

From what has been said previously, the task of articulating a
satisfactory comparative methodology presents itself as central in
importance. Consequently, Chapter two of this study, "Parallels or
Parallelomania?" seeks to clarify the problems inherent in comparative research as well as to offer a constructive means for analyzing
what appear to be, at least superficially, points of correspondence
between the communal laments of Israel and Mesopotamia.

---

[50] *Ibid.*, p. 155, n. 246.

But are these points of correspondence between the two lament traditions only superficial? In order to address that question it will first be necessary to provide a typological description of both the Akkadian *balag/eršemma* laments and their Israelite counterparts. Chapter three identifies and describes the features of the Akkadian materials. What are the structures and constitutive characteristics of the *balags* and *eršemmas*? What is the relationship of these two types of lament to one another? Chapter four, in turn, establishes a typology for Israel's communal laments. The concern here involves, first, a resolution to the question as to whether these often disparate texts do constitute a distinctive genre and, second, an identification of the features characteristic of the Hebrew communal laments.

Finally, Chapter 5 brings the characteristics of the communal laments of both traditions together for purposes of comparison. Points of similarity as well as points of contrast find place in the discussion as does evidence uncovered in related biblical texts.

Standing in the background of this entire investigation are a number of questions relative to the relationship of the Akkadian and Hebrew communal laments: Are these two types of communal laments in fact similar? From what can be described as typologically characteristic of the respective lamentations, how, if at all, do these features correspond to one another? Do either culture's laments provide evidence that one may have influenced the other and, if so, in what direction was that influence? Or is the relationship between the two types of communal laments simply generic so as to preclude the possibility of either a meaningful comparison or a satisfactory answer to the question of literary influence? The final chapter attempts to assay these questions in light of the overall evidence.

This investigation is made possible thanks to the efforts of scholars working in the fields of archaeology and Assyriology who, in the decades since the early debates about the literary influences of other cultures on the psalms of the Bible, have forwarded much new information about the communal laments of Mesopotamia. As a consequence of their diligence, biblical scholars now have more information about Israel's neighbors and their religious practices than ever before. Perhaps Gressmann had a time such as our own in mind when he spoke of "research in the future" that would investigate the extent to which the Hebrew psalms are rooted in those of Babylon.[51] If so, let us hope Gressmann was equally visionary when he continued:

> There is no reason for doubting that the psalms of the Old Testament have been influenced by the psalms of other nations, and it would be exceedingly interesting to state some of the conditions which led to this influence.[52]

Already enough has been said to indicate that a good number of worthy scholars have indeed found reason for doubting the influence of other nations on the psalms of Israel, Gressmann's certitude notwithstanding. If the following pages do not assuage those doubts, the present writer hopes that this investigation at least proves, in Gressmann's words, "exceedingly interesting."

---

[51] Gressmann, "The Development of Hebrew Psalmody," p. 20.

[52] *Ibid.*

CHAPTER 2

PARALLELS OR PARALLELOMANIA?[1]
METHODOLOGICAL CONSIDERATIONS

THE PROBLEM OF ESTABLISHING LITERARY RELATIONSHIPS

Paul Wayne Ferris concludes his study of the genre of communal lament in the Bible and the ancient Near East with the claim that, while the lament tradition in the Near East is both long and widespread, the available data

> does not seem to support the theory that lament was something learned directly from the Babylonians during the exile. . . . The data does support a cultural dependence upon what Mowinckel calls "the common oriental culture" and hence, "participation in a common literary culture."[2]

However, this "participation in a common literary culture" is not understood by Ferris to signal that the biblical laments achieved their form or content by means of any direct modeling on or literary contact with the Sumero-Akkadian tradition. To the contrary, in Ferris's view common human experience, addressed by a similar if not common culture, account for the "coincidental" parallelisms

---

[1] The term "parallelomania" was coined by Samuel Sandmel in his presidential address to the Society of Biblical Literature. As Sandmel uses the term, "parallelomania" refers to "that extravagance among scholars which first over-does the supposed similarity in passages and then proceeds to describe source and derivation as if implying literary connection flowing in an inevitable or predetermined direction." Cf. "Parallelomania," *JBL* 81 (1962), 1.

[2] Ferris, *Genre*, pp. 174–175. Ferris cites Mowinckel, *The Psalms*, vol. 2, p. 178.

evident in the respective lament traditions.[3] Ferris bolsters this conclusion with the claims that (1) features which appear common to the two lament traditions are either significantly distinctive or so widespread as to make a direct connection impossible to demostrate, (2) features regarded as characteristic of the Sumero-Akkadian tradition are noticeably absent in the biblical laments, and (3) the absence of any example of any type of Sumero-Akkadian lament in the West, whether individual or communal, indicates that the biblical writers were unfamiliar with the Mesopotamian lament genre, the cultural intercourse between the two regions notwithstanding.[4]

Ferris's conclusion and the claims that support it are pervious. Indeed the present writer intends to demonstrate that a comparison of the Sumero-Akkadian and Hebrew lament materials points more naturally to a specifically literary connection between the two collections. Nevertheless Ferris's observations have heuristic value in that he illustrates, within the context of a broad sweeping study of the communal lament genre, precisely those criteria which traditionally have been marshalled to argue whether or not the literature of one culture has directly influenced that of another. Discussion on the question of literary influence typically is founded on the two points that Ferris, in fact, assumes:

1. The criterion of cultural contact. Comparisons that serve to specify the literary influence of one text or genre upon another are most profitable where the avenues for cultural contact are demonstrable. Ideally, one should be able to establish that tradition "A" is chronologically anterior to tradition "B"—or at least that the two are simultaneous—as well as to specify historical junctures and geographic locations at which exposure and influence might have taken place.

---

[3] Similarly, James A. Durlesser, "The Book of Lamentations and the Mesopotamian Laments: Experiential or Literary Ties?" in *Eastern Great Lakes Biblical Society Proceedings* 3 (1983), 84, whose examination of the question of a literary relationship between Mesopotamian laments and the Book of Lamentations leads him to conclude: "Commonality of experience seems to this writer to be the best explanation for contacts in theme and content between the important laments of these two greatly divergent cultures."

[4] Ferris, *Genre*, pp. 173–174. In this respect Ferris differs little from the conclusion drawn long ago by Driver, "The Psalms in Light of Babylonian Research," p. 172: "We cannot therefore believe that Babylonian hymns and psalms exercised any real influ-

2. The criterion of comparability. Comparisons should be made between commensurate textual materials whose similarity can be established, at least superficially, on the basis of genre, form, or content.

Ferris tacitly acknowledges these criteria throughout his work. He can, however, be faulted for minimizing the evidence. He regards direct contact between the Sumero-Akkadian cultural tradition and the Hebrew as "limited"[5] but fails to treat the biblical and extra-biblical evidence that suggests a contrary conclusion. Moreover, as will be shown below, his own method of determining what does and does not belong within the genre of communal lament in the Hebrew tradition is fraught with problems that present difficulties when he compares the specific details of the Sumero-Akkadian and Hebrew communal lament traditions.

Even were Ferris's application of the above criteria flawless, however, one suspects that his investigation would be unable to move beyond the negative "cautious answers" he claims as the maximum for comparative study of the lament tradition[6] since he is no more sanguine about isolating cross cultural influences for any

---

ence on the work of the Hebrew psalmists." Instead, Driver claims, a common Semitic origin (his "original Semites") provides the sole sufficient explanation for any similarities between Mesopotamian and Hebrew psalms and hymns. Cf. the rejoinder by George Widengren, *Accadian and Hebrew Psalms of Lamentations as Religious Documents*, pp. 2–12, who argues, among other things, that Driver's claim is nullified by the Amarna materials and their unimpeachable testimony relative to the influence of the Mespotamian cuneiform tradition on Canaan's culture and literature down through the Late Bronze Age. "Israelitic literature probably developed under more or less direct Babylonian influences," Widengren avers (p. 12). Widengren himself relies primarily on the criteria of comparability and cultural contact (see below) in an effort "to demonstrate the similarities of the structure, phraseology, and religious contents of the individual Accadian and Israelitic psalms of lamentation" and to show "that there is no very significant difference between the two literatures, and that Israelitic, being incomparably the younger, must be considered to have developed under the influence of the Accadian, though not directly, but by way of a Canaanitic cult-literature whose existence we are compelled to assume" (p. 315).

[5] *Ibid.*, p. 167. Cf. p. 174.

[6] Ferris, *Genre*, p. 164, writes: "Perhaps more than any other aspect of lament study, the question of influence yields only cautious answers. Granted, sweeping conclusions sometimes have been offered. However, they may not be quite so broad as they may have appeared on the surface."

other genre.[7] Nor is Ferris alone in his skepticism.[8] As the history of this century's discussion on this matter demonstrates, scholars who would attribute at least part of Israel's literary genius to the influence of the traditions of her neighbors by means of the criteria of cultural contact and comparability alone have not convincingly demonstrated their case—at least in the eyes of their critics.[9] Thus the so called "Pan-Babylonian" school of the early 1900s, guided by scholars such as Friedrich Delitzsch[10] and A. Jeremias,[11] soon gave way to an even shorter lived "Pan-Egyptian" school, which in turn fell to those claiming primacy for Ugarit[12] and, more recently, Ebla.[13]

On the other side there are those who use the criteria of cultural contact and comparability to argue with equal vigor for the

---

[7] Cf. Ferris, *Genre,* p. 167, n. 550, where he approvingly cites Mowinckel's pronouncement that the question is "often impossible to decide in any particular case" (*Psalms,* vol. 2, p. 178). Ferris's conclusions and terminology relative to a "common literary culture" seem to be taken straight from Mowinckel.

[8] E.g., Morton Smith, "The Present State of Old Testament Studies," *JBL* 88 (1969), 19–35, who is highly critical of the failure to consider the possible survival of cultural elements in the (mis)use of literary parallels to date biblical materials.

[9] Witness the stalemate in the ongoing discussion regarding the influence of the Sumero-Akkadian flood traditions upon the Hebrew accounts. Essentially the debate remains as it was since the discovery of the Atrahasis tablets (and the parallels in the Gilgamesh Epic), with both sides arguing solely on the basis of comparability and cultural contact. For a bibliography of this discussion and an advance upon it, see Jeffrey H. Tigay, "On Evaluating Claims of Literary Borrowing," in *The Tablet and the Scroll: Near Eastern Studies in Honor of William W. Hallo,* ed. by Mark E. Cohen, Daniel C. Snell, and David B. Weisberg (Bethesda, MD: CDL Press, 1993), pp. 250–255, esp. 251–252.

[10] Friedrich Delitzsch, *Babel und Bibel: ein Vortrag* (Leipzig: J.C. Hinrichs, 1902).

[11] Alfred Jeremias, *Das Alte Testament im Lichte des alten Orients* (3rd ed.; Leipzig: J.C. Hinrichs, 1916).

[12] See Peter C. Craigie, "Ugarit and the Bible: Progress and Regress in 50 Years of Literary Study," in *Ugarit in Retrospect: Fifty Years of Ugarit and Ugaritic,* ed. by G.D. Young (Winona Lake: Eisenbrauns, 1981), pp. 99–111.

[13] For a brief but important summary of the successive "schools" see Tremper Longman, III, *Fictional Akkadian Autobiography: A Generic and Comparative Study* (Winona Lake: Eisenbrauns, 1991), pp. 24–26. Cf. also Robert Gordis, "On Methodology in Biblical Exegesis," *JQR* 61 (1970), 94–95. Gordis is critical of the "imperialist" claims of these schools since, in his view, by paying too little attention to channels of communication and textual transmission, their representatives violate the canons of scientific method. Critical too is Sandmel, "Parallelomania," 7, whose complaint is leveled against scholars suffering from what he calls "parallelomania," i.e., a penchant for discovering "seeming parallels which are so only imperfectly; and statements which can be called parallels only by taking them out of context."

absolute uniqueness of Israel's traditions vis-à-vis her neighbors.[14] Morton Smith[15] for example, eschewing the efficacy of comparative research,[16] begins his discussion of this matter with the assumption that there are "great and important differences between the works in the Old Testament and those of other Near Eastern literatures."[17] His goal is to illuminate the extent of those differences toward which end he employs H.A. Wolfson's "hypothetico-deductive" method. As Smith explains it,

---

[14] This position was heralded already in the seminal article by B. Landsberger, "Die Eigenbegrifflichkeit der Babylonischen Welt," *Islamica* 2 (1926), 355–372 [E.T. "The Conceptual Autonomy of the Babylonian World," trans. by T. Jacobsen, B. Foster, and H. von Siebenthal, MANE 1/4 (Malibu: Undena, 1976)], who argued that cultures are autonomous and should be studied on their own terms. Landsberger was particularly anxious to establish a case for studying Mesopotamian culture as a unique manifestation of human culture and civilization. It was, however, the members of the so called "Biblical Theology" movement who, as Norman Gottwald, "Biblical Theology or Biblical Sociology? On Affirming and Denying the 'Uniqueness' of Israel," *Radical Religion*, 2 (1975), 42, put it, "sought to express the internal unity-in-diversity and the comparative uniqueness-in-environmental-continuity of ancient Israel's faith." A primary exemplar is the work by G. Ernest Wright, *The Old Testament against its Environment*, SBT, Vol. 2 (London: SCM Press, 1950), the title of which volume proclaims its author's thesis. For an objection to the entire premise behind Wright's approach, see H.W.F. Saggs, *The Encounter with the Divine in Mesopotamia and Israel* (London: Athlone Press, 1978), esp. pp. 1–3. Others assailing the view that Israel's religion was unique against its cultural environment include Bertil Albrektson, *History and the Gods: An Essay on the Idea of Historical Events as Divine Manifestations in the Ancient Near East and in Israel*, Coniectanea Biblica; Old Testament Series, Vol. I (Lund: C.W.K. Gleerup, 1967); James Barr, *Old and New in Interpretation: A Study of the Two Testaments* (2nd ed.; London: SCM, 1966); "Revelation through History in the Old Testament and in Modern Theology," Int 17 (1963), 193–205; L. Gilkey, "Cosmology and the Travail of Biblical Language," JR 41 (1961), 194–205. Cf. J.J.M. Roberts, "Divine Freedom and Cultic Manipulation in Israel and Mesopotamia," in *Unity and Diversity: Essays in the History, Literature, and Religion of the Ancient Near East*, ed. by Hans Goedicke and J.J.M. Roberts (Baltimore: Johns Hopkins University Press, 1975), pp. 181–190.

[15] Morton Smith, "On the Differences between the Culture of Israel and the Major Cultures of the Ancient Near East," *JANES* 5 (1973), 389–395.

[16] Smith suggests that demonstrating particular similarities between details of the Old Testament and other ancient Near Eastern works "presents no difficulty: only one instance on either side is needed to prove a positive statement" ("Differences," 389). While he goes on to suggest that someone ought to collect and publish a full collection of these similarities, both the tenor and the specifics of his article suggest his view that little new can be learned from such comparisons.

[17] *Ibid.*

This method dictates that we first determine the differences between the specific situations, geographical and historical, of the Israelites and their neighbors, *and then inquire into the cultural differences which might be expected to follow* as consequences of the historical and geographical distinctions.[18]

From such an embarkation one would expect little attention to the possibility that Israel's traditions were any more than superficially similar to those of her neighbors. Indeed, Smith cedes not an inch of ground on this matter. However, the methodology employed by Smith is even more problematic than the comparative approach he criticizes: if, as he seems to claim, the demonstration of similarities is a facile achievement that demonstrates little of consequence, then a method which is self-confessedly grounded on historical speculation (i.e., his own inquiry "into the cultural differences which might be expected to follow") is, as the following pages of his article illustrate, no improvement. Consider, for example, Smith's discussion of the Israelite attitude toward land possession and exile. According to him Israelite reflection about land possession came about in the following way:

Since the gods of ancient peoples normally helped them in their wars of aggression and conquest . . . we should expect that the Israelites would regularly refer to their land as that which their god had given them—that is, enabled them to conquer—and would celebrate their god as the giver, rather than the creator, of the land. Whether or not they thought he had created it, the creation was comparatively immaterial to them; the important thing was the giving, the conquest. So we should expect myths of creation to be less important in their literature than legends of the conquest.[19]

---

[18] *Ibid.*, 390 (emphasis added).

[19] Smith, "Differences," 391. The widespread assumption that the biblical doctrine of creation never achieved an independent status in Israel, but was instead subordinated to soteriology, evidently owes its origin to Gerhard von Rad's highly influential 1936 essay "The Theological Problem of the Doctrine of Creation in the Old Testament," in *The Problem of the Hexateuch and Other Essays,* trans. by E.W. Trueman Dicken (London: SCM Press, 1966), pp. 131–143. Cf. Richard J. Clifford, "The Hebrew Scriptures and the Theology of Creation," *TS,* 46 (1985), 507; Terence E. Fretheim, "The Reclamation of Creation: Redemption and Law in Exodus," *Int* 45 (October, 1991), 355. The extent of von Rad's impact can be measured by the number of standard Old

However, if (as Smith claims) the divine assistance granted Israel in the taking of the land was "normal" behavior among the gods of ancient peoples, it is difficult to see how he intends to distinguish Israel from her neighbors on these grounds. *Mutatis mutandis*, one would expect to see a de-emphasis of creation myths and a concomitant emphasis on conquest legends in other ancient Near Eastern peoples. Yet that is not the case in either Mesopotamia or Egypt where creation accounts remain foundational to those cultures' respective *Weltanschauungen*. Moreover, and as an increasing number of studies have begun to show, any attempt to divorce the creative and redemptive acts of God in the Hebrew Scriptures or to portray Israel's prior experience with God as Redeemer as the vehicle by which Israel came to understand Yahweh as Creator results in an inaccurate portrayal of ancient Israel's own view of these theological categories. Indeed, as Claus Westermann and others have noted, the biblical evidence indicates that Israel's understanding of God as creator was the *a priori* presupposition of the understanding of the significance of God's redemptive acts in history.[20] Richard J. Clifford summarizes the matter thus:

> The omission of creation from Israelite confessions of faith is not a sign of its unimportance; creation of the world by the gods was so much part of the ancient Near Eastern world view that it was not an explicit item in the Israelite creed.[21]

Testament introductions such as that by Bernhard W. Anderson, *Understanding the Old Testament* (4th ed.; Englewood Cliffs, NJ: Prentice-Hall, 1986), which are ordered around the conclusion that, in spite of contrary evidence, e.g., the canonical ordering of scripture, Israel's understanding of God's soteriological activity was anterior to its understanding of the doctrine of creation. Smith's above-quoted evaluation of the subordinate role of creation theology in the larger horizon of Israel's theological reflection clearly owes more to von Rad's influence that any fresh conclusions reached by the "hypothetico-deductive" method.

[20] See Claus Westermann, *Creation*, trans. by John J. Scullion (Philadelphia: Fortress, 1974), pp. 1–15 and *passim*; H.H. Schmid, "Creation, Righteousness and Salvation: 'Creation Theology' as the Broad Horizon of Biblical Theology," in *Creation in the Old Testament*, ed. by B.W. Anderson (Philadelphia: Fortress, 1984), pp. 102–111; Clifford, "Hebrew Scriptures," 507–523; Terence E. Fretheim, *Exodus* (Louisville: John Knox, 1991), pp. 12–14 and *passim*; *idem*, "Reclamation," 354–365. See also Rolf Knierim, "Cosmos and History in Israel's Theology," *HBT* 3 (1981), 59–123.

[21] Clifford, "Hebrew Scriptures," 507–508.

God's gift of the land, like the deliverance from Egypt, was construed as a continuation of God's creative will for the world.[22]

Like his "hypothetico-deductive" claims for Israel's understanding of land possession, Smith's explanation of the origin of Israel's concern with exile fails to satisfy the evidence. According to him, the idea of the land as a divine gift eventually led to a concern that, should the deity be angered, the gift of the land might be revoked and the land's residents be put in exile. But while he admits the possible antiquity of this notion, Smith maintains that a divine anger that immediately threatens to lead to the punishment of the exile "is not likely to have arisen [in Israel] until there was a real and present danger of such a punishment—that is, after 745," with the revival of Assyria under Tiglath-Pileser III and the attendant development of Assyrian policies of deportation.[23] Moreover, he adds,

> it seems likely that neither of these themes would have played a large part in the literatures of Mesopotamia and Egypt, where the bulk of the population neither looked back to a conquest nor forward to an exile, being too long established for the one and too large for the other.[24]

In point of fact, this claim for Israel's unique attitude toward exile vis-à-vis other ancient Near Eastern people is flatly untenable even as a 'hypothetico-deduction.' As Bertil Albrektson[25] has conclusively demonstrated, there exists a wide variety of textual evidence dating as far back as the Sumerian "Curse of Agade" which leads to the conclusion that

> in Mesopotamia, as in Israel, the idea of historical events as a revelation of divine wrath or mercy for sins or godliness presupposes both that the deity acts in history and that the universe is ruled with justice.[26]

---

[22] Terence E. Fretheim demonstrates with compelling force that creation theology was in fact foundational to Israel's conquest ideology and legends. Specifically, Fretheim maintains that (1) a creation theology provides the cosmic purpose behind God's redemptive activity on Israel's behalf, (2) that God's redemptive activity is a reflex of God's purpose in creation, (3) that God's redemptive activity is cosmic in its effects, and (4) that God's call to Israel is given specifically on a creation-wide scope. Cf. Terence E. Fretheim, *Exodus*, pp. 12–14 and *passim*. Fretheim discusses his case in further detail in his article "Reclamation."

[23] Smith, "Differences," 391.

[24] *Ibid.*

[25] Bertil Albrektson, *History and the Gods*, pp. 100–09.

[26] *Ibid.*, p. 109.

Moreover, Albrektson continues, Israel was not the only ancient people capable of interpreting a defeat and destruction of city and its temple(s) by enemies as a revelation of a god's power and punishing wrath. For example, both the basalt stele of Nabonidus and Sennacherib's account of the ravaging of Babylon center on these themes.[27] Significantly, the latter account interprets Babylon's defeat as a reflex of Marduk's voluntary abandonment of the city and the subsequent disaster that befalls the city because of that leave taking. Contrary to Smith's expectations, this motif of divine abandonment can be traced at least as far as the Sumerian city laments and, as will be seen below, provides a point of continuity between the Sumero-Akkadian lament traditions and those of Israel.

At this juncture, however, it is sufficient to point out that Smith's procedure for comparing—or, more accurately for contrasting—Israelite traditions and those of Mesopotamia and elsewhere suffers from the same lack of control as do those that attempt to establish parallels on the basis of comparability and cultural contact alone. Who is to say what establishes a parallelism or, conversely, a contrast? What qualitative and quantitative similarities must one demonstrate or disprove? How much similarity is needed to prove a parallelism? What sorts of differences are tolerable? Without further clarification on these matters of method, the debate is unlikely to move beyond either Smith's starting point, the presumption of a general cultural and religious chasm between Israel and other people of the ancient Near East, or beyond Ferris's conclusion, the "cautious" and negative answers relative to the specific question of the lament tradition. Hence the following comments address the often-assumed criteria noted above, that of cultural contact and comparability, in an effort to refine further the basis by which the Sumero-Akkadian lament traditions and those of Israel might be compared.

THE CRITERION OF CULTURAL CONTACT

That Israel was never culturally or religiously isolated from her ancient Near Eastern neighbors is a fact which can hardly be gainsaid. Geographically situated between Egypt and a succession of powerful Mesopotamian empires, not to mention the indigenous

---

[27] *Ibid.*, p. 112.

Canaanites and nations of the Transjordan region, Israelites engaged in trade, in warfare, and in political alliances with a host of people whose culture and religion differed dramatically from their own. Whether one conceives of Israel's theology, hymnody, and mythology as a *reaction to* her ancient neighbors or as an *appropriation of* other culture's traditions, Israelite history and the Hebrew Scriptures leave no doubt about Israel's intercourse with other nations. Neither can there be any doubt that cultural contact inevitably found a reflex in the texts of the Bible.[28] The issue, therefore, is not whether Israel was affected by cultural and religious exchanges, but to what extent Israel was affected and, further, how to assay the significance of these exchanges within the biblical tradition. That is, the fact of historical and cultural intercourse demands comparison of Israelite materials with that of her ancient neighbors. The question is what methodological constructs one might employ to effect such a comparison.

Least satisfactory is what Shemaryahu Talmon has called a comparative method on the "grand scale." The comparative method on the grand scale assumes the fundamental unity of the human spirit throughout time and across cultures. Because human beings and their social structures are considered to be intrinsically equal, proponents of this methodology assume that "comparisons can be drawn, therefore, between any two (or more) cultures and social organisms which exhibit some similar features, though they be far-removed from one another in time and space."[29] The potential for non-productive comparisons and erroneous conclusions inherent in this method are self-evident. The presupposition of an intrinsic equality between all human beings and their social organisms means, perforce, a disregard for the specific cultural location of a given phenomenon. But disregard for the specific cultural location of a phenomenon—be that in the arena of *mores,* law, religion, and so forth—means that the comparisons being drawn may in fact be between two disparate features of a culture, and that in spite of their

---

[28] Tigay, "Evaluating Claims," p. 252, remarks: "In the case of the Hebrew Scriptures and the rest of the ancient Near East, frequent contacts between pre-Israelite Palestine and the Israelites, on the one hand, and Egypt, Mesopotamia, and the Syro Palestinian states on the other hand, provide sufficient channels to make borrowing in principle likely."

[29] Shemaryahu Talmon, "The 'Comparative Method' in Biblical Interpretation—Principles and Problems," in *Congress Volume: Göttingen 1977,* VTSup, Vol. 29 (Leiden: E.J. Brill, 1978), pp. 322–324.

superficial similarity. Talmon here echoes a warning articulated earlier by William Foxwell Albright, who, though he saw some value in the "grand scale" approach, specifically cautioned against the temptation to employ analogies which were not truly comparable:

> The use of known human analogies and models for better interpretation of less-known phenomena is entirely legitimate in principle, given the well-documented persistence of basic human drives in all kinds of societies, modern primitive, ancient, and modern. But in employing such analogies or models one must be doubly sure that they are really comparable. In other words, one must be sure that cultural and societal factors are duly considered, and that function as well as external form is really comparable. One must also be clear that an analogy or analogies actually point to a stochastic model (i.e., a working hypothesis put into quasi-mathematical form). Above all, then, we should make use of independently convergent lines of evidence which prove that the analogy or model is valid. Without at least two such independent groups of confirmatory evidence, stochastic models seldom amount to more than eventual working hypotheses.[30]

If anything, however, Talmon is less sanguine than Albright about the utility of using a stochastic model on the "grand scale" since even convergent lines of evidence may point to an erroneous comparison:

> Seemingly identical phenomena which may occur in different cultures are often quite differently weighted in the one in comparison with the other. When dealing comparatively with separate features of social and religious life, or with single concepts, motifs, and idioms, it is imperative to view them in relation to the total phenomena of the groups involved.[31]

Talmon proceeds then to document instances within the sphere of biblical scholarship, including claims of surviving nomadic ideals, Israel's so-called democratic institutions, and a pan-Semitic view of divine kingship, in which he discovers that the ill-considered application of a grand-scale methodological approach has skewed the results of biblical interpretation.[32] He concludes with the dictum, "Comparisons on the 'grand scale' are better avoided."[33]

---

[30] William Foxwell Albright, *Archaeology, Historical Analogy, and Early Biblical Tradition* (Baton Rouge: Louisiana State University, 1966), pp. 5–6.

[31] Talmon, "Comparative Method," p. 324.

[32] *Ibid.*, pp. 329–343.

[33] *Ibid.*, p. 356.

With respect to the question at hand, the articulation of a methodology for comparing Sumero-Akkadian and Hebrew communal laments, Talmon's caution against the failings of the grand scale method are instructive. One cannot simply assume that similar or identical features in the two traditions indicate a common conceptualization within their respective cultures; similar features may in fact be no more than coincidental or superficially similar. Of course, it may well turn out that the Israelite and Mesopotamian traditions *do* share a mutual understanding and that similar phenomena *are* indicative of more than superficial similarity. If such proves to be the case, however, that will necessarily need to be established on grounds other than the supposition of an intrinsic equality between the Sumero-Akkadian and Hebrew communal laments. In any event, and as Talmon has said, it will be imperative to view the respective laments in relation to the total phenomena of the groups involved. In the instance of this investigation, this means a consideration of the origin, cultic use, and literary features of both Mesopotamian communal laments, especially the *balag* and *eršemma* texts, and the communal laments included in the Hebrew Bible.

On the other hand, from a methodological perspective it seems equally illegitimate to employ the grand scale view to deny summarily any literary linkage between the lament traditions under consideration on grounds that features which appear common to them are either significantly distinctive or so widespread as to make a direct connection impossible to demonstrate. This is, of course, one of the conclusions toward which Ferris (among others)[34] would point his readers. Implicit in this conclusion, however, is the presupposition of the grand scale approach, namely, that similarities are explicable owing to the fundamental unity of the human spirit

---

[34] E.g., A. Falkenstein and W. von Soden, *Sumerische und akkadische Hymnen und Gebete* (Zurich: Artemis-Verlag, 1953), p. 51, where the authors discuss the elusive relationship between Israel's psalms and Babylonian prayers in terms of the "altsemitischen Erbe, das für beide Kulturen bestimmend war." For a recent example, see the sophisticated work by Dobbs-Allsopp, *Weep, O Daughter of Zion*, and especially his conclusions on pp. 157–163. In spite of the fact that he is able to muster an impressive array of parallels between the Mesopotamian city-lament genre and the Hebrew Bible as well as evidence indicating that the two genres had some kind of close contact, Dobbs-Allsopp insists that the biblical genre is native to Israel and is no more than generically related to the Mesopotamian genre.

throughout time and across cultures or, in this instance, across the Mesopotamian and Hebrew cultures. Human beings, in both the east and west Semitic worlds, by virtue of their common humanity and a very general similarity of life-style, are assumed to have responded to and reflected upon communal disaster and calamity in similar ways, albeit arrived at independently or as a consequence of "participation in a common literary culture." So, on the one hand, similar expressions, themes, and motifs can be explained by recourse to this "common culture." On the other hand, the "common literary culture" is evidently not pervasive enough to posit any sort of modeling on or literary contact between the cultures since there are distinctions between the traditions of Mesopotamia and Israel. But of what then, one wonders, does "the common oriental culture" consist and what might "participation in a common literary culture" mean? The answers to these questions are elusive because the foundational premise of the comparative method on the "grand scale," namely, the supposition of the intrinsic unity of human culture, is itself so tenuous. In effect, the "common oriental culture" and "participation in a common literary culture" turns out to mean whatever features of the given phenomena are in fact common to Mesopotamian and Israelite writings. But thereby the inherently circular reasoning of the method reveals itself: because any perceived similarities cannot, by definition, be employed to posit modeling or literary contact between the cultures, i.e., they are merely a reflex of the "common oriental culture," it follows that there are *no* similarities and *no* genuine points of comparison between, for example, the two lament traditions. Were any to be discovered, they would, of course, be attributable to the "common oriental culture." It is not therefore astonishing to discover that those applying the "grand scale" method, whether as a basis for comparing the respective traditions or as a foundation for contrasting them, are unable to achieve satisfactory results.

Drawing upon the work of Marc Bloch and M.J. Herskovits, Talmon points to a more felicitous methodological construction for considering the criterion of cultural contact, one dubbed by him as the "historic stream." Bloch defines this method as one

> in which the units of comparison are societies that are geographical neighbors and historical contemporaries, constantly influenced by one another. During the historical development of such societies, they are subject to the same over-all causes, just because they

are so close together in time and space. Moreover, they have, in part at least, a common origin.[35]

Affinities based on geographical and historical proximity as well as cultural origins constitute the "historic stream," and, Talmon avers, the most productive comparisons will be drawn from those waters.

Clearly the conceptual model commends itself for the comparison of cultural features of Mesopotamian and Israelite societies: in every respect just mentioned they are within a continuous "historic stream." Talmon likens this approach to the tenets of comparative philology and draws from James Barr's[36] work in that field a number of corollaries for comparing aspects of societies within the same "historical stream":

> Sources closer to the Old Testament in time take pride of place over considerations of geographic proximity; because of the latter, though, even features observed in relatively late sources may retain traces of earlier common cultural conditions. Thus *date* appears to be more important than *place*. Within this framework, a general closer *affinity* should decide on the actual investigative procedure, i.e., the decision as to which two out of an available selection of compared features, culled from different cultural settings, are most likely to represent a common basic phenomenon.[37]

Thus the comparative priorities for Talmon include (1) proximate date, (2) proximate geography, and (3) other affinities between like phenomena. The last priority persists as the most troublesome one since the identification of the those features which are most likely to represent a common basic phenomenon often become the *crux* of the debate. For example, what comprises the constitutive features of the communal lament traditions in Mesopotamia and Israel? And given that there are some differences between these two in the literary remains of these traditions, how can those affinities which do exist be legitimately compared? These questions, which will be addressed below, hint at some of the problems inherent in the criterion of comparability.

---

[35] Marc Bloch, "Two Strategies of Comparison," in *Comparative Perspectives: Theories and Methods,* ed. by A. Etzioni and F. L. Dubow (Boston: Little Brown, 1970), p. 41. Cited in Talmon, "Comparative Method," p. 325.

[36] James Barr, *Comparative Philology of the Text of the Old Testament* (Winona Lake, IN: Eisenbrauns, 1987).

[37] Talmon, "Comparative Method," p. 325.

William W. Hallo has devoted much of his professional career to the quest for a solution to the problems raised in isolating specifically literary parallels and contrasts between the literature of ancient Israel and Israel's Mesopotamian neighbors.[38] Rather than a methodological procedure, however, Hallo describes his own work as a "contextual approach." Indeed, Hallo seems intent on avoiding extensive discussion of his procedure as a method, choosing instead to illustrate the contextual approach through a series of case studies. Nevertheless it becomes clear that Hallo's "contextual approach" bears certain affinities with Talmon's "historic stream."

Like Talmon's "historic stream," Hallo's "contextual approach" centers on those literary and historical *contexts* which were common to ancient Israel and Israel's Near Eastern neighbors. By "literary contexts" Hallo means to include "the entire Near Eastern literary milieu, to the extent that it can be argued to have had any conceivable impact on the biblical formulation."[39] Historical context is similarly defined as any event in the historical milieu which may have impacted the biblical institution.[40] Hallo intends, however, to

---

[38] A partial listing of Hallo's essays pertinent to this topic include: William W. Hallo, "New Viewpoints on Cuneiform Literature," *IEJ* 12 (1962), 13–26; "Individual Prayer in Sumerian: The Continuity of a Tradition," *JCS* 88 (1968), 71–89; "Problems in Sumerian Hermeneutics," *Perspectives in Jewish Learning* 5 (1973), 1–12; "The Royal Correspondence of Larsa: I. A Sumerian Prototype for the Prayer of Hezekiah?" in *Cuneiform Studies in Honor of Samuel Noah Kramer*, AOAT, Vol. 25 (Neukirchen-Vluyn: Neukirchener, 1976), pp. 209–225; "New Moons and Sabbaths: A Case-Study in the Contrastive Approach," *HUCA* 48 (1977), 1–18; "The Expansion of Cuneiform Literature," in *Proceedings of the American Academy of Jewish Research*, pp. 307–322. 1980; "Biblical History in its Near Eastern Setting: The Contextual Approach," in *Scripture in Context: Essays on the Comparative Method*, ed. by Carl D. Evans, William W. Hallo, and John B. White, John B. (Pittsburgh: Pickwick, 1980), pp. 1–26; "Letters, Prayers, and Letter Prayers," in *Proceedings of the Seventh World Congress of Jewish Studies Held at the Hebrew University of Jerusalem, 7–14 August 1977 Under the Auspices of the Israel Academy of Sciences and Humanities, World Congress of Jewish Studies*, (Jerusalem: World Union of Jewish Studies; Magnes Press, 1981), pp. 17–27; "Sumerian Literature: Background to the Bible," *BR* 4 (June 1988), 28–38; "Compare and Contrast: The Contextual Approach to Biblical Literature," in *The Bible in the Light of Cuneiform Literature. Scripture in Context III*, ed. by Bruce William Jones, and Gerald L. Mattingly, ANETS, Vol. 8 (Lewiston: Edwin Mellen, 1990), pp. 1–30; "The Concept of Canonicity in Cuneiform and Biblical Literature: A Comparative Appraisal," in *The Biblical Canon in Comparative Perspective: Scripture in Context IV*, ed. by K. Lawson Younger, Jr., William W. Hallo, and Bernard F. Batto, ANETS, Vol. 11 (Lewiston: Edwin Mellon, 1991), pp. 1–19.

[39] Hallo, "Compare and Contrast," p. 3; cf. *idem*, "The Contextual Approach," p. 2.

[40] *Ibid.*

do far more than demonstrate the ways in which the respective literary and historical contexts are similar or dissimilar. Rather his goal is

> not to find the key to every biblical phenomenon in some ancient Near Eastern precedent, but rather to silhouette the biblical text against its wider literary and cultural environment and thus to arrive at a proper assessment of the extent to which the biblical evidence reflects that environment or, on the contrary, is distinctive and innovative over and against it.[41]

For Hallo, however, a "proper assessment" is always dependent upon epigraphic and textual evidence. His approach involves the identification of a particular written phenomenon and tracing the development (as well as any transformation of it) through the canons of the cuneiform corpus down to the point where it is temporally proximate with the biblical materials. At that point only will he venture a comparison. Like Talmon, therefore, Hallo values temporal proximity as a prime basis for comparative research.

Also like Talmon, Hallo perceives the necessity of establishing geographic proximity for comparative research. He is concerned to treat not only the history of cuneiform literature, and especially the transmission of Sumero-Akkadian texts and themes, but geographi-

---

[41] *Ibid.* Explicit in this quote is Hallo's recognition, *per contra* the evaluation of his work by Dennis Pardee, "Review of *Scripture in Context: Essays on the Comparative Method,*" *JNES* 44 (1985), 221–222, that some aspects of Near Eastern cultural phenomenon can not be compared to the biblical traditions but instead must be contrasted to them. In fact, the "contextual approach" he champions admits the possibility of a number of relationships, including the negative one: "But for me the method requires only the commensurability of the two terms, not a prejudgment as to their equation. If A is the biblical text, or phenomenon, and B the Babylonian one, I am quite prepared to test the evidence for a whole spectrum of relationships, expressed "mathematically" not only by $A = B$ but also $A \sim B$ or $A < B$ or $A > B$ and even $A \neq B$. The last possibility needs stressing, because a comparative approach that is truly objective must be broad enough to embrace the possibility of a negative comparison, i.e., a contrast. And contrast can be every bit as illuminating as (positive) comparison. It can silhouette the distinctiveness of a biblical institution or formulation against its Ancient Near Eastern matrix" ("New Moons and Sabbaths," 2; cf. a similar statement "Expansion of Cuneiform Literature," 307–308). Even a contrast, however, does not necessarily disprove a literary relationship. To the contrary, and as the next section will show, distinctive aspects of kindred cultural phenomena may demonstrate another feature of the comparative process, namely the recognition that the transmission of cultural materials, not excluding canonical religious texts, often witnessed the adaptation of those texts via the incorporation of local traditions.

cal distribution of that literature as well.[42] Specifically, Hallo has
been successful in describing the ways in which cuneiform literature, including Sumerian texts, survived and spread through scribal
schools which ringed Mesopotamia from Susa to Ḫattuša and Amarna. As he understands the matter, scribal schools were initially
responsible for the transmission of Sumerian literary texts whose
composition dates back to the neo-Sumerian period.[43] These texts
were learned and copied out in the schools of Hammurapi's time
early in the second millennium, with careful attention to liturgical
notations (even when these were no longer understood) and to
"Masoretic" details such as variant readings or the number of lines
in a given composition. When historical circumstance brought about
the demise of the Old Babylonian schools, the traditional texts and
the surviving Sumerian-speaking scholars kept their literary tradition alive, possible by seeking refuge in extreme southern Mesopotamia. Still later, the Kassite conquest of the southern Sealand late
in the second millennium reunited that region and the surviving
scribal traditions with Babylonia and retrieved the older textual
materials. Then, Hallo believes,

> the newly formed scribal guilds of this feudal age took up where
> the earlier scribes had left off. They selected a portion of the surviv-
> ing Sumerian literary corpus, provided it with a literal translation
> into Akkadian and preserved the ancient learning for both Baby-
> lonia and Assyria well into the first millennium.[44]

The significance of these observations exceeds the observation that
even ancient Sumerian literary traditions survived via the scribal
schools. The scribal schools disseminated Mesopotamian *culture*,

---

[42] See especially Hallo, "The Expansion of Cuneiform Literature," 309–316; "Problems in Sumerian Hermeneutics," 5–8.

[43] William W. Hallo, "Toward a History of Sumerian Literature," in *Sumerological
Studies in Honor of Thorkild Jacobsen on His Seventieth Birthday, June 7, 1974*, Assyriological Studies, Vol. 20 (Chicago: University of Chicago, 1975), p. 181ff. On scribes and
scribal schools more generally see Samuel Noah Kramer, *The Sumerians: Their History, Culture, and Character* (Chicago: University of Chicago, 1963), p. 230ff.; Leo A.
Oppenheim, *Ancient Mesopotamia: Portrait of a Dead Civilization* (Chicago: University
of Chicago, 1964), pp. 235–249; H.W.F. Saggs, *The Greatness that was Babylon: A Survey
of the Ancient Civilization of the Tigris-Euphrates Valley* (New York: New American
Library, 1962), p. 389ff.; Joan Oates, *Babylon* (London: Thames and Hudson, 1986),
pp. 163–167.

[44] Hallo, "Problems in Sumerian Hermeneutics," 5.

and that not only within Mesopotamia itself but in diffuse peripheral areas of the ancient Near East.[45] As one scholar has noted: "It must be stressed that the adoption of cuneiform implied the borrowing of an entire cultural tradition, and that, conversely, scribal education was the means by which that tradition was transmitted, both to the native Mesopotamian and to the foreigner."[46] Again Hallo neatly summarizes the facts of the case:

> Even where the harvest of Akkadian or Sumerian texts is minimal, as at Hazor, Megiddo, Taanach, Schechem, Aphek or Gezer, the significant point is that literary texts or, more broadly, school texts regularly constitute an impressive proportion of the epigraphic finds. The implication is that schooling in Mesopotamian cuneiform was a farflung phenomenon throughout the [second] millennium, and that it involved the customary transmission of the Sumerian literary canon, combined with translation into Akkadian and the local vernacular, and sometimes with imitations in the local language and/or in the local script which, notably at Ugarit, did not at once displace Mesopotamian cuneiform for literary purposes. . . . Its further implication is that Sumerian literature survived in the "West" almost to the end of the Bronze Age, i.e., to the very threshold of Israelite literary history. We cannot simply exclude the possibility that the beginnings of that history were somehow influenced by it.[47]

---

[45] See Gary Beckman, "Mesopotamians and Mesopotamian Learning at Hattuša," *JCS* 35 (1983), 98, n. 5, and the bibliography cited there. Beckman mentions evidence from sites as far flung as Emar, Ebla, Qatna, Ugarit, Ras ibn Hani, and Alalakh in Syria, Hazor, Meggido, Shechem, Gezer, Aphek, and Ta'nach in Palestine; Amarna in Egypt and Kültepe Kaneš and Boghazköy-Ḫattuša in Anatolia. See also Aaron Demsky, "The Education of Canaanite Scribes in Mesopotamian Cuneiform Tradition," in *Bar-Ilan Studies in Assyriology Dedicated to Pinhas Artzi*, ed. by Jacob Klein and Aaron Skaist (Ramat Gan: Bar-Ilan University, 1990), pp. 157–170, where the author adduces evidence showing the existence of several scribal centers which persisted down to at least the 13th century: one at Hazor in the earlier period; at least one other, at Megiddo; and perhaps still another at Aphek. Another helpful study is that by René Labat, "Le rayonnement de la langue et de l'écriture akkadiennes au deuxième millénaire avant notre ére," *Syria* (1964), 1–27, who argues that centers of cuneiform literacy existed in each of the city states of Canaan from the Middle Bronze to the close of the Late Bronze ages. Hayim Tadmor, "A Lexical Text from Hazor," *IEJ* 27 (1977), 98–102, agrees with Labat's conclusions and offers a text from Hazor as further proof.

[46] Beckman, "Mesopotamians," 98.

[47] Hallo, "The Expansion of Cuneiform Literature," 312.

Direct proof of such an influence is, of course, difficult to demonstrate, owing in part to the paucity of cuneiform materials yet discovered in Israelite lands.[48] Though cuneiform finds have been sparse, even the small number of discoveries does illustrate cuneiform literacy in Palestine during the second millennium, and most likely during the first millennium as well.[49] A larger sampling would doubtless reveal what changes the canonical Mesopotamian texts underwent as they were translated and interpolated into the local vernacular and culture. That Sumero-Akkadian canonical texts were locally translated and thence interpolated into local cultures, however, leads directly into the complexities of the other commonly posited criterion for establishing a literary comparison between texts from disparate traditions, what we called the "criterion of comparability" above. That second, related criterion will be discussed shortly. For now a brief summary of the criterion of cultural contact is in order.

As defined above, the criterion of cultural contact specified that comparisons which serve to establish the literary influence of a text or genre upon another are most profitable where the avenues for cultural contact are demonstrable. As discussed, however, demonstrable "avenues for cultural contact" are unsatisfactorily treated by recourse to a hypothetical "common oriental culture" or "participation in a common literary culture" when such a common heritage is construed along the lines of a "grand scale" methodology. If it is a fact that the ancient Near East shared such a common literary heritage wherein particular themes, expressions, literary devices, and even whole genres were transmitted from one culture to another apart from literary contact,[50] that fact can neither be proven nor

---

[48] See Tadmor, "A Lexical Text from Hazor," 101–102 and nn. 21–25, where he helpfully lists the various cuneiform materials discovered in Israel. Included in his survey is a fragment of the Gilgamesh Epic, fragments of lexical texts, a liver model, and so forth. The 1995 discoveries at Hazor, however, including four new cuneiform tablets and the identification of what appears to be royal archives, promise to expand the present list considerably. See "Royal Archives of Hazor Near Discovery," *Archaeology in Review* <http://www.serve.com/Bridge/arch996.htm> (12 December, 1995).

[49] Dobbs-Allsopp, *Weep, O Daughter of Zion*, p. 159.

[50] Hallo, "Sumerian Literature," 38. The additional comment by Hallo in this context is thereby made all the more surprising: "The parallels I have drawn [between Sumerian and biblical literature] may in many cases owe more to a common Ancient Near Eastern heritage—shared by Israel—than to any direct dependence of one body of literature on the other." And yet, he asserts, "The evolution of these genres can be

disproven by means of this model. On the other hand, the "historic stream" model, which assumes that societies of at least a partial common origin and which exist close together in time and space will influence one another, appears to be a more promising approach. This would be particularly true if it could be demonstrated that Mesopotamian and Israelite writings, and specifically their respective communal laments, were temporally and geographically proximate. Of these two factors temporal proximity is of greater significance and, as the next chapter will show, relatively easy to demonstrate. Geographic proximity remains more difficult to establish, chiefly because cuneiform texts of any sort remain scarce in Palestine. Nevertheless, the well-established phenomenon of cuneiform scribal schools, located on the periphery of Mesopotamian influence and ubiquitous throughout the second and first millennium, presents the likely possibility that the problems presented in establishing geographic proximity are consequential to the accidental character of the archaeological enterprise.[51] In this regard, Akkadian loan words and especially those that are *hapax legomena* in biblical Hebrew will provide significant further evidence of cultural contact and, possibly, of literary contact as well. At the very least it can be confidently asserted that avenues for cultural contact between Mesopotamia and ancient Israel are demonstrable. The next chapter intends to demonstrate cultural contact along the lines of the "historic stream" model, i.e., an emphasis on time and, in a less direct way, place, can be demonstrated for the respective communal lament traditions of Mesopotamia and Israel.

THE CRITERION OF COMPARABILITY

The second criterion commonly employed in comparing the literature of one culture with another is what was called above the

---

traced over the millennia, and their spread can be followed across the map of the biblical world." One wonders how it is possible to trace the evolution and spread of a particular genre over the millennia and from one location to another and still attribute that development to a "common Ancient Near Eastern heritage."

[51] Again Hallo, "The Expansion of Cuneiform Literature," 313, concisely describes the criterion of cultural contact: "I must of course admit that the scholastic traditions of Mesopotamia did not survive in the West beyond this, i.e., into the Iron Age. For the greater part of the biblical text, therefore, comparativists who would entertain the possibility that a biblical author drew inspiration from a cuneiform text or textual genre must at minimum demonstrate that that text or genre survived in its Mesopotamian homeland far enough into the first millennium to have become familiar to

"criterion of comparability." Simply put, this criterion posits that fruitful comparisons should be made between commensurate textual materials whose similarity can be established, at least superficially, on the basis of genre, form, or content. The self-evident character of this maxim hardly needs explanation. One *may* compare dissimilar literary types and doubtless discover points of commonality (poetics, similar metaphors, identical vocabulary, common tropes, etc.) but the utility of such a comparison will likely be less than were the comparison to be conducted between textual materials that have some formal affinities with one another.

Once the decision has been made to compare commensurate textual materials, however, Talmon's observation relative to affinities between like phenomenon is apposite. A definitive methodology that embraces every stochastic model cannot be had. Instead, within the comparative framework:

> a general closer *affinity* should decide on the actual investigative procedure, i.e. the decision as to which two out of an available selection of compared features, culled from different cultural settings, are most likely to represent a common basic phenomenon.[52]

Unfortunately, the determination of genre, form, and content for both the Mesopotamian and the Israelite communal laments remains a complex and somewhat elusive matter. Which features and which texts represent the "common basic phenomenon" of communal lament? On the Israelite side, scholars have long disagreed as to which psalms ought be numbered among the communal laments and what the criteria of that assignation might be. Part of the task in comparing Hebrew and Mesopotamian communal laments, therefore, will be an articulation of just what comprises that genre and on what grounds. Accordingly, Chapter 5, which compares the communal laments of Mesopotamia and Israel, will be preceded by a

---

that author. (Optimally, they should find, not only a time, but also a place where it might have become familiar, but that is truly asking too much at this stage.)"

[52] Talmon, "Comparative Method," p. 325. Similarly, Longman, *Fictional Akkadian Autobiography*, pp. 12–13, argues for the establishment of generic identity based on similarities between texts on many different levels. His own study is concerned to compare both the "outer form" of texts (including "the structure of the text and the metrical or nonmetrical speech rhythm") and the inner, non-formal aspects of a text (including the mood, the setting, the function, narrative voice, and content of the texts).

discussion of those features that appear to be constitutive of the communal lament in the Hebrew Bible.

The situation is somewhat less complicated in the Mesopotamian tradition if only because the laments are designated as such in the surviving colophons. Communal laments in the Sumero-Akkadian tradition are generally denominated as *balag* and *eršemma* texts. Contained in the collection of canonical *balag* and *eršemma* materials, however, is quite a diverse collection of themes and content. It will be necessary to identify characteristics of these materials, beyond their colophonic designations, that represent their basic attributes. The ancient colophon, however, will be a determining factor relative to which materials will be considered, notwithstanding the occasional thematic or other affinities between this generic designation and other Mesopotamian prayers.[53] As Piotr Michalowski has noted in another context:

> The fact that we are, at present, ignorant of the principles of generic assignation of Mesopotamian texts should not prevent us from recognizing the value of ancient taxonomic labels, if only because "the ethnic system of genres constitutes a grammar of folklore, cultural affirmation of the communication rules that govern the expression of complex messages within the cultural context. . . . It consists of distinct forms, each of which has its particular symbolic connotations and scope of applicable social contexts."[54]

---

[53] See Mark E. Cohen, *Sumerian Hymnology: the Ersemma*, HUCA Supplement, No. 2 (Cincinnati: Hebrew Union College-Jewish Institute of Religion, 1981), pp. 29–35, where the content and structure of *Eršemma* no. 29 (*nam-mu-un-šub-bé-en*) is anomalously *identical* to that of an *eršaḫunga*. On colophons more generally, see Hermann Hunger, *Babylonische und assyrische Kolophone*, AOAT, No. 2 (Kevelaer: Butzon und Bercker, 1968).

Longman, *Fictional Akkadian Autobiography*, p. 14, echoes the caution of A.K. Grayson, *Babylonian Historical-Literary Texts* (Toronto: University of Toronto, 1975), p. 4ff., to the effect that Mesopotamian scribes were not concerned with a precise and self-conscious generic classification of their literature. Nevertheless, with the exception of the *eršemma* just mentioned, the notations *balag* and *eršemma* serve better than is often the case with the cuneiform texts as an identifier for two types of cultic lament. Moreover, Gerald H. Wilson, *The Editing of the Hebrew Psalter*, SBLDS, No. 76 (Chico, CA: Scholars Press, 1985), pp. 17–18, has identified instances where colophons were "frozen" as a fixed part of the literary composition so that it no longer stood as "a variable document appended by each successive copyist-scribe and containing the data necessary for his own particular situation."

[54] Piotr Michalowski, "On the Early History of the Eršaḫunga Prayer," *JCS* 39 (1987), 41. Michalowski quotes D. Ben-Amos, "Analytical Categories and Ethnic Genres," in *Folklore Genres*, ed. by D. Ben-Amos (Austin: University of Texas, 1976), p. 225.

Once the respective literary forms or *Gattungen* have been determined and described, however, an additional step is needed in order to address the comparability of the communal laments. Again it is Talmon who reminds us that by definition a *Gattung* has a specific *Sitz im Leben*, i.e., a delimited location in the cultic and cultural structure of the society which produced it:

> Therefore, the identification of a *Gattung* evidenced in the literature of one society also in the creative writings of another requires the additional proof that in both it had the same *Sitz im Leben*. This means that a comparative study of *Gattungen* must take into account the social context in which the specific literary types and forms arise. What must be shown is that this *Gattung* and what it expresses indeed finds its place in the cultic and conceptual framework of both societies. A *Gattung* cannot be contemplated in isolation from the overall socio-cultural web of a society.[55]

Talmon's forceful statement must be attenuated slightly. The determination of the *Sitz im Leben* for individual Hebrew psalms or *Gattungen* has long been a matter of scholarly debate, as even a cursory glance at major commentaries published in this century reveals. Besides lacking taxonomic designations, which are ubiquitous in the Mesopotamian materials,[56] the Hebrew psalms are characterized by metaphoric language and tropes which, doubtless intentionally, lend themselves to multiplex interpretation. As a consequence, the psalms are time bound neither by their history nor their content[57] and only rarely indisputably display what must have been an original *Sitz im Leben*.[58] Therefore, for the Hebrew psalms, one (or

---

[55] Talmon, "Comparative Method," p. 352. However the reminder by H.W.F. Saggs, *The Encounter,* p. 13, is also pertinent: "The *Gattung* is the framework in which the idea is preserved, not necessarily the setting in which it was created."

[56] Note, however, that Bruce K. Waltke, "Superscripts, Postscripts, or Both," *JBL* 110 (1991), 583–596, has recently argued that this may not be as true as was once supposed. The possible presence of a Hebrew colophon in the communal lament psalms will be discussed in Chapter 5.

[57] Patrick D. Miller, Jr., *Interpreting the Psalms* (Philadelphia: Fortress, 1986), pp. 22–23.

[58] The entrance liturgies of Psalms 15 and 24, for example, seem to be exceptional in that a *Sitz im Leben* for them is relatively easy to discern. Even with these psalms, however, it may be also be the case that Gunkel's notion that each form had one and only one *Sitz im Leben* was overly rigid from the start: a particular form may occupy multiple settings and, by the same token, one particular social setting may generate more than a single specific *Gattung*. Cf. Longman, *Fictional Akkadian Autobiography,* pp. 17–18.

more) *Sitz im Leben* must be deduced, drawing evidence first from the Hebrew Bible itself and only secondarily from ancient Near Eastern analogues.[59] The elusive character of any original *Sitz im Leben* further means that, just as any one using the stochastic model must take into account "the social context in which the specific literary types and forms arise" in each society, one must also be open to the possibility that further clarity regarding the context for Israel's cult and culture, its "socio-cultural web," may emerge as part of the comparative process itself. If, for example, it can be demonstrated that both Israelite and Mesopotamian peoples found a place in their cultic and conceptual framework for routine use of communal laments, that determination lays sufficient groundwork for comparison of the respective compositions. At the same time, however, it may prove to be the case that Mesopotamian cultic employment of those communal laments, and specifically the *balag* and *eršemma* compositions, can be suggestive of ways in which Israel might likewise have employed its own laments.[60]

There are, however, two further considerations in the matter of appraising the relationship of equivalent *Gattungen*, both of which involve peculiarities in the transmission of the cuneiform materials in the scribal schools.

The Creative Adaptation Principle

The first additional consideration has to do with the standardization of the *balag* and *eršemma* texts in a "canonical" form. Generally speaking, there is the problem of what is and is not certain about the "canon" of Mesopotamian literature.[61] Piotr Michalowsi

---

[59] To a lesser extent this same situation pertains to the *balag/eršemma* compositions which, as it turns out, came to be integrated in the Mesopotamian cultic calendar for routine use quite apart from their original *Sitz im Leben*.

[60] The author regards this approach as similar to the theory of probability as discussed by E.D. Hirsch, Jr., *Validity in Interpretation* (New Haven: Yale University, 1967), p. 173ff. Cf. Longman, *Fictional Akkadian Autobiography*, pp. 18–19.

[61] Francesca Rochberg-Halton, "Canonicity in Cuneiform Texts," *JCS* 30 (1984), 127–128, cautions Assyriologists against the inexact application of the terms "canon" and "canonization" in the sense in which the biblical terms are applied to the biblical texts with all of their connotations: "Rather it [canonization] may be viewed in terms of standardization of formal aspects of the text, that is, the number and arrangement of tablets, while a degree of flexibility remained permissible in the content, in terms of exactly what a particular tablet was to include and in what order, thus resulting in only a relative stabilization of the wording of the text. . . . Exact wording does not

discusses the difficulty by noting that reconstructions of even the first millennium "canon" are incomplete and, further, that publications of recent years have only lately made scholars aware of the fact that a greater proportion of Sumerian literary texts were known in later periods than had been expected.[62] This evolving situation prompts Michalowski's call for a thorough reevaluation of the history of textual transmission and of the *Rezeptionsgeschichte* of Mesopotamian literary works in general. In particular he is concerned with the presence and absence of particular texts, questions of transmission, redaction, and intertextuality.[63]

Michalowski's concerns are illustrated by cultic texts such as the *balag*s and *eršemma*s. Even when colophons are missing, these materials are seldom difficult to recognize on the basis of internal criteria.[64] Nevertheless, reconstruction of individual texts remains a notoriously complex undertaking. Miguel Civil enumerates the difficulties:

> One reason is structural: these poems are composed of textual blocks that are repeated within the same *balag*, in other *balag*s, and in *eršemma* compositions making it very easy to combine frag-

---

seem to have been an essential ingredient in textual transmission." Cf. W.G. Lambert, "Ancestors, Authors, and Canonicity" *JCS* 11 (1957), 9 and n. 34; Michalowski, "Early History," 38; Mark E. Cohen, *The Canonical Lamentations of Ancient Mesopotamia* (Potomac: Capital Decisions Limited, 1988), vol. 1, p. 40, for similar opinions. "Canon" and "canonical" as they appear in this context are meant to be understood more loosely, with Rochberg-Halton's comment in mind. For a reconstruction of the "canonical" process with respect to the *balag* texts see J.A. Black, "Sumerian Balag Compositions," *BO* 44 (1987), 34–35.

[62] Michalowski, "Early History," 37–38. Michalowski contrasts the present situation to that when J. Cooper published his "Bilinguals from Boghazköi, I," *ZA* 61 (1971), 7, n. 30, where he was able to list only a handfull of Sumerian texts appearing in later periods. Specific references to the more recently published Sumerian literary texts, which survived in first millennium copies, appear on 38–39, nn. 5–8.

[63] *Ibid.*, 39. Michalowski's concern is shared by authors of several significant studies of cuneiform literary works in various stages of life including Jerrold S. Cooper, "Symmetry and Repetition in Akkadian Narrative," *JAOS* 97 (1977), 508–512; "Gilgamesh Dreams of Enkidu: The Evolution and Dilution of Narrative," in *Essays on the Ancient Near East in Memory of J.J. Finkelstein*, ed. by M. de Jong Ellis (Memoirs of the Connecticut Academy of Arts and Sciences; Hamden, Conn.: Archon Books, 1977), pp. 39–44; Marianna E. Vogelzang, "Kill Anzu! On a Point of Literary Evolution," in *Keilschriftliche Literaturen. Ausgewählte Vorträge der XXXII. Rencontre Assyriologique International*, Münster, 8.-12.7.1985, edited by K. Hecker and W. Sommerfeld (Berliner Beiträge zum Vorderen Orient, no. 6; Berlin: Dietrich Reimer, 1986), pp. 61–70.

[64] *Ibid.*, 40.

ments in an incorrect sequence. A second reason is the complicated textual transmission: a *balag* can be preserved partly in a
tablet of the OB period and partly in NA or NB sources. The text
is modified through the centuries by weak links of oral tradition or poor copies by inexpert scribes. In NA and NB times the
texts were standardized and arranged in a fixed sequence (canonical version). For unknown and possibly accidental reasons some
*balag*s have been abundantly preserved while others we know
only the name.[65]

The discovery of the textual history of individual *balag*s and
*eršemma*s continues as an ongoing project of Assyriologists and is
best left to them. The fact that these ritual texts were standardized
and arranged in a "canonical" version during the first millennium is
a boon to the present investigation: the "canonical" versions are contemporaneous with the Hebrew communal laments and therefore
meet the methodological criteria of temporal proximity discussed
above. Moreover, the known "canonical" versions are readily ac-
cessible as they have been gathered and studied in recent critical
editions.[66] Nevertheless, it is incumbent to bear in mind one result of
critical research into the "pre-canonical" transmission of these materials which has found widespread agreement among specialists,
namely what William Hallo has referred to as the "organic transformation and creative adaptation" of Sumero-Akkadian compositions in the cuneiform tradition.[67] By this phrase Hallo means that,
in general,

> although the original creative impulse [for composition] most
> often arose out of and in response to a specific historical situation,
> the long process of canonization (that is, the incorporation of the
> text in fixed form in the generally accepted curriculum of the

---

[65] Miguel Civil, "The 10th Tablet of úru àm-ma-ir-ra-bi," *Aula Orientalis* 1 (1983),
45; cf. *idem*, "Enlil, The Merchant: Notes on CT 15 10," *JCS* 28 (1976), 72.

[66] Mark E. Cohen, *Balag-compositions: Sumerian Lamentation Liturgies of the Second
and First Millennium B.C.* (Malibu: Undena, 1974); *SH*; *CLAM*; cf. Raphael Kutscher,
Oh Angry Sea (a-ab-ba hu-luh-ha): The History of a Sumerian Congregational Lament, Yale
Near Eastern Researches, No. 6 (New Haven: Yale University, 1975); Konrad Volk,
*Die Balag-Komposition úru àm-ma-ir-ra-bi. Rekonstruktion und Bearbeitung der Tafeln 18
(19'ff.), 19, 20, und 21 der späten, kanonischen Version* (Stuttgart: Franz Steiner Verlag
Wiesbaden GMBH, 1989). The latter two studies trace the textual history of their
respective *balag*s.

[67] Hallo, "Problems," 7.

scribal schools) tended to suppress allusions to these situations. If a composition resisted such sublimation or ideological updating, it tended to disappear from the canon.[68]

Examples of this process include the disappearance of the two Enheduanna cycles of Ninurta hymns after Old Babylonian times,[69] the elements of the Curse of Agade which have been adopted and adapted into the Weidner Chronicle,[70] transformations in the various recensions of the Gilgamesh Epic,[71] and laments, both private and public.[72] Of the latter, Hallo observes that whatever real historical events originally inspired the prayers became sublimated into vague descriptions of the cessation of cultic processes or the flight of the divine presence, with the result that "there is sometimes uncertainty in both as to just what historic event is intended, the more so as there seems to have been no great reluctance about applying older allusions to more recent events."[73]

As with the examples just mentioned, it likewise appears certain that a real historic event, a national disaster, served as inspiration

---

[68] Hallo, "Toward a History of Sumerian Literature," p. 194. Cf. Jeffrey H. Tigay, "On Some Aspects of Prayer in the Bible," *AJS Review* 1 (1976), 376, for a concurring statement.

[69] *Ibid.*, 183–187. Hallo refers to Enheduanna's versions of Inanna and Ebih (in-nin-šà-gur$_x$-ra) and the Exaltation of Inanna, composed under the patronage of Sargon or Naram-Sin in the Sargonic period. The latter composition in particular apostrophizes the temples of Sumer and Akkad "in a manner calculated to put royal solicitude for them in the best possible light" while at the same time portraying the Sargonic kings as defenders of the traditional Sumerian faith. Both cyles disappear after Old Babylonian times, Hallo states, because "they failed to sublimate their historical particulars sufficiently to qualify for enduring and universal interest in the cuneiform curriculum" (187).

[70] *Ibid.*, 188. A. Falkenstein, *Orientalische Literaturzeitung* (1958), 142f., although not mentioned by Hallo, was the first to point out the parallels between the *Curse of Agade* and the *Weidner Chronicle*: in both Naramsin is credited for the destruction of the city and in both Enlil/Marduk send the Guti against Agade to avenge Naramsin's sacrilege. Cf. Jerrold S. Cooper, *The Curse of Agade* (Baltimore: Johns Hopkins University, 1983), pp. 6, 17, and 19, n. 37. Cooper believes, however, that Hallo's claim that the *Weidner Chronicle* is an Akkadian adaptation of the *Curse of Agade*, exaggerates the relationship between the two compositions.

[71] Hallo, "Problems," 7. Cf. Jeffrey H. Tigay, "The Evolution of the Pentateuchal Narratives in the Light of the Evolution of the *Gilgamesh Epic*," in *Empirical Models for Biblical Criticism*, ed. by Jeffrey H. Tigay (Philadelphia: University of Pennsylvania, 1985), pp. 21–52, and especially pp. 35–46; *idem*, "Evaluating Claims," 250–255.

[72] Hallo, "Individual Prayer," 75; "Problems," 7.

[73] Hallo, "Individual Prayer," 75.

for the composition of the Sumerian city laments,[74] compositions which, as will be shown, display a generic relationship with the succeeding *balag* and *eršemma* lamentations. Indeed the *balag* and *eršemma* prayers, developed from these older city laments and used routinely in Mesopotamian cultic worship for the succeeding two millennia, survived because of the tendency to sublimate those precipitating historic events in such a way that the original events became indiscernible within the text, thus allowing ongoing use of the texts in the cult.[75] Kutscher has confirmed that principle in his study of the *balag a-ab-ba hu-luh-ha*, wherein he demonstrates that that lament survived in liturgical usage through its adaptation to more contemporaneous events by means of changes in the names of god, cities, and so forth.[76] As a consequence of the creative adaptation process, one finds in the latest copies of the *balag*s a description of the destruction of the land and city in general terms rather than references to a specific historical occurrence.[77]

The tendency within the Mesopotamian lamentations to lose the specifics of their historical genesis in turn raises the distinct possibility, already proposed by Hallo, that an analogous transformation and adaptation took place in the congregational laments of the Psalter as well as, perhaps, in the Book of Lamentations. That is, the lack of specific mention of historical peoples or events in the biblical material is likewise a consequence of the creative adaptation principle: during the transmission process historical referents were dropped in order that the materials might find use in the ongoing cultic worship of Israel.

The lack of a traceable tradition of the Hebrew compositions makes absolute confirmation of this suggestion difficult. It may well be that the Hebrew communal laments reflect the adaptation and

---

[74] For example, the city laments include references to Elam, the Su-people, the Gutians, and the misfortunes of Ibbi-Sin. Cf. LU 244; LSUr 33–35, 75, 109, 149, 169, 175, 233, 257–260, 264, 404, 495–498; EL, 4th *kirugu* 10; UL 4th *kirugu* 20, 22.

[75] On the origin of the Sumerian city laments and their relationship to the *balag* and *eršemma* lamentations, see Chapter 3.

[76] Kutscher, *Oh Angry Sea*. It is also possible to trace the spread of the cuneiform literature through the shifting allusions and reminiscences which appear in the various copies. See André Finet, "Allusions et réminiscences comme source d'information sur la diffusion de la littérature," in *Keilschriftliche Literaturen. Ausgewählte Vorträge der XXXII. Rencontre Assyriologique International, Münster, 8.-12.7.1985* (Berlin: Dietrich Reimer, 1986), pp. 13–17.

[77] Cohen, *balag*, p. 10; *idem, CLAM*, p. 38.

that original references to historic events have been purged from the compositions. If this is the case, however, it seems that the analogue drawn by Hallo between the Mesopotamian and Hebrew compositions is in need of slight modification. In contradistinction to the type of *Vergegenwärtigung* evidenced in the Mesopotamian materials during their long journey from the Old Babylonian period down through the first millennium, the Hebrew prayers would had to have undergone a sublimation of historical events almost immediately after their composition. For if it is assumed, as is almost universally the case, that at least those laments which mention the destruction of the Temple and Jerusalem (e.g., Pss 74, 79, and Lam 5) were dependent upon the Babylonian invasion in 587 BCE for their inspiration and were written down shortly thereafter,[78] the analogue would lead one to expect references to the Babylonians or, at the very least, some indication of the historic circumstances which inspired the composition—similar, perhaps, to what one finds in Psalm 137. It may be that the factors involved in sublimating any historical references took place quickly for reasons that remain unclear. The very similarity between this aspect of the Hebrew tradition and the Mesopotamian laments, however, suggests other possibilities. On the one hand, the Hebrew poets might have borrowed from or modelled their compositions upon late standardized

---

[78] In this connection it is interesting to note a recent comment by Claus Westermann, *Lamentations: Issues and Interpretation,* trans. by Charles Muenchow (Minneapolis: Fortress, 1994), pp. 102–104. Locating the historical impetus for the composition of Lamentations within the context of the disaster of 587 BCE, Westermann contends that there was a period of oral transmission of these texts before they were written down in their (mainly) acrostic form. Proof for the oral phase rests in a) sentence structures which reflect original oral delivery, e.g., Lam 1:9c, 11c, and b) the pathos of the suffering in the book which could only have come from eyewitnesses. Still, the period of oral transmission could not have been a lengthy one since, he writes, "As many interpreters of Lamentations have discerned, the descriptions of the decimated city and its suffering inhabitants are often so vivid and gripping that they could only have come from eyewitnesses. This much is certain. Many voices, finding expression in diverse ways, echo throughout these laments. The initially chaotic, multi-voiced nature of such laments finds an impressive parallel in the Lamentation over the Destruction of Ur, with its frequent repetitions." Here and elsewhere in his volume the parallels discerned by Westermann are at once nearer and further away than he imagines. On the one hand, there are impressive continuities between the LU and Lamentations. On the other hand, it is certain that eyewitnesses to the destruction were not responsible for the LU or, for that matter, any of the other Sumerian city laments. It is no less likely that the same situation obtains for the author(s) of the Book of Lamentations.

editions of the older *balag*s and *eršemma*s, wherein metaphors and descriptions had already been stripped of specific historic referents and which, in turn, could be applied to national disasters— not excluding the destruction of the city and Temple—at any time in Israel's history. Alternatively, the presence of archaic and other features within some of the psalms—features discussed in the following chapters which remain difficult to explain if 587 BCE is the *terminus post quem* for their composition—suggest that the analogue proposed by Hallo is correct after all: the Hebrew compositions could have originally included historical references which, like those of the Mesopotamian counterparts, had already disappeared from the text prior to 587 BCE. This suggestion would naturally necessitate a reconsideration of the dating of the Hebrew communal laments, including especially Psalms 74 and 79 which are, as noted, widely regarded as originating shortly after the destruction of Jerusalem. It is, incidently, the presence of those same peculiar features, particularly in those two psalms, when coupled with the absence of specific historic references, that make unlikely the suggestion that the composition of these psalms took place in a period far removed from the events of 587 BCE such as the Maccabean era or, alternatively, that they underwent a final redaction at that time. The first alternative does not explain the lack of specific historic referents in these psalms—it simply projects the same problem into the Maccabean period—and the second proposal does not make understandable other parallels with the Mesopotamian materials. Nor does either of these propositions address what will prove to be archaic features of these materials, even assuming they were composed in 587 BCE.

One could, of course, reach another solution by simply dismissing a direct or indirect relationship between the two traditions: perceived similarities are said either to be accidental (Ferris's view), or it is claimed they represent Israel's indigenous version of the city lament genre (Dobbs-Allsopp). It is noteworthy, however, that Dobbs-Allsopp concerns himself with a comparative study of city-laments in the ancient Near East and what he perceives to be reflections of that in the Hebrew scriptures, especially in prophetic texts and the Book of Lamentations. He leaves open the possibility that a comparative investigation of the *balag*s and *eršemma*s with the communal laments in the Psalter might lend themselves to different results.[79] It is the present writer's contention that different conclusions are obtained when such a study is executed: parallels between the psalms and the *balag*s and *eršemma*s, not excluding the more general "organic transformation and creative adaptation" effecting each, prove significant. Indeed, the thesis of the present work is that those psalms which apparently treat the destruction of the Temple and Jerusalem are not specifically dependent on the events of 587 BCE for their inspiration but instead represent prayers which were patterned on, or perhaps specifically adopted from, older Mesopotamian *balag*s and *eršemma*s—and that some time prior to the destruction of Jerusalem by Babylon. This proposal, if sustainable, would explain the "organic transformation" of the psalms while still accounting for their other parallels with the *balag*s and *eršemma*s as well as the archaic features present in these psalms.

This thesis will be taken up in greater detail later in this study. It suffices for now to point out a further ramification of Hallo's "organic transformation and creative adaptation" concept. If the communal laments in the Psalter do represent an adaption or even an adoption of the Mesopotamian materials, one might anticipate that discerning that relationship would be complicated by the very process of "creative adaptation" by the Hebrew poets. That is, it would not be at all surprising to discover that part of the transformation process included not simply the sublimation of historical events so that the composition might be used in subsequent generations, but the incorporation of themes and motifs that are peculiar to the faith of Israel as well. Indeed, if nothing else, Israel's Yahwism demanded such a transformation.

As it turns out, Jeffrey Tigay has documented instances within the cuneiform scribal tradition where an identical principle was at work in the transmission of Mesopotamian epic materials into non-Mesopotamian hands. For purposes of clarity, this principle will be referred to as the "creative *adoption*" principle in order to distinguish it from Hallo's "creative *adaptation*" concept.[80] Clearly the two notions overlap. Both involve redactional activity in the text in order to "re-present" and contemporize it for its hearers or readers.

---

[79] Dobbs-Allsopp, *Weep, O Daughter of Zion*, p. 155, n. 246.

[80] Note, however, that neither Tigay nor Gütterbock, whose contributions are discussed below, use the term "creative adoption."

The difference between the two is that with Hallo's "organic trans-formation and creative adaptation" principle the emphasis rests on the adaptation of the text within a continuous culture or tradition. As we will see, however, the "creative adoption" principle attempts to describe what transpires when a literary text is borrowed and received by a second culture.

The Creative Adoption Principle

Recently, in a brief but pivotal article, Tigay has again taken up the difficult problem of evaluating claims of literary borrowing.[81] The criterion of cultural contact or, in his words, the "channels of transmission" he regards as established. The real difficulty, in his estimation, lies in the evaluation of the *content* of apparent literary borrowing. Scholars have reached an impasse: those who would advocate a literary relationship between Israel and other cultures, willing to accommodate some differences in detail and content, are countered by those who view those very differences as evidence that borrowing did not occur. Tigay sees a way out of this conun-drum through an "empirical approach," by which term he means the observation and study of the changes that take place in Meso-potamian texts that have multiple copies and translations. Since, however, the early symbiotic relationship between Sumerians and Akkadians *within* Mesopotamia often makes it impossible to dis-tinguish two separate cultures, he judges a study of the many in-teresting instances where Sumerian literature was borrowed into Akkadian as less helpful.[82] Tigay instead wants to know in what form Mesopotamian materials were known *outside* of Mesopotamia and "How much do the peripheral versions resemble the native Mesopotamian versions to which they are *indisputably* related?"[83] Discerning any changes between the Mesopotamian texts and those versions and translations discovered on the cultural boundaries

---

[81] Tigay, "Evaluating Claims," pp. 250–255.

[82] An exception to this difficulty is the clear case of adoption in the instance of *eršemma* 13 [NBC 1315 (RA 16 208) reverse 15–14], an Old Babylonian *eršemma* to Marduk copied into the first millennium. This *eršemma* appears as the eleventh and final *kirugu* of an Old Babylonian recension of *balag* 12, a *balag* of Enlil. Cf. Cohen, *SH*, p. 135.

[83] *Ibid.*, p. 253. Emphasis his.

would provide an analogue to the way in which Israel may have borrowed Mesopotamian literature.

In many respects, Tigay's "empirical approach" was anticipated almost forty years ago in a now-famous study by H.G. Gütterbock. Gütterbock's examination of Hittite prayers to Šamaš revealed, on the one hand, an abundant number of Babylonian elements present in the prayer [84] and, on the other hand, a series of concepts that were peculiar to the Hittite religion.[85] The combination of Babylonian and Hittite features results in a composition without exact parallel in Babylonian literature:

> It may be called a free composition for which the Hittite poet has taken a great deal of inspiration from Babylonia. He has made free use of these borrowed motifs, mixing them with others that are Hittite, and has thus produced a work of literature that, in spite of some rather clumsy repetitions, is not without force.[86]

The Hittite prayer to Šamaš, therefore, appears as clearly "Hittite" in character, including aspects of Hittite religion unique to that people. And yet, just as clearly, the Hittite text had a Babylonian precursor that served as a model. Gütterbock himself regarded the Hittite prayer as a concrete example of "the main characteristic of

---

[84] H.G. Gütterbock, "The Composition of Hittite Prayers to the Sun," *JAOS* 78 (1958), 241–242. Quite apart from the fact that the Hittite prayer follows a Babylonian pattern, Babylonian features identified by Gütterbock include the following: Šamaš is addressed as "lord of judgment" and he is called kind and merciful. Šamaš allots portions. He passes through the gates of heaven and illuminates the below and above. In both cultures Šamaš is described as having a lapis lazuli beard, as well as being the son of Ningal, the wife of Sin. Both Babylonian texts and the Hittite prayers include the statement that Enlil put the four corners of the world into his hands although, Gütterbock notes, the rule over the four corners of the earth is given to other deities in Babylon.

[85] *Ibid.* Unique to the Hittite prayers, Gütterbock reports, is the mention of group of deities called the Former Gods, the inclusion of animals (and especially of the dog and pig) among those persons whom the Sun deity judges, and the notion that man can feed the animals harnessed to the god's quadriga. Moreover, Gütterbock remarks, "the elements [of the prayer] are Babylonian as that of the personal god 'who turned his face elsewhere'; also prayers are found in which a great god is asked to order the personal god to be friendly again. But the idea that Shamash should find the god and transmit man's prayer to him is not known from Babylonian texts and thus seems to be a Hittite innovation."

[86] *Ibid.*

the Hittite civilization, namely, the way in which this people adapted and transformed elements of the high civilization of Mesopotamia according to its own way of thinking."[87] Gütterbock's observations make it clear, however, that the Hittites *adapted and transformed* these materials in order to *adopt* them as their own texts and traditions. And the *adoption* process involved creative innovation on the part of the Hittite poet: the form and the particulars of Babylonian prayers to Šamaš were modified so as to be more suitable for the Hittite's particular culture and religious understanding.

It is this process of creative adoption by means of adaptation and transformation of Mesopotamian texts in peripheral territories that interests Tigay. Although he is able to cite numerous examples of this phenomenon,[88] his particular focus, like Gütterbock before him, rests on those features of Hittite materials that differ from their Babylonian counterparts. Specifically, Tigay evaluates the Hittite version of the *Gilgamesh Epic* as compared to the Old Babylonian and Standard Babylonian versions of that same tale.[89] He notes that, while in general the Hittite account is an abridgment of the Mesopotamian versions, the episode describing the journey to the Cedar Mountain and its guardian Huwawa receives more attention in the Hittite text, presumably because that mountain's location was supposed to be near Anatolia and the events described there would be of more interest to Anatolian listeners or readers. Another Hittite distinction is the mention of the storm-god, popular among Hittites, who in their version was numbered among those who gifted Gilgamesh with his attributes at birth. This deity performs no such corresponding function in the Babylonian copies. Yet another theme which finds modification in the Hittite account concerns the early life of Gilgamesh's companion Enkidu. Unlike the Babylonian

---

[87] *Ibid.*, 245.

[88] Tigay, "Evaluating Claims," p. 253, mentions the omen series *Šumma Alu*, versions of *Nergal and Ereshkigal* found at Amarna and Sultantepe, fragments of the *Atrahasis Epic*, prayers to Ištar discovered in Anatolia, a trilingual hymn to Iškur-Adad, copies of *Anzu* found in Assyria, Sultantepe, and Susa, and versions of *Etana* from Assyria and Susa.

[89] For the following, see "Evaluating Claims," 254. Many of Tigay's observations regarding the changes in the Hittite version of *Gilgamesh* are drawn from his earlier study *The Evolution of the Gilgamesh Epic* (Philadelphia: University of Pennsylvania Press, 1982), especially pp. 110–129, and pp. 198–200.

versions, the Hittite text says nothing about Enkidu's hairiness, clothing, or nakedness; it shares with the Babylonian versions only the claim that Enkidu grazed and drank waters with the animals. Comparing the Old Babylonian, the Standard Babylonian, and the Hittite versions of the description of Enkidu's early life, Tigay states,

> It cannot be denied that these descriptions are related, since they are each other's counterparts in two versions of the same composition. But if we did not know that, and if we were to apply the exacting criteria exemplified in the arguments against borrowing . . . we might have to conclude instead that the two passages are independent crystallizations of the popular wolf-boy or hairy anchorite themes."[90]

The implications of Tigay's and Gütterbock's studies for the question of literary borrowing should not be dismissed. Both studies indicate that, on those occasions when scribes and poets on the peripheral areas of Mesopotamian influence adopted texts into their own tradition, they did so by simply abridging, expanding, or otherwise modifying the original material to better suit their own setting, local interest, and ideology.[91]

Did the Israelite authors similarly creatively adopt the texts of others, modifying those texts to suit their own interests and ide-

---

[90] *Ibid.* Cf. his *Evolution of the Gilgamesh Epic*, p. 204.

[91] The cuneiform texts from Emar provide yet another example. Besides evidencing a number of morphological, presumably dialectal variations (cf. Miguel Civil, "The Texts from Meskene-Emar," *Aula Orientalis* 7 (1989), 8), the texts from Emar reveal, as Hoskisson has observed, "a full range of possibilities, from seeming dependence on Old Babylonian tablets, through commonality with other peripheral Middle Babylonian texts, to similarities with the late lexical canon, and in most cases with indications of local scribal conceits. The literary texts with only one possible exception display knowledge of or dependence on parallel recensions of Mesopotamian canonical texts. Yet here again, the local scribes or scribal tradition in Emar did not slavishly ape the Sumero-Akkadian posited Vorlagen." Cf. Paul Y. Hoskisson, "Emar as an Empirical Model of the Transmission of Canon," in *The Biblical Canon in Comparative Perspective: Scripture in Context IV*, edit. by K. Lawson Younger, Jr., William W. Hallo, and Bernard F. Batto, ANETS, Vol. 11 (Lewiston, Edwin Mellon, 1991), p. 26. See also Claus Wilcke, "Die Emar-Version von "Dattelpalme und Tamariske"—ein Rekonstruktionsversuch," *ZA* 79 (1989), 161–190; Guy Bunnens, "Emar on the Euphrates in the 13th Century B.C.: Some Thoughts about Newly Published Cuneiform Texts," *AbrN* 27 (1989), 23–36.

ology? There is no intrinsic reason to suppose they did not, and examples exist to suggest that such was precisely the case for many biblical texts,[92] including some psalms.[93] Tigay summarizes:

> If these data appear to weaken the grounds for opposing claims of literary borrowing—and I believe that they do—then this has some unsettling implications. For it means that an alleged relationship between a Biblical text or motif and some ancient Near Eastern counterpart cannot be refuted simply by pointing to differences between the two, even if they are numerous.[94]

For the purposes of the present study, the principle of creative adoption indicates that differences between the Hebrew communal laments and those of Mesopotamia likewise do not necessarily indicate that borrowing from the latter to the former was unlikely. To the contrary, if borrowing took place, one would expect to find the incorporation of distinctively Israelite traditions within the laments, alongside Mesopotamian elements. This is especially so because, as another scholar has observed:

---

[92] One thinks in particular of the texts included in the Wisdom writings, and especially of Proverbs 22–24, as well as the various mythologies incorporated in Genesis. The latter, of course, remain a constant source of scholarly debate. Of the alleged parallels between the biblical and Mesopotamian primeval stories see the representative but opposing statements by Theodore Gaster, *Myth, Legend, and Custom in the Old Testament* (Harper & Row: New York and Evanston, 1969), p. xxvii, and A.R. Millard, "A New Babylonian 'Genesis' Story," *TynBul* 18 (1967), 17. See, also the more moderate discussion by Patrick D. Miller, Jr., "Eridu, Dunnu, and Babel: A Study in Comparative Mythology," *HAR* 9 (1985), 227–251, in which the similarities of Genesis 1–11 and the Eridu Genesis are discussed. Miller does not, however, claim a literary dependence of Genesis 1–11 on the Mesopotamian model. The burden of his article is instead to illustrate ways in which the biblical writer adopted the theogonic and cosmogonic elements and structures of the Mesopotamian tradition, as well as the first city tradition, while at the same time subordinating the older culture's emphasis on the antediluvian cities.

[93] For example, Psalm 29 which long ago was identified by H.L Ginsberg, *ktby 'wgryt* (Jerusalem: The Bialik Founday, 1936), p. 129ff., as an ancient hymn to Ba'al which had been adopted and modified for use in the Yahweh cult. Cf. Frank Moore Cross, *Canaanite Myth and Hebrew Epic* (Cambridge: Harvard University Press, 1973), pp. 151–159, esp. p. 152, n. 22, and the bibliography cited there. Other psalms where literary dependence seems probable include Psalms 19 and 104. On these psalms see Helmer Ringgren, "The Impact of the Ancient Near East on Israelite Tradition," in *Tradition and Theology in the Old Testament*, ed. by Douglas A. Knight (Philadelphia: Fortress, 1977), p. 39.

[94] Tigay, "Evaluating Claims," 254.

Above all it should be stressed that foreign ideas were never taken over unchanged but were adapted to suit their new Israelite context. The important task of research in this area, therefore, is to assess the Israelite use of the foreign material and the reinterpretation it underwent in the framework of Yahwistic religion.[95]

SUMMARY

The question is, of course, how does one critically examine the claims of literary borrowing? To be more specific, how does one measure the possibility of Israel's having borrowed the communal laments of Mesopotamia? The discussion above suggests that a satisfactory investigation involves a collocation of a number of factors. Opportunities for cultural contact and, hence, for the borrowing of literary traditions must be established, with special attention given, first, to the temporal and, second, to the geographic proximity of the respective texts. It is also requisite to focus attention on those materials in the two traditions that present similarity of content, form, and especially of *Gattung*, while keeping in mind the likelihood that if borrowing indeed took place the cultic use of lament materials likely also meant that transformation and adaptation took place both *within* the respective texts and *between* them as one culture adopted and transformed the literary traditions of another. Similitude in style and the presence of foreign words or concepts will factor in the latter consideration as they provide the raw material for a comparison of form and content. In short, what is sought is a general pattern of relationships that avoids both the errors inherent in the extremes of the pan-Semitic cultural perspective—and its attendant tendency towards "parallelomania"—and a one-sided insistence on ancient Israel's literary genius, conceived in such a way that Israel is viewed as pristinely removed from the culture and religions that surrounded it.

---

[95] Ringgren, "The Impact of the Ancient Near East," p. 46.

CHAPTER 3

THE MESOPOTAMIAN LAMENT TRADITIONS

COMMUNAL LAMENTS AND THE CRITERION OF COMPARABILITY.

The criterion of comparability, discussed in the last chapter, holds that if literature from two or more cultures are to be compared, the most fruitful comparisons will be made between like types or genres of literature. Therefore, before any attempt can be made to analyze the Mesopotamian *balag/eršemma* compositions and the communal laments in the Hebrew Book of Psalms, one must first necessarily discern the characteristic components of each. The present chapter will discuss the distinguishing features of the *balag/eršemma* in an effort to develop a descriptive grid or typology which, in turn, will aid in the comparative process. Since, however, the *balag/eršemma* texts appear to be the literary progeny of the slightly older Sumerian city laments, it remains incumbent first to call to mind what is known about these other Mesopotamian texts.

THE SUMERIAN CITY LAMENTS: "VORLÄUFER" OF BALAGS AND ERŠEMMAS

Most of the five primary examples of the Sumerian literary genre known as the city lament[1] have now been published in critical editions:

---

[1] For a general introduction to the discovery and significance of Sumerian literature as well as the types of literature so far uncovered see Samuel Noah Kramer, "Sumerian Literature and the Bible," in *AnBib*, Vol. 12; Studia Biblical et Orientalia, Vol. 3 (Rome: Pontificio Istituto Biblico, 1959), pp. 185–204. *idem*, "CT XLII: A Review

Lamentation over the Destruction of Ur[2] (LU)
Lamentation over the Destruction of Sumer and Ur[3] (LSUr)
Lamentation over the Destruction of Nippur[4] (LN)
The Eridu Lament[5] (EL)
The Uruk Lament[6] (UL)

Article," *JCS* 18 (1964), 35–48; "Sumerian Literature: A General Survey," in *The Bible and the Ancient Near East: Essays in Honor of William Foxwell Albright,* ed. by G. Ernest Wright (2nd ed.; Winona Lake: Eisenbrauns, 1979), pp. 249–266; and, more recently, Thorkild Jacobsen, *The Harps that Once . . . : Sumerian Poetry in Translation* (New Haven; London: Yale University Press, 1987), pp. xi–xiv. One should also note the important essay by H.L.J. Vanstiphout, "Some Thoughts on Genre in Mesopotamian Literature," in *Keilschriftliche Literaturen. Ausgewählte Vorträge der XXXII. Rencontre assyriologique internationale. Münster, 8.-12.7.1985,* ed. by K. Hecker and W. Sommerfeld (Berliner Beiträge zum Vorderen Orient, 6; Berlin: Dietrich Reimer, 1986), pp. 1–11, where that author catalogues the main specific difficulties in Mesopotamian literature from the perspective of genre analysis and hints at ways a systematic approach to the generic system(s) of the literature could be initiated, i.e., via historically oriented genre criticism.

[2] S.N. Kramer, *Lamentation over the Destruction of Ur,* Assyriological Studies, Vol. 12 (Chicago: University of Chicago Press, 1940); "Lamentation over the Destruction of Ur," in *ANET*[3], ed. by James B. Pritchard (3rd ed.; Princeton: Princeton University, 1969), pp. 455–463. In addition one can find a complete and beautiful translation of this lament in Jacobsen's *The Harps that Once . . . ,* pp. 447–474.

[3] S.N. Kramer, "Lamentation over the Destruction of Sumer and Ur," *ANET,* pp. 611–619; Piotr Michalowski, *The Lamentation over the Destruction of Sumer and Ur* (Winona Lake: Eisenbrauns, 1989). LSUr includes those texts formerly referred to as the Second Lamentation of Ur, the Lamentation over the Destruction of Sumer and Akkad, and the Ibbi-Sin Lamentation, all of which have been shown to be a part of a single composition. See Michalowski (pp. 3–4) or Kramer (*ANET*[3], p. 612 and n. 9) for a summary of the history of research and the relevant bibliography. In addition, see C.J. Gadd and S.N. Kramer *Literary and Religious Texts, Ur Excavation Texts, 6, Part 2* (London: British Museum, 1966), p. 1, who have demonstrated the joins and thus the unity of the texts.

[4] A critical edition of this text has yet to be published although one has been promised by H.L.J. Vanstiphout. A portion of the text can be found in Dietz Otto Edzard, *Die Zweite Zwischenzeit Babyloniens* (Wiesbaden: O. Harrassowitz, 1957), pp. 86–90. For a description of the contents, however, see S.N. Kramer, "Sumerian Literary Texts from Nippur in the Museum of the Ancient Orient at Istanbul," AASOR, no. 23 (New Haven: American Schools of Oriental Research, 1943–44), 34, and especially, "Lamentation over the Destruction of Nippur: A Preliminary Report," *ErIsr* 9 (1969), 90–93.

[5] M.W. Green, "The Eridu Lament," *JCS* 30 (1978), 127–167.

[6] M.W. Green, "The Uruk Lament," *JAOS* 104 (1984), 253–279.

A sixth text, "The Curse of Agade," (CA) is sometimes included in discussions of Sumerian city laments. Michalowsky, *The Lamentation,* pp. 5–6, for example, argues that the precursor for LSUr was CA: "The switch of accent, from guilty to innocent protagonist, from curse upon the destroyed city to a curse upon those who fulfilled

There exists a growing scholarly consensus relative to the origin and history of these laments.[7] During the twenty-fourth year of the reign of Ibbi-Sin, the last king of the Third Dynasty of Ur, established some one hundred years previously by Ur-Nammu, the city of Ur fell under the onslaught of an army from the east (Elam and Simaski). The exact causes and effects which precipitated the kingdom's gradual erosion of power are difficult to gauge;[8] already

---

the destiny pronounced by the gods and who took part in the destruction of Sumer, is a fundamental element in the relationship between the two compositions and is the key to the intertextual nature of this type of writing. LSUr cannot really be understood without recourse to CA, for the relationship between the two is truly dialectical with mutual contradictions bound to similarities." Nevertheless, the scholarly community generally judges CA to be uniquely historiographic and not properly a sixth city lament. Cf. Jerrold S. Cooper, *The Curse of Agade* (Johns Hopkins Near Eastern Studies; Baltimore: Johns Hopkins University, 1983), pp. 20–28; M. Lambert, "La littérature sumérienne à propos d'ouvrages récents," *RA* 56 (1962), 81–82; S.N. Kramer, *The Sumerians: Their History, Culture, and Character* (Chicago: University of Chicago, 1963), pp. 62–66; "The Curse of Agade," *ANET*[3], p. 646; A. Falkenstein, "Fluch über Agade," *ZA* 57 (1965), 43ff..

Cohen, *CLAM*, p. 34 and n. 97, points out that CA contains several lines in common with the *balag*s: 152 = *u⁴-dam ki àm-ús*, line 15 (and others); 212–214 are similar to the recurring theme as found in *am-e am aš-a-na*, lines 83–84; 219 is somewhat similar to *am-e am aš-a-na*, line 134; 244 occurs in *e-lum gu⁴-súm-e*, line 14; 234–238 are paralleled in *abzu pe-el-lá-àm*, lines 109–111. In spite of these affinities, however, and unlike his assessment of the other Sumerian city laments, Cohen does not believe that this standard (*emigir*) composition served as a direct antecedent to the *balag* laments.

7 For an overview of the Sumerian city laments and their history, see S.N. Kramer, "The Weeping Goddess: Sumerian Prototypes of the *Mater Dolorosa*," *BA* 46 (1983), 69–72. The summary above is drawn from those pages as well as Thorkild Jacobsen, "Review of *Lamentation over the Destruction of Ur* by Samuel N. Kramer," *AJSL* 58 (1941), 219–224; *The Harps that Once . . .*, pp. 147–148; Michalowski, *The Lamentation*, pp. 1–3; William W. Hallo, *Origins: The Ancient Near Eastern Background of Some Modern Western Institutions*, edited by B. Halpern and Weippert M.H.E. Studies in the History and Culture of the Ancient Near East, vol. 6 (Leiden: E.J. Brill, 1996), 224–25; *idem*, "Lamentations and Prayers in Sumer and Akkad," in *Civilizations of the Ancient Near East*, vol. 3, ed. by J.M. Sasson (New York: Scribners, 1995), 1871–74.

8 Several theories have been forwarded. Cf. Thorkild Jacobsen, "The Reign of Ibbi-Suen," *JCS* 7 (1953), 36–47; W.W. Hallo, "A Sumerian Amphictiony," *JCS* 14 (1960), 88–114; and T. Gomi, "On the Critical Economic Situation at Ur Early in the Reign of Ibbisin," *JCS* 36 (1984), 211–242. Michalowski, citing P. Steinkeller, "The Administrative and Economic Organization of the Ur III State: The Core and the Periphery," in *The Organization of Power: Aspects of Bureaucracy in the Ancient Near East*, ed. by M. Gibson and R.D. Biggs (Chicago: Oriental Institute of the University of Chicago, 1987), pp. 19–41, believes the root cause rested in a decline begun already in Ibbi-Sin's predecessor, Šu-Sin, and his structuring of the state, rather than external forces. Recently, Robert McC. Adams, "Contexts of Civilizational Collapse: A Mesopotamian

in the reigns of Ibbi-Sin's two predecessors, however, there are reports of serious incursions by nomadic Amorites from the Syro-Arabian desert. Whatever the precise circumstances of Ur's fall, it is clear that shortly afterward Ishbi-Erra, a former underling of Ibbi-Sin, founded a new dynasty at Isin. Once the invaders had with-

---

View," in *The Collapse of Ancient States and Civilizations,* ed. by Norman Yoffee and George L. Cowgill (Tucson: University of Arizona, 1988), pp. 20–43, has suggested a more multiplex paradigm for understanding the rise and fall of Mesopotamian civilizations, including a consideration of "patterns of differentiation in productivity, security, population density, resource potential, and many other variables that preceded urbanism" (p. 31). In a companion essay appearing in that same volume, Norman Yoffee, "The Collapse of Ancient Mesopotamian States and Civilization," pp. 44–68, argues more generally against the idea that cultural heterodoxy accounts for the demise of Mesopotamian civilizations.

The least likely explanation for the demise of Ur III, however, is the theory offered by H.L.J. Vanstiphout, "The Death of an Era: The Great Mortality in the Sumerian City Laments," in *Death in Mesopotamia: Papers Read at the XXVIe Rencontre assyriologique internationale,* ed. by B. Alster (Copenhagen: Akademisk Forlag, 1980), pp. 83–89 (cf. *idem,* "Was een Pestepidemie de Oorzaak van de Ondergang van het Nieuw-sumerische Rijk?" *Phoenix* 20 [1974], 351–370), who argues that the effects of the devastating "storm" described in both the LU as well as in the LSUr ought to be interpreted as a "combination of drought, famine, and an epidemic, leading up to the foreign invasions" (p. 86). Vanstiphout believes that a reference to drought and famine can be discerned in the second song of LSUr where canals are said to be silted up (line 224). He argues further that the sixth *kirugu* of LU indicates that the bubonic plague came upon Ur: the description of dead bodies in the city that "lay (spread-eagled) head over shoulders, although they had not taken strong drink" point to apparent drunkenness generally and specifically connected with the loss of control of the nervous system over the muscles—two symptoms of the plague. The fact that these bodies "were like fish whose water is taken away" (line 229) and were found mostly in elevated places suggests to him the breathing difficulties associated with the plague. Vanstiphout tentatively associates "Those afflicted by the Weapon, the Weapon did kill" with the characteristic *bubo* of the plague. Finally, the swiftness of the plague left no time for the care of victims, a circumstance indicated by LU line 219–223 (p. 87). The storm metaphor was, in his view, generated by a short wet period which must have come upon Ur after a prolonged drought; this wet period enhanced the virulence of the plague.

In fairness to Vanstiphout it should be noted that he does not see the outbreak of plague as the *only* cause of the downfall of the Ur III empire. But, he points out, "there are enough features of the description of what happened to say that the plague may have been *one* of the factors of the catastrophe, along with famine, drought, internal upheavals and almost inviting foreign invasions" (p. 88). Against all this, however, it seems that Vanstiphout makes too much out of what, after all, may be no more than poetic metaphor. It is instructive to consider, by way of contrast, that not all the city laments utilize the storm metaphor: the destruction at Uruk is wrought by a divinely

drawn, Ishbi-Erra's son, Shu-ilishu, began the restoration of Ur, which work continued through his successors Iddin-Dagan and Ishme-Dagan. The work, it seems, was completed in the latter's reign. It was sometime between the fall of Ur (2004 BCE) and its restoration—the usually accepted *terminus ante quem* is 1925 BCE[9]—that the city laments were composed. Because of to the vivid memory within LU, Edzard thinks that composition was written within a generation of the events described;[10] Kramer makes the same claim

---

fashioned monster (cf. *kirugu* 1 and 2), the effect of whose assault is described as the onslaught of flood, war, and storm, all in cosmic proportion (cf. *kirugu* 3. 1–21). Nothing in this lament would seem to suggest a plague. Nor, frankly, does any of the evidence adduced by Vanstiphout seem definitely to indicate a record of pestilence. A similar evaluation of Vanstiphout's thesis has been expressed by Robert M. Martinez, "Epidemic Disease, Ecology, and Culture in the Ancient Near East," in *The Bible in the Light of Cuneiform Literature. Scripture in Context III* ed. by William W. Hallo, Bruce William Jones, and Gerald L. Mattingly, ANETS, Vol. 8 (Lewiston: Edwin Mellen, 1990), pp. 437–444. Martinez remarks: "Vanstiphout's ideas, though interesting, are at variance with the known manifestations of the disease" (p. 437). Specifically Martinez notes that the description of the location of the bodies in LU, lines 218–219, follow the description of the enemy's breach of the walls and, consequently, "death at the hand of the enemy is a reasonable interpretation" (p. 438). Moreover Kramer's translation of line 229 ("like fish were carried off by the waters," *ANET*[3], p. 459), though contrasting with Vanstiphout's rendering ("were like fish whose water was taken away," "Death of an Era," p. 86), implies no breathing difficulties, and, in any event, dehydration was not a major symptom of the plague. Martinez also takes issue with Vanstiphout's interpretation of the Weapon, noting that the description, which follows a description of deaths by spear and battle mace is better taken literally. Against Vanstiphout's suggestion that the swiftness of the plague left no time for the care of victims, Martinez responds that the texts give no hint of those symptoms characteristic of pneumonic or acute septicemic plague, yet only these two forms of plague even approach lending credence to Vanstiphout's thesis. Also medically inaccurate is Vanstiphout's claim that a period of long drought interrupted by a short wet period increases the virulence of plague and that nomads would therefore be less susceptible. Martinez summarizes: "However, even if Vanstiphout is correct in his reading of disease symptoms into the poetry of the city laments, the constellation of symptoms described are not unambiguously those of black plague. There is, therefore, no reasonable basis on which to conclude that the black plague contributed to the downfall of Ur III" (p. 444).

[9] W.C. Gwaltney, "The Biblical Book of Lamentations in the Context of Near Eastern Lament Literature," in *More Essays on the Comparative Method: Scripture in Context II*, ed. by William W. Hallo, J.C. Moyer, and L.G. Perdue (Winona Lake: Eisenbrauns, 1983), p. 196. Cf. Cohen, *Balag-compositions*, p. 9.

[10] Edzard, *Zwischenzeit*, p. 57: "Die Entstehung der Ur-Klage ist kaum später als eine Generation nach dem Ereignis anzusetzen."

for both LU and LSUr.[11] Two of the remaining three laments have been associated with the regnal years of Ishme-Dagan, mentioned by name in the Uruk Lament (12.9) as well as LN (*kirugu* 6). The Eridu Lament is somewhat more problematic, since Ishme-Dagan is not cited in the text. Nevertheless, Green also locates the Eridu Lament within that king's reign, based on the text's affinities with other city laments.[12]

But areas of consensus reach well beyond the dating of the materials. Scholars are also largely agreed on the purpose, character, and subsequent history of these city laments. In general terms, the following can be affirmed:

1. The lamentations describe particular historical events, namely, the destruction of Sumer's major cities.[13]
2. The lamentations were associated with the *emesal* dialect of Sumerian,[14] a dialect which has been particularly connected to the rituals of the *gala*-priests.[15]

---

[11] Kramer, "Weeping Goddess," 71. Jacobsen at one point appeared willing to have left the date of LU's composition within the seventy to eighty year window between Ur's destruction and its final restoration under Ishme-Dagan ("Review," 221). More recently, however, he seems to have fallen in line with Edzard and Kramer in viewing LU as having "been written soon after the events it records, while they were yet fresh in memory" (*The Harps that Once . . .*, p. 447).

Vanstiphout, "Genre in Mesopotamian Literature," pp. 7–8, confirms the historical priority of LU and LSUr from a different perspective. He sees LU and LSUr as representing a primary or aggregation phase of genre development when all features of a genre assemble and a formal type emerges. The remaining three laments occupy what he describes as the secondary or classical phase which "shows the format resulting from the primary state as an almost mandatory, normative prescription for composing new texts consciously after a given and approved model."

[12] Green, "Eridu," 129–130.

[13] Cohen, *balag*, p. 11; *CLAM*, p. 38; cf. W.C. Gwaltney, "The Biblical Book of Lamentations," p. 196.; Ferris, *Genre*, pp. 48–50.

[14] Note, however, that whether all the city laments were written in *emesal* rather than the "main" dialect of *emegir* remains a point of dispute between Kutscher (*Oh Angry Sea*, p. 3) and Cohen (*balag*, p. 11); the latter appears to have modified his earlier position somewhat inasmuch as he states in his more recent *CLAM* (p. 38) that LSUr, UL, and EL are in standard *emegir* rather than *emesal*. On the *emesal* dialect, see Joachim Krecher, *Sumerische Kultlyrik* (Wiesbaden: Otto Harrassowitz, 1966), pp. 12–14.

[15] For the relationship of *emesal* compositions to the liturgies of the *gala* priests see Cohen, *SH*, p. 4; *idem*, *CLAM*, pp. 13–14. See also F. Thureau-Dangin, *Rituels accadiens* (Paris: E. Leroux, 1921), p. 1.

3. The lamentations were composed and recited for a specific occasion, namely, the razing of Ur and Nippur sanctuaries in anticipation of their restoration.[16]

4. The lamentations incorporate a political ideology which finds expression in both positive and negative terms. Negatively, the destruction of Sumer is explained as a consequence of divine decision, unrelated to human behavior,[17] which included the abandonment by the deities of their various temples.[18] As Green has pointed out, however, the laments are not filled with an attitude of hopelessness: the city laments proclaim the

---

[16] Cohen, *balag*, p. 11; *idem*, *CLAM*, p. 39 Cf. Jacobsen, "Review," 223; William W. Hallo, "The Cultic Setting of Sumerian Poetry," in *Actes de la XVIIe Rencontre Assyriologique Internationale* (Ham-sur-Heure: Universite Libre de Bruxelles, 1970), p. 119; Kutscher, *Oh Angry Sea*, p. 6.

[17] Green, "The Uruk Lament," 253. Cf. LSUr 359–379 where the focus is on divine causation and the human factor is disregarded entirely.

[18] E.g., LU 1–39, 237–238, 373–384; LSUr 58–64, 115–284, 370, 373–376, 475–477; EL 1:11–15, 5:1–2, 6:2'–27', 7:1–83a; UL 2:21'–26'; LN 80–81, 89, 208–209, 214; CA 60–65, 67–76, 209. On the theme of divine abandonment in Mesopotamia see Albrektson, *History and the Gods*, pp. 24–41, 98–114; Mordechai Cogan, *Imperialism and Religion: Assyria, Judah, and Israel in the Eighth and Seventh Centuries B.C.E.* (Missoula: Scholars Press, 1974), pp. 9–21; J.J.M. Roberts, "Nebuchadnezzar I's Elamite Crisis in Theological Perspective," in *Essays on the Ancient Near East in Memory of Jacob Joel Finkelstein*, ed. by Maria de Jong Ellis, Memoirs of the Connecticut Academy of Arts and Sciences, Vol. 19 (Hamden: Archon Books 1977), pp. 183–187; Patrick D. Miller, Jr. and J.J.M. Roberts, *Hand of the Lord: A Reassessment of the "Ark Narrative" of I Samuel* (Baltimore: Johns Hopkins University Press, 1977), pp. 9–17, 41–43; Daniel Isaac Block, *The Gods of the Nations: Studies in Ancient Near Eastern National Theology* (Jackson: Evangelical Theological Society, 1988), pp. 125–161. Block points out, p. 132, that in LU, 230ff., "The abandonment of the city is the consequence, not the cause of its destruction." But Block makes too much of this chronology: the reticence of the goddess to leave expressed earlier in the composition seems more likely to involve a literary device designed to enhance the pathos of the city's destruction. And, in any event, the lament *begins* with a lengthy recitation of the lists of those cities which have been abandoned by their gods. More correct is the following assessment of the meaning of divine abandonment from Peter Machinist, "Literature as Politics: the Tukulti-Ninurta Epic and the Bible," *CBQ* 38 (1976), 464, comparing the Sumerian laments to the Tukulti-Ninurta Epic: "Earlier, as the Sumerian city lamentations illustrate, the motif in whatever form appeared in compositions of disaster victims—of poets trying to explain why their cities, sanctuaries, or lands suffered political collapse and devastations. For them, in short, disaster was on the way when their gods left. The Epic, however, is the work of a victor, aiming to justify and explain his king's conquest. For him, victory is on the way when the gods of the enemy abandon that enemy." For a recent discussion of the theme of divine abandonment in relationship to the city laments, see Dobbs-Allsopp, *Weep, O Daughter of Zion*, pp. 45–51.

royal accomplishments in the reconstruction of Sumer, urging the deities to return home and to bless, and thereby legitimate, the current king.[19]

5. The lamentations were not reused in subsequent ceremonies but were immediately retired to the scribal curriculum whence they were copied until the first millennium.[20]

It should be added that there is general agreement in taking the five lamentations as constituting a genre.[21] As Green has summarized:

> The two pivotal issues of the laments, the collapse and revival of Sumer, are presented in five major themes: destruction, assignment of responsibility, abandonment, restoration, and return. Each of the five known city laments follows this general thematic pattern, with individual differences in focus and elaboration.[22]

---

[19] Cf. Green, "The Uruk Lament," 253. Michalowski, *Lamentation*, p. 6, describes the situation thus: "The dynasty founded by the *homo novus* Isbi-Erra at Isin had little claim to traditional forms of ideological legitimization. Moreover, new historical circumstances required a claim of continuity with the state that had just toppled—the 'empire' ruled from Ur. To create the fiction that Isbi-Erra and his followers were the true sovereigns of Sumer and Akkad, his scribes imitated the style of Ur III propaganda and composed literary texts that stressed connections with the successors of Ur-Namma."

[20] Gwaltney, "Lamentations," p. 196; cf. Kutscher, *Oh Angry Sea*, p. 6.

[21] This in spite of objections by Jeremy A. Black, "A-še-er Gi₆-ta, a Balag of Inana," *ASJ* 7 (1985), 13, and Michalowski, *The Lamentation*, pp. 5–6. The latter scholar writes: "From the formal point of view the texts that have been grouped together under the label of "city laments" are not homogeneous. Except for the fact that they depict in great detail the fall and destruction of cities and states, as well as a decision by the gods to undo the disaster, they have little in common. All the known examples are divided into sections called *kirugu* but the number and size of these sections differ in individual compositions, although the fragmentary state of *LE* [= EL, W.C.B.] and *LW* [=UL, W.C.B.] makes it difficult to generalize in this matter." Michalowski's observations serve as a helpful reminder that the determination of genre depends on the identification of similarities between texts on many levels. Tremper Longman III, *Fictional Akkadian Autobiography*, p. 13, notes that the similarities to be considered are not only features of the outer form (e.g., the structure of the text and the metrical or nonmetrical speech rhythm), but also those non-formal characteristics such as mood, setting, function, narrative voice, and content. Longman calls the latter the "inner form" of the genre. It is the interpreter's artful assimilation of similarities between texts on these two levels that constitutes the work of genre identification. Obviously this also means that a certain subjectivity in the elucidation of genre remains inescapable since "genre exists at all levels of generality" and "the make-up and nature of a particular genre depend on the viewpoint the critic adopts" (p. 11).

[22] Green, "The Uruk Lament," 253. Cf. also M.W. Green, "Eridu in Sumerian Literature," (Ph.D. dissertation, University of Chicago, 1975), pp. 277–325, where she provides a typology of the Sumerian laments.

These themes, as well as the lament mode, persisted in literature which subsequently evolved from the larger city laments already in the Old Babylonian period, namely the important *balag* and *eršemma* compositions. These two forms are directly related to the Sumerian city laments, bearing both outer and inner formal similarity to them and, evidently, having been inspired by them. They should, in fact, be considered as subgenres of the city lament.[23]

The generic relationship of *balag*s and *eršemma*s is born out by the following considerations.

Temporal Continuity

The city laments appear to be the inspiration for the *balag* and *eršemma* laments, the latter two forms having appeared just subsequent to the former. According to Cohen, *balag* compositions emerged around 1900 BCE as a literary outgrowth of the (slightly) older city laments. He subjectively judges the *eršemma* materials to be modestly more ancient than the *balag*, supposing that the compact focused structure of the former compositions is more original than the lengthy, rambling quality of the latter.[24] Nevertheless, since in some cases entire *eršemma*s have been incorporated as *kirugu*s of Old Babylonian and first millennium BCE recensions of *balag*s, there is no way to determine which direction the borrowing went or even if the borrowing took place in both directions.[25] What can be determined is that the *balag*s and *eršemma*s, already closely identified with one another in the Old Babylonian period, came to be formally joined for purposes of recitation or cultic use during the Middle Babylonian period. Cohen observes:

> During the Middle Babylonian period the two genres [*balag* and *eršemma*] had apparently been so closely identified with each other, presumably on the basis of ritual function, that each *balag* was assigned one *eršemma* as its new conclusion. The *eršemma* was

---

[23] Longman, *Fictional Akkadian Autobiography*, p. 11, suggests that the term sub-genre be employed for narrower genres, i.e., those texts sharing more specific traits, in contradistinction to those broader common features found in texts. Following this suggestion, it is appropriate to speak of the Sumerian city lament genre as encompassing the various so-called city laments as well as the *balag*s and *eršemma*s, while the latter two type compositions are subgenres of the broader classification.

[24] Cohen, *SH*, p. 37.

[25] *Ibid.*

then reworked, adopting a second concluding unit which contained the plea to the heart of the god and the concomitant [*sic*] list of deities, although this list was drastically reduced in size from the final *kirugu* of the Old Babylonian lamentation.[26]

Evidence that this joining did occur during the Middle Babylonian period consists of the fact that while the Old Babylonian period has no examples of catalogues in which a *balag* is joined to an *eršemma*,

by the time of the editing of the neo-Assyrian catalogue for the library of Asshurbanipal, however, the coupling of an *eršemma* with a *balag* had already occurred (though not every *balag* was assigned an *eršemma* and not every *eršemma* was assigned to a *balag*).[27]

Whatever the causes accounting for the joining of these two subgenres, (Cohen's suggestion that its basis was ritual function seems likely), it is clear that by the first millennium BCE, many of the *eršemma*s came to be understood as appendages to *balag* lamentations and, therefore, in some sense constituted a single unit.[28] Supporting this is the fact that from the neo-Assyrian period down through the Seleucid era, whenever a ritual text joins the *balag* and *eršemma* compositions, the lamentation is called *ér* and the joined text is called *eršemma* and, further, it is only after the *eršemma* that the colophon indicates that the *balag* is finished.[29] This circumstance led Thorkild Jacobsen to suggest that in the first millennium the term *balag* may have designated the combination of *ér* and *eršemma*, though in some instances the *eršemma* does not appear.[30]

---

[26]Cohen, *balag*, p. 9. Cf. J.A. Black, "Sumerian Balag Compositions," *BO* 44/1,2 (1987), 35.

[27]Cohen, *CLAM*, p. 43.

[28]Nevertheless, not all *eršemma*s were appended to *balag*s. Catalogue *4R² 53* (= K_1 in Cohen *SH*), for example, in which column i lists the incipits of *balag*s and column ii the incipits of the corresponding *eršemma*s, also includes third column, labeled *kidudû*, which lists *eršemma*s which are unrelated to *balag* lamentations. Several of the *eršemma*s appear in both columns ii as well as column iii, but a number appear in column iii only. Thus, it appears, the *kidudû eršemma* could find use in various cultic rites apart from the *balag*. Cf. Cohen, *SH*, pp. 42–43. For a discussion of *4R² 53* in relationship to Cohen's numbering, as well as corrections of the latter, see Black, "Sumerian Balag Compositions," 32, n. 1.

[29]Cohen, *CLAM*, p. 43.

[30]Thorkild Jacobsen, "Review of *Lamentation over the Destruction of Ur* by Samuel N. Kramer," *AJSL* 58 (1941), 223. Cf. Cohen, *CLAM*, p. 43. Green, "Eridu,"

Structure and Form

The five aforementioned city laments are divided into structural units labeled *kirugu* and *gišgigal*. The exact significance of these terms remains a mystery.[31] Nevertheless it does not appear coincidental that Old Babylonian *balag*s are also divided into units labeled *kirugu* and at least one text, which seems likely to be an Old Babylonian *balag* to Dumuzi,[32] contains a *gišgigal* unit. Given the fact that Sumerian compositions containing *kirugu* and *gišgigal* units are limited almost exclusively to laments,[33] it seems likely that the Old Babylonian *balag*s did in fact evolve from the Sumerian city laments. Nor were the structural conventions lost during the long period of textual transmission. The neo-Assyrian *balag*s, while lacking the term *kirugu*, have instead an incised heavy line drawn across the tablet which appears to correspond to the *kirugu* of the Old Babylonian texts.[34] Moreover, the neo-Assyrian *balag*s frequently include a one-line section, also set off by heavy lines,[35] which Cohen has

---

pp. 282–283, suggests that *ir/ér* might be the term that designates the genre to which the city laments belong, but then dismisses the idea as unlikely. Cf. Ferris, *Genre*, pp. 18–19, for a partial listing of twenty-two entries of laments prefixed with *ir/ér* extrapolated from a text of Tiglath-pileser I. See also B. Landsberger, *Materials for the Sumerian Lexicon*, ed. by M. Civil, vol. 13, pp. 222–223.

31 C. Wilcke, "Formale Gesichtspunkte in der sumerischen Literatur," *AS*, Vol. 20 (Chicago: University of Chicago, 1975), p. 285f., discusses the various rubrics, as does A. Falkenstein, "Sumerische religiöuse Texte," *ZA* 49 (1950), 84–105. Nevertheless Cohen, *CLAM*, p. 29, reports that there is as yet no satisfactory meaning for Sumerian *ki-ru-gú*, a term which appears in the Sumerian city laments as well. Lacking any common or unique structure, the *kirugu* is "either an arbitrary title for the unit of a *balag*, an instruction on how to recite the unit or, perhaps, an act to be performed between the recitation of *balag* sections." *Gišgigal*, on the other hand, may signify a choral term; it is frequently translated "antiphony." Cf. Green, "Eridu," pp. 283–286.

32 CT 42, no. 15. Cf. Cohen, *CLAM*, p. 31.

33 Cohen, *CLAM*, p. 34, can identify just three texts which are not laments but which also contain *kirugu* and *gišgigal* units: TCL 15, no. 8, a Dumuzi work which he regards as almost surely a *balag*; a *širnamgala* published in UET 6/1 96 and 97 which contains the units in question as well as another type called a *šabatuk*; CT 36, pl. 28–30, a hymn to Inanna on behalf of Ur-Ninurta, king of Isin. A translation of the last mentioned text appears in A. Falkenstein and W. von Soden, *Sumerische und akkadische Hymnen und Gebete* (Zürich: Artemis-Verlag, 1953), pp. 105–109.

34 J.A. Black, "Sumerian Balag Compositions," 35.

35 Cohen, *CLAM*, p. 28 and n. 78. The line in question reads *ma-a a-ba u_4-me-na-gin$_7$ ma-a-a-di-di-in* which appears in $4R^2$53 *balag*s 1, 3, 5, 11, 13, 24, 26, 31, 48, and 50. Only *balag*s 5 and 57 from the Old Babylonian period contain this line.

tentatively associated with the typically brief *gišgigal* sections of the city laments.[36]

Equally significant to the shared skeletal structure is the fact that both the *balag* and *eršemma* lamentations, like LU and LN, were predominantly written in *emesal*, a dialect of Sumerian peculiar to the *gala* priest which, evidently, was regarded as particularly fitting for lamentations.[37] Indeed, the catalogue of *emesal* writings (4R²53) compiled for Asshurbanipal's library in the mid-seventh century BCE includes a notation in the colophon to the effect that the *emesal* literature there listed was the province of the *gala* priests. Likewise the colophons of *emesal* texts associate the *gala* priesthood with *emesal* compositions in first millennium Uruk and in Old Babylonian Mari. In the latter text a *gala* priest is instructed to recite an *emesal* composition.[38] Moreover, while information about the religious duties of the *gala* priest during the third and second millennium remains otherwise scarce,[39] the priesthood's association with *emesal* texts is confirmed both by the frequent references to the *gala* priests in the *emesal* texts themselves as well as the fact that *gala* priests are known to have played the *balag*, an instrument associated with the *emesal* literature.[40] Given the close association of *emesal* with the *balag/*

---

[36] *Ibid.*, p. 31.

[37] Krecher, *Kultlyrik*, pp. 12–14, Cohen, *balag*, p. 32, Green, "Eridu," pp. 288–289, and Hallo, "Lamentations and Prayers, p. 1872, also provide discussions of this dialect. The latter scholar reports that "'*Emesal*' (literally 'thin' or 'attenuated speech'). . . . was affected, in literary texts, by women or goddesses and by the liturgical singers (GALA = *kalû*) who specialized in reciting lamentations."

[38] G. Dossin, "Un rituel du culte d'Istar," *RA* 35 (1938), 1–13. Cf. Joachim Krecher, *Sumerische Kultlyrik*, p. 34; Cohen, *SH*, pp. 40–41; *idem*, *CLAM*, p. 13. Cohen, who corrects Dossin's reading of the cuneiform, believes that the text is the only extant Old Babylonian text detailing the cultic implementation of the *eršemma*.

[39] Cf. Cohen, *SH*, pp. 4–6, and *CLAM*, pp. 13–14, for a discussion of what little further evidence is available.

[40] Most likely the *balag* instrument was a drum. Cf. v "*balaggu*," *CAD*; Cohen, *balag*, p. 31 (excursus on the *balag*-instrument); F.W. Galpin, *The Music of the Sumerians and Their Immediate Successors, the Babylonians and Assyrians*. (Cambridge: University Press, 1937), pp. 2–7, and plates II and III. See, however, Hallo, *Origins*, p. 226, who understands the instrument to have been a harp or lyre. On the other hand, the instrument associated with the performance of the *eršemma*, the ŠEM (= Akkadian *halhallatu*) has not been securely identified. S. Langdon, *Babylonian Liturgies* (Paris: Paul Geuthner, 1913), p. xxxii, understands the instrument to have been a double flute. *CAD*, "*halhallatu*," associates it with a percussive instrument, "a kind of drum." H. Hartmann, *Die Musik der sumerischen Kultur* (Ph.D. dissertation, Johann Wolfgang

eršemma, the laments LU and LN, and the *gala* priests, it is reasonable to suppose that the *gala* priests developed the *balag* lamentations from these two city laments.[41]

The neo-Assyrian *balag*s do exhibit one structural distinction in comparison to the city laments. Whereas the latter contain no rubric or descriptor at the end, the *balag*s of the first millennium always include a standardized closing line:

```
=================================================
```
šùd-dè še-eb-TN ki ne-en-gi$_4$-gi$_4$
```
=================================================
```
ki-šú-bi-im

A supplication that the brickwork of the . . . temple should be restored. It is its *kišu*.[42]

This closing is likely connected to the cultic use of the *balag*s which, as will be seen below, differs significantly from the use to which the ancients put the city laments.

Contents

Both the content and tone of the *balag*s and the city laments are remarkably similar. As Jacobsen remarks of LU:

Comparing the present texts [LU] more carefully, it will be seen that not only does it correspond to the *balag* in general character (lament for public disaster) but it also seems to exhibit the same division into two parts.[43]

The two parts to which Jacobsen refers are the plea of the weeping goddess, who bewails the fate of her city, and a description of the city's destruction by means of an evil storm sent by Enlil. Both features appear also as distinguishing characteristics of the *balag*s. Indeed, the description of the weeping goddess, the basis of the

---

Goethe Universität, 1960), pp. 56, 86, equates *halhallatu* with *tigi*, a "concussion instrument," or drum. Cf. Ferris, *Genre*, pp. 85–86, n. 291. Finally, Hallo, *Origins*, p. 225, claims the instrument in question was a tambourine.

[41] Cohen, *CLAM*, p. 38. Cohen, p. 39, notes that although LSUr, EL and UL were composed in standard *emegir* rather than the *emesal* dialect, "their existence may have added impetus for the development of the *gala*-priest's *balag* laments from the Ur and perhaps the Nippur Lament."

[42] *Ibid.*, p. 29.

[43] Jacobsen, "Review," p. 223, cited by Cohen, *CLAM*, p. 34.

LU, is "one of the most essential and pervasive themes in the *balag* lamentations."[44]

In addition to the shared tone and weeping goddess motif, *balag*s and city laments also appear to share entire passages, as the following chart demonstrates:[45]

Accusation of Damgalnuna: Enki hides while Eridu is destroyed	EL, l. 11f. // cf. LSUr 68, 136	*balag* 20:111–117
Description of the merciless destructive storm	LU 400–403 //	*balag* 43:16–19
Long list of the same deities	LU 25–35 //	*balag* 43:82–105
Importunities: calming of the heart and restoration of city or temple	LU 430–435 //	*balag* 5:225–266

Once again, however, a key difference exists between the city laments and the *balag*s. The former reflect the historic circumstances which inspired their composition, including references to the cause of the catastrophe that befell the cities, mention of Elam, the Su-people, the Gutians, and especially the misfortunes of Ibbi-Sin.[46] The *balag*s, on the other hand, evidence the principle of adaptability: they "do not portray any one specific historical occurrence, but rather describe the destruction of the land in general terms."[47] As is the case with the closing line of the neo-Assyrian *balag*s, this distinction reflects a difference in cultic use. Kutscher's comment in regard to *a-ab-ba-hu-luh-ha* pertains to other *balag*s as well:

---

[44] Cohen, *CLAM*, p. 35.

[45] The chart is based on parallels identified by Cohen, *CLAM*, pp. 36–38. *Balag* numbers refer to the NA catalogue 4R²53.

[46] Cf. LU 244; LSUr 33–35, 75, 109, 149, 169, 175, 233, 257–260, 264, 404, 495–498; EL 4th *kirugu* 10; UL 4th *kirugu* 20, 22.

[47] Cohen, *balag*, p. 10; *CLAM*, p. 38.

The dissimilarity between the neo-Sumerian city laments and *a-ab-ba-hu-luh-ha* is a dissimilarity in ritual function. The former were written to be recited in a ceremony marking the restoration of ruins, of temples or other structures, or even of whole cities, destroyed during a major disaster. Their detailed description of the disaster which caused the destruction, and their allusions to peoples and personages involved, bear directly upon the occasion for which they were written. But their use in the liturgy was limited: having fulfilled their unique purpose at the particular ceremony for which they were written they were scrapped from cultic use and were retained as secular literary works, appreciated for their belletristic values only.[48]

That is, whereas the city laments were written and used for a single occasion and then retired from use, *balag*s and *eršemma*s were incorporated into the ongoing liturgy of the Babylonian and Assyrian cults and, specifically, into the liturgies of the *gala* priesthood.

Ritual Use

Another line of correspondence is drawn with the ritual use of the *balag*. It turns out that the use of *balag*s in the cult corresponds to that which has been deduced for the city laments, namely the razing of sanctuaries in anticipation of their restoration. As both Jacobsen[49] and Hallo[50] have pointed out, the Sumerian city laments were composed and recited before the restoration of the cities rather than as a commemoration of that restoration.[51] Corresponding to this is the ritual use of *balag*s. Cohen writes:

---

[48] Kutscher, *Oh Angry Sea*, p. 6. Cf. Gwaltney, "Lamentations," p. 196.

[49] Jacobsen, "Review," 223.

[50] Hallo, "The Cultic Setting of Sumerian Poetry," p. 119.

[51] Note, however, that M. Green, *The Eridu Lament*, pp. 309–311 posits that the lament was recited by the king at the installation ceremony when the deity's statue returned to its refurbished shrine, reasoning that "The god's leaving may not always have been caused by foreign devastation but may have been forced by needed renovations of the temple in peacetime." Gwaltney, "The Biblical Book of Lamentations," p. 203, thinks the violence depicted in the city laments not conducive to Green's alternative although, he allows, "Perhaps Green's suggestion has merit in explaining the function of Old Babylonian *balag*s and *eršemma*s."

Although we possess no Old Babylonian texts detailing the specific occasion in which the *balag*-lamentation was involved, the closing line 'This supplication . . . return the 'x-temple' to place' strongly advocates that the *balag* was also involved in the restoration of sacred buildings. And, as with the three city laments, the continual references to the destroyed temples in the *balag's* indicate that they too were recited ruing the demolition of sacred structures. In fact, the first millennium B.C. ritual texts ascribe just such a function to these laments.[52]

Specifically, texts from the Seleucid period specify the use of these lamentations in two separate rituals, one preparatory to the laying of a temple foundation[53] and the other in a ritual transpiring before the demolition of a buckling temple wall.[54] Moreover, the recitation of *balags* in connection with offerings and libations presented during the demolition of old sacred edifices in the later period clarifies their meaning: the laments served the same function as the offerings, i.e., to assuage the divine anger over the demolition of the temple.[55]

At this juncture it is important to recognize the specifically public character of these laments. While leadership in the recitation of the compositions and the cultic activities that accompanied them undoubtedly was restricted to the *gala* priesthood, it is difficult to imagine that the restoration of a temple wall could be anything other than a communal concern. The *balags* and *eršemmas* are communal laments, i.e., laments spoken on behalf of the whole community. This last statement is evidenced not only by the subject matter of the materials themselves, the lamentation over ruined cities and temples, but also by the diverse ways these lamentations came to be used. As it turns out, the ritual function of *balags* was not restricted to the demolition of sacred structures or, therefore, to a single *Sitz im Leben*. To the contrary, *balags*, formally coupled by the first millennium with the *eršemmas*,[56] came to be used on other occa-

---

[52] Cohen, *balag*, p. 11; cf. *CLAM*, p. 39.

[53] Thureau-Dangin, *Rituels accadiens*, pp. 41–45.

[54] *Ibid.*, p. 34ff., 40. Cf. A. Sachs, *ANET*[3], pp. 339–342.

[55] Cohen, *balag*, p. 14; cf. *SH*, p. 48 and *CLAM*, p. 39, where he adds: "The ritual recitation of the city laments during the razing of sacred buildings apparently appealed to the ancients, who determined to incorporate lamentations into any further such rituals, whereupon new laments were composed for razing ceremonies, lest the god become angry at the tearing down of his sacred house."

[56] Cohen, *SH*, p. 25; *CLAM*, p. 45.

sions as well. A Mari *balag* to Inanna appearing in association with the festival of a new moon[57] as well as subsequent mention of *balag/eršemma* laments in texts detailing the rituals of the *gala* priests,[58] in calendar texts,[59] as a part of the *akîtu* festival at Uruk,[60] and even in a *namburbi*[61] indicate that the lamentation remained a means by which the priests maintained an ever-constant vigil against the inadvertent evocation of the gods' anger. Cohen says it well:

> In summary then, the *balag*-lamentation was originally composed to placate the wrath of the gods during the razing of sacred structures. As early as the Old Babylonian period the laments also became part of a fixed liturgy for certain days of the month, presumably to pacify the gods over unknowingly committed offenses that may have been totally unrelated to the demolishing of temple buildings. This dual usage of the *balag*-lamentation was maintained throughout the first millennium B.C. when the *balag* was even used in rituals to avert portended evil.[62]

This last quote illuminates yet another significant fact: the *balag-eršemma* compositions, copied again and again in the *emesal* dialect and used by *gala*-priests throughout the second and first millennium, represent a living literary and cultic link between the Sumerian city laments and those laments in use in Mesopotamia in the sixth century BCE and beyond.

W.C. Gwaltney[63] has used this literary and cultic chain to demolish an earlier argument raised by Thomas McDaniel with respect to the biblical Book of Lamentations. McDaniel denied a connection between Lamentations and the Sumerian city laments partially on the basis that there was too great a gap between them in terms of

---

[57] Cohen, *CLAM*, p. 43.

[58] An example is the use of *balag*s in a ritual to be followed when covering the temple kettle drum. Cf. A. Sachs, *ANET*[3], pp. 334–338. Cohen, *CLAM*, p. 17, noting the oddity of the use of a *balag* after the covering of the drum (rather than before its repair, as the case with the temple wall), suggests that the *balag* was recited as a means of testing the drum.

[59] S. Langdon, "Calendars of Liturgies and Prayers: I. The Assur Calendar," *ASJL* 42 (1926), 110–127.

[60] Cf. Mark E. Cohen, *The Cultic Calendars of the Ancient Near East* (Bethesda, MD: CDL, 1993), p. 433.

[61] Richard I. Caplice, "Namburbi Texts in the British Museum: IV," *Or* NS 39 (1970), 121.

[62] Cohen, *balag*, p. 15; cf. Cohen, *SH*, p. 49.

[63] W.C. Gwaltney, "The Biblical Book of Lamentations," pp. 191–211.

both time and space.[64] Gwaltney demonstrated the temporal link by showing that the city laments lived on through the *balag-eršemma* laments. McDaniel's corollary objection, that the physical distance between Mesopotamia and Israel precluded influence on the latter's Lamentations, was countered by Gwaltney's demonstration of the correctness of a suggestion originally made by Gadd,[65] namely that the Babylonian Exile provided the opportunity for the Jewish clergy to encounter Mesopotamian laments. To Gadd's observation Gwaltney added, "the exiles of the Northern Kingdom also had similar opportunities to observe or participate in those rituals."[66] To counter McDaniel's further objection that the Book of Lamentations lacks the elements of the Mesopotamian laments, Gwaltney developed a typology of the Mesopotamian laments. He discussed that typology under four headings: ritual occasions, form/structure, poetic techniques, and theology; Gwaltney found significant points of correspondence on each level.[67] What emerges from this comparison is a startling and seemingly undeniable relationship between the laments of Mesopotamia and the Book of Lamentations.[68] While acknowledging some differences between the laments of the two cultures, Gwaltney concludes:

> Because of the polytheistic theology underlying the Mesopotamian laments and their ritual observance, they could not be taken over without thorough modification in theology and language. Still the biblical Book of Lamentations was more closely associated with the Near Eastern lament genre than simply borrowing the 'idea' of a lament over the destruction of a city as McDaniel conceded.[69]

---

[64] Thomas F. McDaniel, "The Alleged Sumerian Influence Upon Lamentations," *VT* 18 (1968), 207–208.

[65] C. J. Gadd, "The Second Lamentation for Ur," in *Hebrew and Semitic Studies Presented to Godfrey Rolles Driver*, ed. by D.W. Thomas and W.D. McHardy (Oxford: Oxford University Press, 1963), p. 61.

[66] Gwaltney, "The Biblical Book of Lamentations," p. 210.

[67] *Ibid.*, pp. 205–210.

[68] This in spite of the conclusions reached by Dobbs-Allsopp, *Weep, O Daughter of Zion*, pp. 5–8, who rejects what he perceives as the unidirectional approach of Gwaltney since that posture, in his view, ignores the possibility of polygenesis for a given genre, underestimates the difficulties in establishing literary dependence between two cultures' writings, and, even assuming the fact of some kind of literary influence, represents a too simplistic view of the way that influence could take place.

[69] Gwaltney, "The Biblical Book of Lamentations," p. 211.

As there appears to be a valid link between the Mesopotamian laments and the Book of Lamentations, can similar lines be drawn between the *balag/eršemma* compositions (and ultimately the city laments) and the communal lamentations of the Psalter? That an affirmative answer may be possible has already been suggested by the permanence and pervasiveness of the Mesopotamian lament form and its potential influence on Israel's Book of Lamentations. The challenge to demonstrate specific points of correspondence between the culturally and theologically divided laments remains. To meet this challenge, the next section attempts to develop a typology of the *balag/eršemma* lamentations.

TYPOLOGY OF BALAG AND ERŠEMMA LAMENTATIONS

The flexible structure of the first millennium *balag/eršemma* compositions complicates any construction of a typological model. The examination ahead is aided, however, by the fact that a good deal of overlap exists between the Sumerian city laments and their successor documents, the *balag*s and *eršemma*s. Beyond the *kirugu* divisions discussed above—and apart even from the evident borrowing of whole passages between *balag*s and city laments—a host of themes, motifs and matters of content remains common to both the *balag*s and the city laments. This happy circumstance makes it possible to draw heavily from those scholars whose attention has focused more specifically on identifying determinative features of the city laments.[70] The goal of this examination, once again, is to isolate those aspects of the materials which are characteristic of the *balag* and *eršemma* texts in order that, at a future point in this investigation, those features may be compared to the communal laments of Israel's psalms.

General Structure

The *balag/eršemma* texts consist of three basic elements including (1) praise, (2) a narrative description of the disaster and destruction

---

[70] The present author's debt to Cohen, *CLAM*, 11–44; Michalowski, *The Lamentation*, pp. 409; Gwaltney, "The Biblical Book of Lamentations," 194–205; M. Green, "Eridu," 277–325; Krecher, *Kultlyrik*, pp. 45–51, and especially Dobbs-Allsopp, *Weep, O Daughter of Zion*, pp. 30–96, will be obvious.

which has fallen upon the nation including various laments, and (3) importunities or pleas to the deity.[71] Often further descriptions of the ruin will follow the importunities. Of these elements the majority of the content is normally devoted to the praise of the deity addressed by the *balag*, there being at least one *balag* for each major deity.[72] Gwaltney has helpfully demonstrated these structural elements in his tripartite outline of the first millennium form of *balag* 16.[73] Another example is *balag* 5, which can be outlined as follows:[74]

I. Praise of Enlil's Word, lines 1–52
   A. The Word is like a storm, earthquake, and flood, lines 1–24
   B. The Word destroys, lines 25–52

II. Lament over Nippur's fall, lines 52–126, [127–200], b+142–+f 224
   A. The Word destroys city, temple, and environs, lines 79–107
   B. Enlil called upon to look at the destroyed city, lines 110–119
   C. Enlil assigned responsibility, lines 120–128
   D. The goddess laments, lines 129–200(?)
   E. The Word destroys social structures, including temple worship, commerce, lines b+142–f+224

III. Importunities and Intercessors, lines f+225–f+277
   A. Plea for "heaven and earth" to calm Enlil, lines f+225–f+226
   B. Plea to listed deities for intercession, lines f+227–f+265
   C. Prayers/pleas of the deities: May Enlil not abandon! lines f+266–f+277

---

[71] Cohen, *balag*, p. 7; cf.Dobbs-Allsopp, *Weep, O Daughter of Zion*, pp. 37–38; Gwaltney, "The Biblical Book of Lamentations," p. 206.

[72] Cohen, *balag*, p. 7.

[73] Gwaltney, "The Biblical Book of Lamentations," 203. Gwaltney's outline is based in turn on the investigation of that *balag* by Kutscher, *Oh Angry Sea*, pp. 143–153. Cf. Cohen, *CLAM*, pp. 374–401, however, who disagrees with Kutscher's reconstruction of the composition. Some texts which Kutscher has assigned to this *balag* have been placed by Cohen in *am-e bará-an-na-ra* (cf. *CLAM*, pp. 319–341, especially p. 320).

[74] The outline follows Cohen's suggestion, *CLAM*, p. 146, that K.2881+2786 (Bl pl LXIX obv.), K.3288 (BL 164), and MLC 1864 were a part of *u₄-dam ki àm-ús* and ought be included after line 126.

While the *balag*s remained relatively stable during the long history of their transmission,[75] the *eršemma*s witnessed a development between the Old Babylonian period and the first millennium. Whereas all known Old Babylonian *eršemma*s consisted of a single literary unit addressed to a deity,[76] by the first millennium the *eršemma* could consist of one, two, or even three units, the scribe indicating the division by a heavy line drawn across the tablet.[77] Characteristic of those later *eršemma*s with more than one unit is the inclusion of a so called "heart-pacification" section in which a prayer is offered to the effect that the deity's heart (or heart and liver) might be pacified. Cohen believes that the unit owes its origin to the last two *kirugu*s of an Old Babylonian *balag* to Enlil and that it came to be associated with the *eršemma*s during the Middle Babylonian period when *balag*s and *eršemma*s were joined.[78] Whatever its genesis, by the first millennium the heart-pacification unit, when it was included, assumed three basic properties:[79]

1. At the beginning of the unit is the refrain *šà-zu ḫé-en-ḫun-gá bar-zu ḫé-en-šed$_7$-dè.* (or some variation thereof), "May he pacify your heart, may he calm your liver!"[80] followed by
2. a short list of gods, and
3. either (a) a repetition of the refrain *šà-zu ḫé-en-ḫun-gá* or an alternation with *bar-zu ḫé-en-šed$_7$-dè* or (b) the repetition of the refrain *a-ra-zu dè-ra-ab-bé*, "May a prayer be uttered to you!" followed by the formulaic lines *na-an-šub-bé-en dè-ra-ab-bé a-ra-zu dè-ra-ab-bé me-na-šè GN na-an-šub-bé-en dè-ra-ab-bé a-ra-zu dè-ra-ab-bé*, "May 'You should not desert!' be uttered to you! May a prayer be uttered to you! May 'Enough! You

---

[75] Cohen, *CLAM*, pp. 40–42, discusses briefly the redactional activity of the Old Babylonian *balag*s as they came to be known in the first millennium. Already in the Old Babylonian period, however, variance between versions of a *balag* existed. Still, the first millennium *balag*s "are reasonably accurate editions of their Old Babylonian antecedents, taking into account phonetic variants which are to be expected with any long literary composition passed on during a thousand year span." Exceptions to this are the *balag*s *a-ab-ba hu-luh-ha* and *e-lum gu$_4$-sún*, both of which appear to have undergone more significant revisions.

[76] Cohen, *SH*, p. 18: "The compositions concern only deities; there are no *eršemma*s involving kings."

[77] *Ibid.*, p. 21.

[78] *Ibid.*, pp. 22–26.

[79] *Ibid.*, pp. 21–22.

[80] Cf. *Ibid.*, p. 22, n. 123, for examples.

should never desert GN!' be uttered to you! May a prayer be uttered to you!"

Given the absence of a parallel unit in the Hebrew laments, it is important to note that not all first millennium *eršemma*s include this feature. Cohen argues that the exceptions, those one-unit *eršemma*s which lack the heart-pacification section, are the very *eršemma*s which have not been joined to a *balag* in the first millennium catalogues[81] and are distinguished there by the designation *kidudû* ("outside").[82] But what was the role of the *kidudû eršemma*s? Interestingly, those *eršemma*s lacking the heart-pacification unit and employed independently of the *balag* lamentation came to be part of a fixed liturgy for certain days of each month, every month, as well as a part of ceremonies centered around certain cultic activities in precisely the same way as did those *eršemma*s which *were* joined to a *balag*.[83] Thus, while the heart-pacification unit of the joined *balag* and *eršemma*s reveals explicitly the ritual purpose of the recitation of these texts, assuaging and soothing the anger of the gods, even those *eršemma*s not recited in connection with a *balag* (and therefore *sans* the heart-pacification unit) were employed toward the same end.

Subject and Mood

Like the city laments, *balag*s and *eršemma*s praise the deity and the deity's power, but that in the context of lamenting the city's destruction. Descriptions of the devastation include the effects the disaster has had upon the city environs as well as the temple(s), the cessation of cultic activities, the disruption of the normal functions of society and its *me*.[84] Jeremy Black has suggested that the subject

---

[81] *Ibid.*, pp. 22–27. Cohen is forced to admit, however, that a few *eršemma*s labeled *kidudû* nevertheless contain the heart-pacification unit. In these instances, he believes, the exceptions include only those *eršemma*s that have been "poorly reworked or composed, their slipshod craftsmanship being further exemplified in that the heart-pacification units have been erroneously appended, despite the fact that these works were not recited along with lamentations" (p. 27, n. 136). The disturbing circularity lurking in this last observation notwithstanding, it appears generally true that the "heart pacification" section typifies many of the first millennium *eršemma*s and that it seems characteristic of those *eršemma*s which have been joined to *balag*s.

[82] v *kidudû*, *CAD*.

[83] Cohen, *SH*, pp. 49–50.

[84] Samuel Noah Kramer, *The Sumerians: Their History, Culture, and Character* (Chicago: University of Chicago, 1963), p. 115, writes that while an exact meaning for the

matter of the *"balags* of Enlil" differ slightly from those *"balags* of Inanna." The former "stress the destructive power of the deity or deities held responsible," while the latter "focus . . . on the destruction wrought, especially [on] the temple and its patron goddess."[85] The mood of each, however, is mournful and somber.

Poetic Techniques and Devices

Again, like the city laments, the *balags* and *eršemmas* incorporate a number of poetic techniques and devices including the use of a theme word or phrase to link lines or stanzas together, various devices of parallelism such as couplets and repeating lines with one word changed from line to line, antiphonal responses, refrains repeated at intervals, and the use of *emesal*, evidently to simulate high-pitched cries of distress.[86] Green correctly observes:

> All the laments employ such compositional devices. They are used throughout Sumerian literature and are a basic tool of poetic composition found in the literature of all cultures, especially in oral literature. There is no apparent restriction to their use in Sumerian lamentations.[87]

Nevertheless, at least two compositional devices are worth special mention since their presence or absence in the Hebrew laments could be judged particularly significant.

First, one should note the shift of speakers within the texts. Various "voices" are heard as the authorial point of view alternates. Primarily, of course, one hears the voice of the omniscient narrator who impartially describes the course of events. However, because the *balags* and *eršemmas* are directed to specific deities, the narrator frequently intrudes as a "privileged" observer who is able to speak

---

term *me* is unknown, "In general it would seem to denote a set of rules and regulations assigned to each cosmic entity and cultural phenomenon for the purpose of keeping it operating forever in accordance with the plans laid down by the deity creating it." See the extensive treatment of the term by Gertrud Farber, "Me, (ĝarza, parṣu)," in *Reallexikon der Assyriologie und Vorderasiatischen Archaologie*, vol. 7 (Berlin: W. de Gruyter, 1990), 610–613. Examples of the disruption of the *me* may be found in *balags* 4:76–77; 5:62; 25:c+66; 50:a+82–83; *eršemma* 171:7–11.

[85] Black, "A-še-er Gi₆-ta," 12.

[86] Gwaltney, "The Biblical Book of Lamentations," p. 206; cf. Green, "Eridu," pp. 286–289.

[87] Green, "Eridu," p. 288.

directly to the god/goddess and yet not enter into the action of the narrative.[88] For example:

> Lord, you have destroyed the faithful house. You have [killed] the men of the faithful house.
> Father Enlil, (your) eyes never tire.
> Your neck does not straighten up. Why do you wander about? (*balag* 5:f+222–225)

> How he has destroyed it! How he.has utterly destroyed! How he has defiled you!
> Princess, how he has destroyed your cella! How he has defiled you!
> How he has handed you over to the enemy!
> How he has handed over to the foreigner! (*balag* 50:b+177–180)[89]

Within the *eršemma*s the "heart-pacification" units exemplify the same phenomenon. Other speakers who find voice in the lamentations include the city goddess[90] or antagonistic male deities[91] and, more rarely, members of the beleaguered community.[92] This change in narrative perspective accounts for the often abrupt grammatical change in persons within the text. The shifting authorial perspective purposes to build pathos in the reader/auditor by articulating the praise and lament of the various *dramatis personae* including, most notably, the goddess who weeps over the destruction of her city and temple.[93]

---

[88] Dobbs-Allsopp, *Weep, O Daughter of Zion*, p. 33; cf. Adele Berlin *Poetics and Interpretation of Biblical Narrative* (Winona Lake: Eisenbrauns, 1994), 43–82.

[89] Other examples include *balag*s 4:1–14, 108–127, 171–176; 6:30–95; 7:b+73–85; 10:a+45–46, 49–51; 12:62–74; 25:f+109–134.

[90] E.g., *balag*s 1:60–63; 7:1–25; 8:b+58–82; 26:38–59; 43:g+335–361; 39:a+71–89; *eršemma*s 79:29–32; 32:36–48; 171:30–38.

[91] Dobbs-Allsop, *Weep, O Daughter of Zion*, p. 37, notes that as in the city laments, Enlil sometimes is given a voice in *balag*s, e.g., 12:d+117–130; VAS 2 16 rev. col v:1–15. Cf. Cohen, *CLAM*, pp. 266–267, and *eršemma* 171:40–45. Since not a few of the *balag*s and *eršemma*s are addressed to other male deities, these gods too are occasionally given a voice in the texts, e.g., Enki in *balag* 3:f+187–189; Nabû in *balag* 29:d+153–163; Nergal in *balag* 31:a+136–161; Iškur in *eršemma* 185:33–36.

[92] E.g. *balag*s 12:e+161–71; 15:a+177–187.

[93] William F. Lanaham, "The Speaking Voice in the Book of Lamentations," *JBL* 93 (1974), 41–49, and Barbara Bakke Kaiser, "Poet as Female Impersonator: The Image of Daughter Zion as Speaker in Biblical Poems of Suffering, *JR* 67 (1987), 164–182, recognize that the poet throughout Lamentations takes on several "speaking voices" (Lanaham) or personae (Kaiser) as a means of heightening the pathos of the poems. Neither author, however, relates this phenomena to the older city laments. Cf. Pamela

A second notable characteristic of these materials is the appearance of sundry lists within the texts. The various cities and temples that have suffered devastation frequently find enumeration, long lists of deities are called upon to intercede, epithets are amassed, and the like. The characteristic opening section of all *eršemma*s is, in fact, a list of epithets and/or cities and buildings.[94] The use of refrains with lengthy, repetitive lists is also a common stylistic feature of the *balag*s and account for the repetitive and monotonous character of many of those compositions.[95]

The Weeping Goddess Motif

Doubtless the most distinctive features of all Mesopotamian lamentations is the figure of the weeping goddess.[96] The goddess is given voice to rue the destruction of her temple and city and its environs. She laments the cessation of cultic activities and pleads before Enlil for pity. The motif appears in all of the city laments, and is especially prominent in LU. The weeping goddess is likewise ubiquitous in the *balag*s. The motif also occurs regularly in many *eršemma*s. The first millennium *eršemma me-er-ra-mu-dè* of Baba serves as a typical example:[97]

> My destroyed house! Tears on her behalf, heart felt sighs on her behalf!
> My ruined city! Tears on her behalf, heart felt sighs on her behalf!
> Its destroyed cattle pens! Tears on her behalf, heart felt sighs on her behalf!

Jean Owens, "Personification and Suffering in Lamentations 3," *Austin Seminary Bulletin, Faculty Edition* 150 (1990), 75–90, whose investigation of Lamentations 3 indicates that the speaker in that chapter remains dramatically multiplex.

[94] Cohen, *SH*, pp. 27–28; cf. Dobbs-Allsop, *Weep, O Daughter of Zion*, p. 44.

[95] Cohen, *CLAM*, p. 15.

[96] On the origin and development of the weeping goddess motif in Sumerian literature see Samuel Noah Kramer, "The Weeping Goddess: Sumerian prototypes of the *Mater Dolorosa*," *BA* 46/3 (1983), 69–80; *idem*, "BM 98396: A Sumerian Proto-type of the Mater-Dolorosa," *ErIsr* 16 (1982), 141–146; *idem*, "Lisin, the Weeping Goddess: A New Sumerian Lament," in *ZIKIR ŠUMIN: Assyriological Studies Presented to F.R. Kraus on the Occasion of his Seventieth Birthday*, ed. by G. van Driel, Th.J.H. Krispijn, M. Stol, and K.R. Veenhof (Leiden: E.J. Brill, 1992), 133–144, and especially 133, 136–137, where Kramer lists and references cuneiform texts which report the weeping goddess.

[97] *Eršemma* no. 10 in Cohen, *SH*, pp. 139–143. Except where otherwise noted, the translations of *balag*s and *eršemma*s in this volume are, respectively, from Cohen, *CLAM* and *SH*.

> Its uprooted sheepfolds! Tears on her behalf, heart felt sighs on her
> behalf!
> *His (?) destroying of* the house! Tears on her behalf! Who can calm me?

Not all *eršemma*s include the speech of the weeping goddess.[98]
Nevertheless, given the predominance of this motif in the *balag*s and
many of the *eršemma*s, one would expect to find at least vestiges
of the weeping goddess tradition associated with Israel's laments,
particularly if the claim is to be maintained that Israel's traditions
found their inspiration in these Mesopotamian materials.

The Destruction

As literary successors to the city laments, the *balag/eršemma*
compositions generally concern themselves with the destruction of
cities and temples. The specific content of these lamentations and
their description of the devastation can be conveniently considered
under three headings: (1) the agents of destruction, (2) the assign-
ment of responsibility for the destruction, and (3) the description of
the destruction.

The Agents of Destruction

The characteristic causes of the city's destruction, already well-
established in the city laments, continue in the *balag*s and *eršemma*s.

Prominently featured is the annihilating storm, sent by Enlil,
which wreaks havoc on the city, cult, and society. In the city laments,
the storm, along with the enemy invasion, provides the means for
Enlil to carry out the judgment of the divine assembly to destroy
the cities of Sumer.[99] Likewise in the *balag*s the storm of Enlil is occasionally associated with the invasion of enemies and divine judgment,[100] though more often the storm seems to take on a life of its

---

[98] E.g., 1.1, an *eršemma* to Enlil and 34.1, an *eršemma* to Inanna consisting entirely
of praise.

[99] LU 173; LW 3:2–3.

[100] E.g. *balag* 50:a+74–80, describing the destruction and defilement wrought by
the enemies is followed by a description of various cities which have been washed
away by the storm's flood (b+108–113). The invasion, flood, and even a fire (b+114)
befall

> That city whose fate has not been decided (favorably)!
> That city whose lord does not care for it!

own,[101] falling capriciously, without warning, and apart from any divine judgment on the hapless citizens. As an expression of divine anger[102] the storm is lethal: it generates flood, fire, famine, homelessness and, above all, human death.[103]

While the storm of Enlil serves as the dominant agent of destruction within the city laments, in *balag*s the destructive power of the word of Enlil appears as the more prevalent image.[104] The annihilating force of Enlil's word is as powerful as the storm with which it is frequently identified:

> It touches the earth like a storm. Its meaning is unfathomable.
> His word touches the earth like a storm. Its meaning is unfathomable.
> The word of great An touches the earth like a storm. Its meaning is unfathomable.
> The word of Enlil touches the earth like a storm. Its meaning is unfathomable. (*balag* 5:1–4)[105]

> That city against which Enlil rushes!
> That city with which Enlil has started a quarrel!
> At which An frowns! (b+115–119)

[101] Dobbs-Allsopp, *Weep, O Daughter of Zion*, p. 57.

[102] E.g. *balag* 43:a+8–10:

> Storm, heart of the heavens! Heart . . . !
> Storm, angry heart of great An!
> Storm, destructive heart of Enlil!

[103] E.g., *balag* 43:1–a+57. Other examples include *balag*s 5:1–12; 9:c+156, 162; 11:a+93–97, 109–19; 12:b+93–101, a+99–108; 13:a+28–45; 43:1–a+57.

[104] The word of Enlil as a destructive power is a motif not well represented in the city laments. It appears in LSUr 165; otherwise destruction comes as a consequence of a decision of the divine assembly, as in LU 139ff.; UL 1.8.

[105] The simile continues through lines 5–24. Other examples linking the word of a deity with the storm include *balag*s 3:c+90–99, 106; 11:b+109–118; 13:a+28–45; 29:c+43–81; 31:a+69–90. Note as well the parallelism in *balag* 43:d+254–255; d+264–270:

> Let the word of great An not release it! You, the storm, have been released!
> Let the word of Enlil not release it! You, the storm, have been released! . . .
> . . . the storm is released, . . .
> When the word of great An goes out, . . .
> When the word of Enlil goes out, . . .
> . . . the storm is released, . . .
> When the word of great An goes out, . . .
> When the word of Enlil goes out, . . .
> My little ones are killed. My adults are killed.

Nor is the understanding of the relationship of the storm of Enlil and that deity's word limited to simile. In the *balags*, the word of Enlil becomes the storm itself, and the effects of the deity's powerful word are indistinguishable from those of the storm. The word of Enlil generates flood, fire, and destruction of the land, city, and temple.[106] Of course, as Albrektson has demonstrated,[107] the destructive power of the divine word is common throughout the ancient Near East. Even the specific associations of the deity's word/voice with the effects of a violent storm appears frequently in other cultures. Enlil's word, for example, equated as it is to meteorological phenomenon and the tempestuous power of the thunder storm, finds a close analogy in the *qol YHWH* of Israel's Psalm 29. The background of this ancient hymn is generally considered to be Canaanite,[108] as is much of the storm god imagery found in the Hebrew scriptures. Nevertheless, the presence in Israel's *lament* tradition of any examples connecting Yahweh to a storm, or Yahweh's word with storm imagery may prove significant, especially given the prominence of those motifs in the *balag* compositions. As Dobbs-Allsopp has noted in connection with his study of Lamentations, there are lines to be drawn between Enlil and Yahweh: "Both deities are storm gods of sorts," and therefore "the Israelite poet placed Yahweh in the role filled prototypically by Enlil in the Mesopotamian city laments."[109]

---

[106] A few representative examples are to be found in *balag*s 9:1–17; 12:17–20, b+93–101 (cf. 12:a+99–108 [First Millennium]); 16:a+31–32; 31:39–46, a+52–67, a+70–90;

[107] Albrektson, *History and the Gods*, pp. 53–67.

[108] Cf. Cross, *CMHE*, pp. 151–157, and especially p. 152, note 22, and the bibliography cited there.

[109] Dobbs-Allsopp, *Weep, O Daughter of Zion*, p. 56. The context of these statements involves Dobbs-Allsopp's attempt to refute McDaniel, "Sumerian Influence," 202, who claims that the absence of storm imagery in Lamentations negatively affected the attempt to locate that book's origins in the laments of Mesopotamia. Dobbs-Allsopp denies that claim, but then lessens the strength of his own observation as he immediately continues by stating, "He [the poet] did not have to import Enlil imagery into his work, because he could make use of his own traditional stock of imagery about Yahweh." Once again one notes Dobbs-Allsopp's curious effort to establish specific and particular associations between aspects of Lamentations and the city laments, on the one hand, while trying to maintain the idea that Israel's city laments represent a separate indigenous generic phenomenon on the other.

A third major cause of destruction in the city laments is the invasion of enemies from abroad. Reference has already been made to the distinction between this aspect of the *balag/eršemma* lamentations and their predecessor city laments: the city laments reflect the historic circumstances which inspired their composition while the *balag/eršemma* materials tend to speak of enemies in more general terms. Indeed, "within the *balag* lamentations there is no historical evidence concerning the cause of the destruction of the land and its temples."[110] Nevertheless the descriptions of the enemy's activities sparkle with images vivid enough to leave one with the erroneous impression that they are in fact rooted in a particular historical event. As Black helpfully remarks: "Quite extensive detail may be given, but need have no reference to specific experience, since the emotions expressed and the events described are part of an artistic convention which is accepted because it is regarded as only too plausible an account of reality."[111] References to invading enemies in these materials, therefore, can be considered ahistorical. Their described behavior is typical and their destructive activities are simply extensions of the destructive power of Enlil's storm and word.

In the following examples, the goddess Inanna laments the enemy's activities and especially the plunder of her temple and its statues:

> My (house), the cult center of mankind!
> My (house), the storehouse of all the lands!
> (When) it was built, the land was also built up.
> (But when) it was destroyed, so, too, was the land destroyed.
> The enemy has carried off the good spouse.
> The enemy has carried off the good child.
> Its great feast is no longer carried out. (*eršemma* 106:11–16)[112]

---

[110] Cohen, *CLAM*, p. 38.

[111] Black, "A-še-er Gi$_6$-ta," 12.

[112] The monotonous character of these materials finds illustration by the comparison of this citation with *balag* 50:a+74–80:

> My (house) which the enemy has destroyed!
> My house which the enemy has defiled!
> My city and house which the enemy has ruined!
> When my house had been built, so too had the land been built up.
> When my house was destroyed, so too the land was destroyed.
> The enemy has carried off the lovely wife of the house.
> The enemy has carried off the lovely child of the house.

They carry off my house and my city from me.
They carry off the lady (of) my house from me.
They carry of my cella, my treasure house from me.
They carry off my property, my possessions from me.
They carry off my property of the Eshumesha from me.
They carry off my property of the Erabriri from me.
They carry off my throne, my seat from me.
They carry off my glistening bed from me.
They have locked up my spouse in my dwelling house.
They have locked up my Shumahanna.
They have locked up what I hold closest to my heart.
   (*balag* 26:168–178)

That enemy has caused men wearing shoes to enter (my) cella.
That enemy has brought the unwashed into the chamber.
He has laid his hands on it and I am afraid.
That enemy has laid his hands on it and I am full of fear.
I am afraid, but he is not afraid of me.
He has stripped off my clothing and dressed his wife with it.
That enemy has cut out the lapis-lazuli and hangs it about his child.
   (*balag* 50:a+155–162)

Despoiled of cultic images and rites, Inanna can no longer occupy
her cherished temple. In the lines following the last quotation,
Inanna describes herself as a bird, flying around temple and city,
before deciding to renounce and abandon both:

How I pour out in my house, "You are no longer my house!"
How I pour out in my city, "You are no longer my city!"
How I pour out in my cella, "You are no longer my cella!"
"I can no longer enter it!" I utter. Its wealth has been consumed.
"I can no longer . . . !" I utter. Its laughter has dried up.
   (*balag* 50:b+172–176).

As in the present example, the desolation of her residence is often
said to force the goddess to abandon her habitation and enter into a
sort of exile.[113]

This theme of divine abandonment features prominently in
all of the Mesopotamian communal laments.[114] Mordechai Cogan

---

[113] E.g., *balags* 27:58; 50:b+252–257; *eršemma* 32:49–54; 159:26–28; 171:51–55. Cf.
Kretcher, *Kultlyrik*, 8:37–54.

[114] See above, note 18. Other examples within the *balag/eršemma* compositions
include *balag* 4:100–127; 5:f+266–277; 6:84–95; b+179–192; 16:c+158–69; *eršemma*
166.1:16–17.

has shown how the idea of divine abandonment gives a practical answer to the questions posed by the capture of divine images by a nation's enemies. As in the present example, spoilation of the temple and city by an enemy did not necessarily lead to the idea that the deity had been defeated and captured and was therefore subordinate to the enemy's gods.[115] That theological explanation was occasionally given,[116] but more often the defeated peoples attributed disaster to a decision by the local deity to abandon his or her place, thus accounting for defeat while still allowing the god/goddess to retain power and autonomy vis-à-vis the gods of the enemy.[117]

The Assignment of Responsibility

If the goddess was thought to retain her authority by a willful decision to abandon her cella, her exercise of power and autonomy in relation to the superior gods of her own pantheon remained a different matter. As her various importunities make clear, the destruction of the city and temple were not of her choosing but, instead, were a consequence of the decision of gods of a higher rank than her own. These gods, in fact, were inevitably responsible for any and all destruction which fell upon the cities: "The destruction may be by natural forces or by human agents, in either case the gods are seen, in their impenetrable wisdom, as ultimately responsible."[118] Specifically, the destruction most often was understood to be sanctioned by the gods Enlil and An, who exercised supreme power. The principle is indicated in *balag* 50, in the lines immediately following those quoted above describing the activity of the enemy and the goddess' subsequent abandonment of her city and cella. Overwhelmed by happy memories of the place, she decides to return, in spite of her misgivings, whereupon an unnamed interlocutor asks:

> How could you ruin it, how could you destroy it, how could you
> yourself humiliate it?
> Lady, how could you destroy your dwelling, how could you yourself
> humiliate it?

---

[115] Cogan, *Imperialism and Religion*, p. 11.
[116] *Ibid.*, p. 40.
[117] Roberts, "Nebuchadnezzar," pp. 183–187.
[118] Black, "A-še-er Gi₆-ta," 11.

How could you yourself hand it over to the enemy?
How could you hand it over to the enemy? (b+177–180)[119]

In response the goddess relates that she had no part in the humiliation or destruction. She would not have handed her city and residence over to the enemy nor willingly defiled it. Rather the decision had been wrested from her by An:

> As for me, I have not defiled it. My father has defiled it.
> The lord, great An, has defiled it. My father has defiled it.
> The lord of all the lands has defiled it. My father has defiled it.
> The lord whose word is true has defiled it. My father has defiled it.
>   (b+181–184).

Just as An and Enlil had earlier cast storm and word against Inanna's house and city (lines b+139–154), so also these deities were responsible for sending enemies to defile the goddess's cella. Indeed, the goddess does not mention the enemies as responsible agents; they have simply been the means by which An and Enlil have exercised their decision to destroy.

Within the Sumerian pantheon An was the chief god, representing the personified heaven, while Enlil, the storm god, was the executive power in the universe and ranked next to An in power and authority.[120] Both of these deities were adopted into the pantheon of the Sargonic empire, evidently in order to legitimate Akkadian hegemony over the cities of Sumer.[121] In the majority of the *balag*s and *eršemma*s, however, it is Enlil, and not the highest ranking god An, who exercised authority. In this respect *balag* 50:181–184 cited

---

[119] The translation of these lines is that of Black, "A-še-er Gi₆-ta," 36–37 (cf. 55), who sees *a-gin⁷* as an interrogative, used in the sense 'how did it come about that?' He further suggests that Cohen's translation of a similar set of questions in *eršemma* 32:57ff. (*SH*, p. 68) ought be modified accordingly. Cohen, *CLAM*, p. 722, reads the passage not as questions but as a series of declaratives, "How he has destroyed it! How he has utterly destroyed!" etcetera.

[120] On the deities An and Enlil, see especially Thorkild Jacobsen, *The Treasures of Darkness: A History of Mesopotamian Religion* (New Haven: Yale University, 1976), pp. 95–104, and Samuel Noah Kramer, *The Sumerians*, pp. 118–121.

[121] J.J.M. Roberts, *The Earliest Semitic Pantheon: A Study of the Semitic Deities Attested in Mesopotamia Before Ur III* (Baltimore: Johns Hopkins University, 1972), pp. 147–148. Cf. Thorkild Jacobsen, *The Intellectual Adventure of Ancient Man*, ed. by Henri Frankfort (Chicago: University of Chicago, 1946), pp. 140–144; *idem*, *Toward the Image of Tammuz and Other Essays on Mesopotamian History and Culture*, ed. by William L. Moran, HSS, Vol. 21 (Cambridge, MA: Harvard University, 1970), pp. 139–140.

above, where An is blamed by Inanna for the defilement of her residence, emerges as a somewhat atypical example.[122] The god An far more often appears as a mere symbol of authority and a figurehead[123] while Enlil is vested with responsibility for the destruction of land, city, and temple.[124] Consequently, when various city gods petition to stop the destruction, it is Enlil they approach,[125] and the sundry importunities uttered are addressed to him.[126]

An interesting and significant aspect of these entreaties to Enlil lies in the total absence of any mention of human indiscretion or sin which might have caused the calamity. The disaster which has come upon the city and its environs stems not from human neglect of cultic duties. Calamity strikes, rather, simply as a consequence of the capricious decision of the deities, whose reason and purposes remain inscrutable to human beings. Jeremy Black posits that, in this respect, the *balag*s forward a theological outlook and point of view which, while present in other Sumerian literature, finds a particular, unremitting expression in the *balag*s:

> It is a view of the world which says: the gods are all-powerful; they have their own wisdom, but it is utterly beyond the reach of human understanding. Divination of the future or of the gods' will is impossible. Man can only stand in awe of their unlimited power, which is exercised in what often appears a brutal, savage, violent, and irrational manner.[127]

---

[122] So too is *eršemma* 168:8–12 (Old Babylonian) where, according to Cohen, *SH*, p. 51, An appears to bestow the power of the storm god upon Iškur. The fragmentary character of the passage in question makes judgment on this point difficult. Note, however, that it is Enlil who vests Iškur with this power in *eršemma*s 23.1:15–30; 184:13–23; 185:8–18.

[123] Dobbs-Allsopp, *Weep, O Daughter of Zion*, p. 52.

[124] E.g. *balag*s 4:b+253–256; 5:59–60, b+155–162; 6:19–23; 10:a+30–36; 43:c+224, d+269–277; 30; 50:b+181–184, 224–228.

[125] E.g. *balag*s [Inanna]; 9 [Ninurta]; 31 [Nergal]; 43 [Ninisina]; *eršemma*s 32 [Inanna]; 171 [Ninisina]. Cf. Cohen, *balag*, pp. 16–30; Dobbs-Allsopp, *Weep, O Daughter of Zion*, p. 59.

[126] Note, however, that in a number of *balag*s other gods are addressed, although usually this is achieved by employing motifs taken over from Enlil. Dobbs-Allsopp, *Weep, O Daughter of Zion*, p. 59, points out that *balag* 9:4–16, addressed to Enlil, correspond exactly to *balag* 31:a+50–67, addressed to Nergal, while the following line (a+68) simply includes Nergal's name rather than Enlil's (cf. 9:17). Other examples discovered by Dobbs-Allsopp include *balag*s 3:c+89–109; 25:1–a+26; 26:61–97; 29: c+43–64, 65–81, and *SBH* 7:37–57.

[127] Black, "A-še-er Gi$_6$-ta," 11.

Black's statement perhaps overstates the case, especially since it appears in connection with a general discussion of *balag*s, the cultic *raison d'être* of which was in part to shield the worshipers from an accidental exercise of divine power directed against them.[128] Nevertheless, Black's comment points toward the inevitable conclusion that, from the Sumerian theological perspective, disaster frequently had nothing to do with the concept of corporate or personal sin: the gods, whose hands held weal or woe, sent calamity and did so without a necessary association with human sin. Perhaps it was this perspective which accounts for the conspicuous absence in either these materials or the city laments of statements of confession or penitence on the part of persons given voice by the poets, be they human or divine. Penitential appeals will not persuade Enlil to relent, since sin had no necessary causal bearing on the described calamity. On the other hand, the lack of confessional or penitential elements in the *balag/eršemma*s could be explained simply as a consequence of their cultic use. As noted above, these materials evidently had their origins in rituals designed to placate the deities lest the destruction of a temple wall for renovation be misunderstood. In such a situation it seems unlikely that confession or penitence would play a large role: the priests were, after all, attempting to remain faithful by renovating the temple for the sake of the gods. If a wall had crumbled, this too was within the purview of the gods since it was the gods who ultimately caused its deterioration by means of arraying their cosmic forces (depicted as storm, word and enemies), against the temple wall. Regardless of whether the lack of confessional or penitential elements in the *balag/eršemma*s stems from cultic use or whether it can be traced back to a hyperextended aspect of the Sumerian *Weltanschaung*, it remains a fact that these materials lack penitential elements. This lack is particularly striking when one considers that not even the various appeals that the deity's heart (and liver) might find pacification include motivating penitential clauses. That divine wrath could be associated with personal sins of commission or omission is, of course, amply witnessed by several other types of prayers including some *ki'utukam* (= Akkadian *šuilla*) prayers and especially the penitential *dingiršadibba* prayers. A perti-

---

[128] Note, however, that Black, "A-še-er Gi₆-ta," 13, seems to object to what he calls Cohen's "functionalist" interpretation.

nent example is the bilingual *šuilla* to Anu (= Sumerian An) used in royal lustration rituals:

> May my wickedness, [sin, and grave mis]deed
> Be absolved with your [life-giving] incantation,
> And all that I have committed or neglected against my (personal) god
> [and my (personal) goddess] be absolved.
> May the angry hearts of my (personal) god and [my (personal)
> goddess be re[conciled to me,]
> May your furious heart b[e calmed],
> And [your] feelings be eased, have mercy! (lines 8–13)[129]

The juxtaposition of a statement of personal confession and penitence with this heart pacification petition only makes the absence of penitential statements in the *balag/eršemma*s that much more striking.

Nevertheless a motive for the deity to relent is implicit in a number of the *balag*s inasmuch as the materials are also characterized by large sections of praise. The praise itself may be construed as an effort on the part of the poet or the *gala* cult to motivate, manipulate, and direct the favor of the gods.[130] But, interestingly, appeals are not directed to the compassionate nature of the gods, or to their concern for the well-being of the humans who suffer at the fate of the storm, word, or enemies. Instead praise addresses the potency of the deity, recognizing the god's creative power and rule. Whether or not the praise elements reflect specific mythical creation accounts involving An or Enlil unfortunately cannot be determined since, as yet, no Sumerian myths dealing directly and explicitly with the creation of the universe have been uncovered.[131] The poets frequently employ cosmogonic images such as one would expect in a creation myth, however, and they regularly depict the deity as a sort of divine warrior. The following examples are representative:

---

[129] The translation is by Benjamin R. Foster, *Before the Muses: An Anthology of Akkadian Literature*, Volume 2: *Mature, Late* (Bethesda, MD: CDL Press, 1993), p. 549. The text, with critical notes, may also be found in Marie-Joseph Seux, *Hymnes et prières aux dieux de Babylonie et d'Assyrie*, Littératures anciennes du Proche-Orient, Vol. 8 (Paris: Les Éditions du Cerf, 1976), pp. 270–271.

[130] Patrick D. Miller, *They Cried to the Lord: The Form and Theology of Biblical Prayer* (Minneapolis: Fortress, 1994), p. 14.

[131] Samuel Noah Kramer, "Mythology of Sumer and Akkad," in *Mythologies of the Ancient World*, ed. by Samuel Noah Kramer (Garden City: Doubleday, 1961), p. 95.

Father Enlil has made the bond of heaven, which no one can reach.
The lord of the nation has made the vault of the sky, to which no one
    can ascend.
The great mountain, Enlil, the important one, has torn down the great
    doors and wall. (*balag* 6:17–19)[132]

Wise 'en,' planner, what has one known about you?
Granted strength (by) the lord of the Ekur,
born by the mountain, lord of the Eninnu,
storm, great strength of father Enlil,
reared by Dingirmah wildly poised for battle,
dispersing the mountains like meal, reaping (them) like grain,
you rushed headlong. To the land rebellious against your father
you approached. In order to destroy the mountain-land
you trample down the enemy land like a single planted reed.
You make all countries harmonious,
(saying), "I am the towering wall (of) the lands! I am their bolt!"
You beat down the mighty.
You dislodge the door of heaven,
strip away the bar of heaven,
tear off the lock of heaven,
and pull out the bolt of heaven.
You pile the disobedient land into heaps.
The rebellious land which does not hearken you do not restore.
    (*eršemma* 163.1:1–18)

What in the depths, what are you not able to reach?
What can stride with you in the sea?
Your foot smashes the rocks. Your foot tramples down the vegetation.
Those who were reared alongside you, the gods, they glean adversity
    (*var*: destruction)
The gods of heaven stand (before you).
The gods of earth gather (before you).
The Anunna-gods pay homage to you.
You killed the six-headed wild sheep in the mountain.
You trampled upon the gypsum in the mountain.
You slipped by the . . . in the standing water.
You called forth at the corner. The people in the corner were killed.

---

132 Dobbs-Allsopp, *Weep, O Daughter of Zion*, p. 68, understands similar statements
in *eršemma*s 163.1:13 and 163.2:a+14 to refer to the destruction of the city gates, walls,
and buildings, such as is standard in the city laments. The context of these passages
suggests that Dobbs-Allsopp errs on this point. In *eršemma* 163.1 one reads:

You called forth at the side. The people at the side were killed.
You called forth to every well. You filled it with blood. . .
You called forth to the dry land. . . . excrement.
. . . excrement, you have heaped it on everything. (*balag* 26:36–51).

The various deities, as warriors, also are praised as ones who guard the city, rally troops, defeat the enemy and pile their bodies in a heap, fell trees, conquer and contain the seas, control the nations and their warfare, and kill various mythological chaos monsters.[133] *Balag* 29 provides an interesting example of a divinely wrought defeat of several monsters in the context of a cosmogonic struggle:

His (word) which carried the battle up to the heavens!
His (word) which did battle on earth!
His (word) which stopped up the waters for An!
His (word) which drowned the harvest for Enki!
His (word) which cut down the oak in the road!
His (word) which snared the *anzu*-bird with a net!
His (word) which (enabled) the ruler to pile high the enemy in battle!
His (word) which killed the seven-headed snake!
His (word) which trampled upon the gypsum in the mountain!
His (word) which tred upon the *kushu*-animal in the standing water!
(d+144–153).

In praising the deities as cosmogonic divine warriors, the Meso-potamian poets generally also meant "to remind them of their spe-cial attributes, whose exercise may have caused the distress of the worshiper or may be the cause of salvation later to be invoked in

---

You beat down the mighty.
You dislodge the door of heaven,
strip away the bar of heaven,
tear off the lock of heaven,
and pull out the bolt of heaven.
You pile the disobedient land into heaps. (lines 12–16 //*eršemma* 163.2:a+13–17)

In both instances cited by Dobbs-Allsopp, Enlil is praised as the one who exercises dominion over the heavenly realm and who, consequently, has authority to deter-mine the fate of rebellious nations. Nothing in these lines suggests that reference is being made to the physical structures of the city. To the contrary, these passages more naturally point to the potency of Enlil as cosmogonic creator.

[133] E.g., *eršemma*s 1.1:1–9; 1.2:10–19 (variant version based on UET 6/2; cf. Cohen, *SH*, p. 116); 163.2:a+3–19; 13:10–14; 45:1–11; *balag*s 5:1–24; 8:1–22 (//CT 42 15:39–56, Old Babylonian); 12:e+81–90; 16:a+74–98; 21:1–48; 23:a+26–35; 27:36–51; 39:1–28.

the prayer."[134] In the case of the *balag*s and *eršemma*s the "special attribute" typically centered on the divine potency of the deities; the gods who brought storm, enemy, and a destructive word against the community were clearly powerful enough, if properly reminded and motivated, to withdraw those agents of destruction.[135]

While it cannot be determined if these materials contain explicit references to creation myths, other recognizable mythic tales emerge in many of the texts. Cohen reports that of the Old Babylonian *eršemma*s, those with narratives are based upon seven recognizable mythological backgrounds: (1) the destruction of the Eanna-temple and Uruk during Inanna's detention by Ereškigal in the netherworld (79, 32, 106), (2) the capture and death of Dumuzi (97, 88, 165, 60), (3) the capture and death of Nergal (164), (4) the plight of Ninisina (171, 159), (5) the plight of Šerida (30), (6) the investiture of Iškur (23.1, 168, 184, 185), and (7) Iškur ends a famine. However, he continues, to date no post-Old Babylonian copies of these narrative *eršemma*s have been discovered, a fact that he speculates may be attributed to their lack of suitability and adaptability in servicing a wide range of cities.[136] Significantly, however, one well known myth does persist, if not in the known first millennium *eršemma*s, then in *balag*s copied through the first millennium. The goddess Inanna mourning over Dumuzi's death provides the subject matter for *balag*s 42, 48,[137] and 49.[138] The importance of the Dumuzi myth's

---

134 E.R. Dalglish, *Psalm Fifty-One in the Light of Ancient Near Eastern Patternism* (Leiden: E.J. Brill, 1962), p. 23.

135 The various "special attributes," moreover, tend to be leveled in these materials as different gods are praised in nearly identical terms. Compare, for example, a *balag* of Asarluhi with a *balag* of Utu:

Your word is a huge net spread over heaven and earth.
When you stretch over the sea, it rages.
When you stretch over the swamp, the swamp moans.
When you are an onrush of water stretching across the Euphrates
the word of Asarluhi roils those subterranean waters. (*balag* 21:39–43)

Your word is a huge net spread over heaven and earth.
You, the hero, . . . children . . . throat . . .
When you, the hero, stretch over the sea, it rages
When you, the hero, stretch over the swamp, its moans.
When you are an onrush of water stretching across the Euphrates, . . .
You, the hero, . . . the mes-trees . . . road . . . canal . . . (*balag* 23:a+30–35)

136 Cohen, *SH*, pp. 20–21.

137 See especially lines e+140ff.

138 See especially lines c+66–96 (Old Babylonian), 1–18, a+20–e+99, e+106–130 (First Millennium).

continuance within the living cultic literature of the *gala* priesthood and of its spread to the west should not be underestimated. The east Semitic cult of Dumuzi/Tammuz was known in the west Semitic sphere already in the Bronze Age; active cultic devotion continued, in the east and in the west, through almost the entirety of Israel's history.[139] The cult was widely enough practiced in sixth-century Jerusalem that it could represent, to Ezekiel at least, a pressing danger to orthodox worship of Yahweh:

> Then he brought me to the entrance of the north gate of the house of the LORD; women were sitting there weeping for Tammuz. (Ezek 8:14).

Ezekiel's condemnation of the cult does more than testify directly to the migration of the "abomination" of the Tammuz cultic traditions into Judah; Ezekiel provides certain evidence that Judah was intimately acquainted not only with the subject matter which occupies the just mentioned first millennium *balag*s, but also with the one motif which pervades the *balag/eršemma* compositions from the Old Babylonian period down through the first millennium and which is their hallmark, namely, the motif of the weeping goddess. Whether the weeping goddess tradition came to the west from Mesopotamia with the Dumuzi/Tammuz cult or whether it represents an indigenous phenomenon is a question to which this study will return. Should the former possibility be proven likely, however, the association of the Dumuzi myth with both the first millennium *balag*s and cultic practices in sixth-century Judah would provide strong circumstantial evidence that the Mesopotamian communal lament tradition did directly affect the communal laments of Israel. Should it further prove to be the case that the weeping goddess motif can be more directly linked with Israel's own lament traditions, circumstantial evidence could be viewed instead as compelling.

The Description of Destruction

Both the city laments as well as the successor *balag/eršemma* compositions focus on the terrible destruction wreaked by Enlil's

---

[139] Susan Ackerman, *Under Every Green Tree: Popular Religion in Sixth-Century Judah*, HSM, No. 46 (Atlanta: Scholars, 1992), pp. 79–93. Ackerman believes that sixth-century Jerusalem could be receptive to the Tammuz cult because it resonated with the indigenous worship of Queen Ištar-Astarte as well as the cult of the dying and rising fertility god Baal.

various agents of annihilation. Basically no aspect of urban life remains unaffected: the city itself and its physical environs are leveled, social life is disrupted, and the temple is ruined and its rites terminated.

Like an approaching storm, the tempestuous word of the deity devastates the land surrounding the city. References to floods drowning the harvest,[140] quaking earth,[141] famine[142] and a general disruption of the elements necessary to support the Mesopotamian agrarian economy make their occasional way into the texts. An example of the latter appears in the praise Ninurta heaps upon himself:

> Hostile land! Oh! Oh you! Oh you! Oh! Oh I! Oh I!
> Hostile land, when will your clay return to its ground?
> Hostile land, when will your reeds return to their canebrake?
> Hostile land, when will your beams return to their forests?
> (*balag* 26:88–91)

The destruction of the city occupies a greater portion of the poets' imagination. Whether the agency is storm, word, or a nameless enemy, the city itself is said to be demolished by fire, "carried away," and knocked off its foundation.[143] The city becomes an abandoned tell, a haunted place inhabited by wild beasts.[144]

Naturally the destruction of the land and the city have dramatic, deleterious effects on the normal workings of society. In a few instances it appears that the armies defending the city have been defeated because the divine warrior has not preceded them onto the battlefield.[145] Defeat by the enemy or the tempestuous word of the god both lead to the same result: a general disorder prevails. Robbers plunder without consequence:

> On my road hostile bandits commit murder. In my street during
> the night thieves break into (the homes). (*balag* 42)

Nor is lawlessness the only consequence of the calamity. People, including merchants, craftsmen, shepherds and prostitutes, find

---

140 E.g., *balags* 12:34; 47.

141 E.g., *balags* 31:a+65; *SBH* 7. Cf. Cohen, *CLAM*, p. 531.

142 E.g., *balags* 8:36–37; 13:b+64–65; 43:a+42–43, c+214–215.

143 *Balag* 25:A+19–20; cf. *balag* 42.

144 E.g., *balags* 4:a+210, 223; 5:d+179, 194; 10:a+22–27, 31, 122–125; 13:f+212–15.

145 E.g., *balag* 8:77–82; *eršemma* 53:8; cf. 1.1:8; 1.2:8.

themselves unable to pursue their normal occupations.[146] Young and
old alike go mad even as wild dogs carry off the dispersed citizenry.[147] Whether the texts intend to refer literally to dogs or if they
are metaphorical descriptions of the enemy taking captives into
exile remains indeterminable from the context. The laments, however, clearly were not unfamiliar with the horrors of exile. *Balag* 42,
for example, includes the notice that

> The patrician men, the patrician mothers have been led away.
> The plebeian men, the plebeian mothers have been led away . . .
> Its fleeing men who have been captured . . .[148]

Those not dragged away into captivity remain to face decimating
famine,[149] and the corpses of those who perished by hunger, disease,
or sword are stacked in heaps.[150]

Surpassing in length the description of the fall of the city and the
effects on its population is the attention given by the poets to the
details surrounding the fate of the city temple, its heart and center.
The condition of the temple is a particular concern to the weeping
goddess who articulates, frequently in great detail, its destruction
and desolation. *Balag* 50, quoted at some length above, has already
indicated a common theme of lament: the plunder of the temple
treasures and the removal of its sacred images. These acts, perpe-
trated by an enemy, would doubtless seem especially odious as
the sacred precincts were not to be gazed upon, let alone violated,
by foreigners.[151] But the plunder was only the beginning of the goddess's complaint. Her residence, abandoned in the wake of the destructive agents, came to be the abode of birds and beasts, unfit for
her habitation. Its walls and brickwork collapsed into ruin. The
sentiments expressed by the goddess in *balag* 10 typify many similar
passages:

> Lamentation! My treasure house which is (in the hands of) the enemy!
> Its crenelated wall has been destroyed. Its dove hovers about.

---

[146] E.g., *balags* 4:a+196–197, 198–200, 231–232; 5:d+165–169, 183; PBS 10/2 no. 12 +
VAS 2 12, obv. ii:1–2 (Cohen, *CLAM*, p. 264); 42:85–89

[147] E.g., *eršemma* 1.1:30–35; 1.2:45–49.

[148] Cf. *balag* 25:f+130; *eršemma* 1.1:30–35; 160:25.

[149] E.g., *balags* 8:36–37; 13:b+64–65; 43:a+42–43, c+214–215.

[150] E.g., *balags* 2:27–31; 43:a+36; *eršemma* 35.2:27–31.

[151] Dobbs-Allsop, *Weep, O Daughter of Zion*, p. 69. This concept likewise finds expression in LSUr 151–152, 197–198, 442; EL 4:9–10, 6:12'; CA 129–130.

Its door-frame has been torn down. What was once a place of marvel
   is no more.
Its rafters lie exposed to the sun like a man felled by a disease.
Its jutting brickwork is crouching in tears like a mother in mourning.
Its reed eaves are lying on the ground like plucked hairs.
Its reed mat is contorted like a person (suffering) from colic.
Like a flying bat, its . . . has disappeared within the ruin mound.
In closing (the door), its doorposts have fallen like a man bathing . . .
(The inhabitants) of my house have abandoned it. Outside they just
   pass by.
(The inhabitants) of my house, the faithful house, he [Enlil] has made
   unclean. (lines a+11–19, 37–38)[152]

Most distressing of all, however, was the cessation of cultic activities
within the temple. The songs and sacred rites of the *gala* priesthood
came to an end, as did the celebrative feasts:

Oh house, my tasty food which is not being eaten!
Oh house, my sweet water which is not being drunk!
My house of the good seat where no one is sitting!
My house of the good bed chamber where no one is lying down!
My house of the holy plate where no one is eating!
My house of the holy bronze (vessel) where no one is drinking!
My house of the holy offering table which no one carries!
My (house) of the holy vessel where no one libates water!
My (house) of the holy kettledrum where it is not set up!
My (house) of the holy balag-instrument which no one plays!
My (house) of the holy halhallatu-drum which does not resound!
My (house) of the holy manzu-drum which does not sound sweet!
My reed pipe which does not thunder forth!
My instruments which are not being distributed!
My gala-priest who no longer soothes my heart!
My gudu-priest who no longer speaks happily!
My house! My happy spouse who no longer is present there!
My house! My sweet child who no longer is present there!
My house! I, its lady do not majestically pass through it.
I do not majestically pass through it. I am no longer majestically
   present there. (*eršemma* 159:9–28)[153]

In this context one should also note a similar, often-spoken complaint that the diviners and dream interpreters either lie (e.g., *balag*s

---

[152] Other examples include *balag*s 3:1–28; 4:137–70; b:155–161
[153] Cf. *eršemma* 106; *balag*s 1:81–89; 3:a+51–54; 4:a+198–232; 5:d+165–201;
6:214–246; PBS 10/2 no. 12 + VAS 2 12:obv. col. ii 1–31; 25:60–68' 50:a+81–86.

5:35–36, 9:4–5) or are unable to perform their respective functions (e.g., *balag* 13:f+160). Similarly *balag* 12:b+100 states, "His word has no diviner. It has no interpreter." As Dobbs-Allsopp correctly notes, these sentiments invariably find expression in the context of the praise of Enlil's word and its incomprehensibility.[154] The reasons why these statements seem to appear only in the context of praise remain perhaps as mysterious as Enlil's word itself. The larger context of the *balag*s suggests, however, that these statements were not descriptive of the normal state of affairs; deceit by diviners or their inability to discern the divine purposes was a consequence of the total disruption brought about by the onslaught of the word of the god.

Importunities

A final characteristic of the *balag* and *eršemma* compositions finds expression in the array of importunities expressed to the deity. Once more the pleas have their precedents in the city laments upon which these materials were modeled.

Chief among these importunities, of course, stands the heart pacification unit discussed above, which, though not present in all of the *balag*s, appears as a ubiquitous feature of *eršemma*s. Frequently these units also include appeals for lesser gods to intercede with the god/goddess to whom the work is addressed. For example, *eršemma* 13, addressed to Marduk, includes requests that Panunanki, Mudugasa, Ningutešasiga, and Nanâ all "utter a prayer" to the deity that his heart might be pacified and his liver calmed.[155]

Importunities are not limited to the heart pacification units, however, and scattered throughout the materials one often finds statements which either explicitly or implicitly urge the deity to action. The deity may be urged simply to change his mind[156] or to "rise up" or awaken from his slumber, in order to consider the disaster:

---

154 Dobbs-Allsopp, *Weep, O Daughter of Zion*, p. 75, n. 194. The conclusion he draws from this, however, that similar statements in Lamentations should not be directly compared since "the image seems to function quite differently in the two contexts," does not obviate the fact that both Lamentations and the *balag*s clearly describe the disruption of normal cultic functions.

155 Cf. lines 22–31.

156 E.g., *balag* 16:48–50.

> Let the resting bull arise!
> Let resting Enlil arise!
> Let the resting bison arise! (balag 16:a+60–63)[157]

Similar to the call for the deity to awaken, and here linked to it, is the characteristic woe-cry "How long?":

> How long will the sleeping one sleep?
> How long will the great mountain father Enlil sleep?
> How long will the shepherd of the black-headed sleep?
> How long will he who witnesses everything first hand sleep?
> How long will the bull who causes the troops to wander sleep?
> How long will he who sleeps a false sleep? (balag 8:77–82)[158]

The "how long?" of the woe cry implies a request that the deity might consider the circumstances of the city and its temple and thereby be moved quickly to alleviate the distress. The desire for divine action becomes explicit as the poets urge the deity to rise up or walk about and look upon the havoc.[159] Again in *balag* 13 Enlil is encouraged to "go about!" and to "watch over" his city (f+166–192). The context makes plain that the request intended Enlil to perceive that his city had been flooded (f+192–202) and its people driven mad by grief (f+203–215). Implicit in this petition is the expectation that Enlil will be sufficiently disturbed by what he sees that he will bring relief. What remains of the next *kirugu* (f+216–246) reports that the deity is disturbed; his "heart is not calm" and he recites dirges in the wilderness. Unfortunately, any further action the deity might have taken at that point has not been preserved.

A final common importunity appears in the pleas that the god and goddess either not abandon their cities and their proper residences in the temples or, having done so, that they return. *Eršemma* 13 provides an example of the plea that the god, in this case Marduk, not abandon his city:

> "You should not desert your city!" may he utter to you! May he utter
>   a prayer to you!

---

[157] Cf. *balag* 13:71–73. Also note *eršemma* 1.1:9 where Enlil is described as "He who sleeps a false sleep."

[158] The lament occurs frequently; other examples are to be found in *balag* 6:24–29, a+107–119; 16:a+33–34. Cf. 13:b+47 where the another woe-cry, "When . . . the land?" (presumably 'when [will be the restoration of] the land?') is repeated.

[159] E.g., *balags* 5:108–119, 120; 6:25, b+121–132, b+193–209; 10:a+52–67; 13: c+119–122; CT 42 26: 1–2; *eršemma* 1.1: 1–20; 1.2:1–27.

"You should never desert Tinter!" may he utter to you! May he utter a
prayer to you! (lines 30–31).

Elsewhere the god/goddess is said to have already deserted the city,
and the deities are encouraged to return:

> Sir, you have turned away from your city. When will you return?
> Enlil, you have turned away from your city. When will you return?
> You have turned away from Uruk, from the Eanna. When will you
> return? (*balag* 6:b+247–249)

The petitions are urgent ones as the return of the deity to his or her
place signals a restoration of divine favor and order.

All of these importunities are motivated by the understanding
that, just as calamity has come as a result of the god/goddess's decision and will, so too relief will arrive only when the deity is moved
to remedy the situation. Against the inscrutable purposes of the
gods and against the exercise of divine power human beings can do
little more than implore the god or goddess to act, and quickly.

SUMMARY

In the discussion above, an attempt has been made to outline
those aspects of the *balag/eršemma*s which are characteristic of the
sub-genre. In most respects the *balag*s and *eršemma*s show themselves to be the literary progeny of the earlier city laments. A number of consistent features appear throughout these materials. While
no single text contains all of the elements, the following can be said
to be typical of the *balag/eršemma*s:

1. Structure and content
   A. Large sections of praise in which the chief deity is
      frequently described as a powerful cosmogonic
      divine warrior who is held responsible for the
      destruction
   B. Narrative descriptions of the disaster in which
      (1) the chief deity, responsible for the fate of the city
          and temple, issues destructive agents, described
          mainly as storm, divine word, and alien invaders
      (2) cities and their environs are destroyed and
          transformed by fire, flood, and earthquake into
          abandoned tells

      (3) society is disrupted as city residents are indiscriminately slaughtered or driven into exile

      (4) the temple is plundered and destroyed which results in divine abandonment and the cessation of cultic activities

   C. Importunities that disaster might end and order be restored, including

      (1) petitions that the deity awaken

      (2) petitions that the deity might gaze upon the disaster

      (3) petitions that lesser gods would intercede

      (4) petitions that the god/goddess would return to the temple

      (5) the woe cry "How long?"

2. Various poetic devices, the most notable being

   A. A shift in speakers; various *dramatis personae* are given voice

   B. Lists, including names of the destroyed temples, epithets of the deity, names of gods said to intercede, etc.

3. A weeping goddess figure who articulates a detailed lament over the destruction of her city and temple; in the *balag*s she is not infrequently linked to the Dumuzi myth

4. The absence of penitential motifs

Some differences have been noted between the *balag/eršemma*s and the city laments. In particular the texts are distinguishable by the lack of historic specificity within the later *balag*s and *eršemma*s when compared to the city laments. While sometimes giving the appearance of treating historic moments when the city and temple fell at the hand of an enemy or was destroyed by a natural disaster, the *balag/eršemma*s were not inspired by any such historic event. This distinction has been explained as likely the result of a difference in the cultic use to which the materials were employed: whereas the city laments were composed for a specific occasion and then almost immediately retired from use, the *balag*s and *eršemma*s found employment in the ongoing cultic activities of the *gala* priesthood who composed them and preserved them.

Although the *balag*s and *eršemma*s evidently had an original ritual purpose to appease the potential wrath of a deity prior to temple renovations, the ritual calendars and other extant references indicate that these texts came to be used on other occasions as well. Rather than a single *Sitz im Leben*, it appears the laments were recited routinely, as a way to prevent the inadvertent invocation of the wrath of the various gods whom they addressed. That these materials could be and were adapted for cultic purposes which varied somewhat from those for which they were first composed doubtless accounts for their tenacity in Mesopotamian worship practices.

The fact that the *balag*s and *eršemma*s were commonly and broadly used down to the close of the first millennium BCE means that they were contemporaneous with the cult in Israel for essentially the entire course of Israel's history. In Chapter 2 of the present investigation it was shown that temporal proximity and geographic proximity are among the first important criteria for comparing texts from two separate cultures. The *balag*s and *eršemma*s provide an example of a specific type of literature, the communal lament, which was temporally and geographically proximate to the writings of Israel. But did these writings impact the Hebrew lament tradition and, if so, in what way? This question has already been vigorously pursued vis-à-vis the question of the potential influence of the Sumero-Akkadian lamentations upon the Book of Lamentations, although no consensus has yet been reached. The task ahead is to discover what influences the Mesopotamian traditions may have had on Israel's psalms. In order to further this matter attention first must be given to the scope and substance of the Hebrew communal laments.

CHAPTER 4

THE HEBREW COMMUNAL LAMENTS

The Difficulties of Definition

Any effort to discuss the characteristic features of the Hebrew communal lament psalms immediately encounters a fundamental difficulty, namely, the problem of the classification and enumeration of the psalms to be included in the *Gattung*. Which psalms shall be considered? What constitutes a communal lament? What are its normative features? Is the *Gattung* identifiable by its formal characteristics, by content, or by some combination of content and form? These are, of course, the essential questions of form criticism[1] which, in spite of occasional criticisms,[2] continues to benefit biblical studies in general and psalm studies in particular. And yet, as Table 1

---

[1] A full rehearsal of the tenets of form criticism lies outside the scope of this presentation. Moreover, the need for such a review is obviated by the vast number of publications on the subject including, especially, Klaus Koch, *Was ist Formgeschichte?* (2nd ed.; Neukirchen-Vluyn: Neukirchener Verlag, 1967), [Eng. *The Growth of the Biblical Tradition: The Form Critical Method*, trans. by S.M. Cupitt, (2nd ed.; New York, Charles Scribner's Sons, 1969)]; Edgar V. McKnight, *What Is Form Criticism?* (Philadelphia: Fortress, 1969); Gene M. Tucker, *Form Criticism of the Old Testament* (Philadelphia: Fortress, 1971); John H. Hayes, ed., *Old Testament Form Criticism* (San Antonio: Trinity University, 1974); John Barton., *Reading the Old Testament: Method in Biblical Study*, (Philadelphia: Westminster Press, 1984), pp. 30–44; *idem*, "Form Criticism (OT)," *ABD*, Vol. 2, pp. 838–841.

[2] See especially James Muilenberg, "Form Criticism and Beyond," *JBL* 88 (1969), 1–18; R. Knierim, "Old Testament Form Criticism Reconsidered," *Int* 27/4 (1973), 435–468.

Table 1. Hebrew Communal Laments in the Psalter as Identified by Various Scholars*

Pss.	HG	SM	OE	CW	AW	JD	AA	LS	BA	MD	HK	EL	MH	Totals
9/10												x		1
12		x				x		x	x			x		5
14		x												1
36												x		1
44	x	x	x	x	x	x		x	x	x	x	x	x	12
58	x	x				x		x	x			x		6
60	x	x	x	x		x	x	x	x	x	x	x	x	12
74	x	x	x	x	x	x	x	x	x	x	x	x	x	13
77								x			x	x		3
79	x	x	x	x	x	x	x	x	x	x	x	x	x	13
80	x	x	x	x	x	x	x	x	x	x	x	x	x	13
82								x						1
83	x	x	x	x	x	x	x	x	x	x	x	x	x	13
85						x	x	x	x		x	x		6
89	x	x	x	x			x	x	x				x	8
90						x	x	x	x		x	x		6
94	x					x		x			x			4
106								x						1
108								x						1
123								x	x		x			2
124							x							1
126						x	x	x	x		x			5
129									x	x	x			3
137					x	x	x	x	x		x	x		7
144		x												1
Totals	9	11	7	7	6	13	11	19	15	7	14	14	7	

*Scholars

HG = H. Gunkel	AW = A. Weiser	BA = B. Anderson	MH = M. Haar
SM = S. Mowinckel	JD = J. Day	MD = M. Dahood	
OE = O. Eissfeldt	AA = A. Anderson	HK = H.-J. Kraus	
CW = C. Westermann	LS = L. Sabourin	EL = E.A. Leslie	

indicates, when attempting to discern which psalms ought to be classified as communal laments, critical scholarship finds little consensus.[3]

At least two reasons for the divided opinion relative to the determination of this *Gattung* can be identified. First is the methodological problem inherent in the discipline itself. As H. Gunkel long ago recognized, while *Gattung* identification consists primarily of

---

[3] Sources for the table include Gunkel, "Psalmen," *RGG* (1913), col. 1934; Mowinckel, *The Psalms*, vol. 1, p. 194; O. Eissfeldt, *The Old Testament: An Introduction*, trans. by P. Ackroyd (New York: Harper & Row, 1965), p. 112; Claus Westermann, *Praise and Lament in the Psalms*, trans. by Keith R. Crim and Richard N. Soulen (Atlanta: John Knox Press, 1981), pp. 173–174; Artur Weiser, *The Psalms: A Commentary*, trans. by Herbert Hartwell (Philadelphia: Westminster Press, 1962), p. 66; J. Day, *Psalms* (Sheffield: Sheffield Academic Press, 1992), p. 33; A.A. Anderson, *The Book of Psalms* (London: Oliphants, 1972), vol. 1, p. 39; Leopold Sabourin, *The Psalms: Their Origin and Meaning* (New York: Alba House, 1974), p. 297; Bernhard W. Anderson, *Out of the Depths: The Psalms Speak for Us Today* (Philadelphia: Westminster, 1983), p. 235; Hans-Joachim Kraus, *Psalms 1–59*, trans. by Hilton C. Oswald (Minneapolis: Augsburg, 1988), p. 50; E.A. Leslie, *The Psalms: Translated and Interpreted in the Light of Hebrew Life and Worship* (New York: Abingdon Cokesbury, 1949), pp. 217–258; Joseph Murray Haar, "The God-Israel Relationship in the Community Lament Psalms" (Ph.D. dissertation, Union Theological Seminary, 1985), p. 59. The three-volume commentary of Mitchell Dahood, *Psalms*, (New York: Doubleday, 1970), while not including a list of the psalms in question, does describe the psalms listed below as lamentations of the community.

The recent major commentary by James Luther Mays, *Psalms* (Louisville: John Knox Press, 1994), has been intentionally omitted from Table 1. Although Mays does list (p. 25) Psalms 44, 74, 79, 80, and 83 as "clear examples" of a corporate prayer for help, including his work in the table would violate that author's purposes. While acknowledging the significant contributions of form critical research, Mays's commentary appears to be written in direct response to the call of Muilenberg, *op.cit.*, for critical scholarship to move "beyond" form criticism. Muilenberg notes that form criticism has an inherent penchant to stress the typical and representative to the exclusion of individual, personal, and unique features of any given particular pericope. Form criticism is, in his view, "by its very nature bound to generalize because it is concerned with what is common to all the representatives of a genre, and therefore applies an external measure to the individual pericopes" (p. 5). Mays echoes Muilenberg's position (pp. 19–21), refusing to "bind the interpretation of a psalm to a definite setting" since "identifying a psalm by type does not necessarily determine a context of composition and use in which it is to be interpreted." Leery of the "temptation to take form critical identification as the final and decisive goal and guide in interpretation," he refuses to provide a complete list of psalms according to classification by type. Instead he advocates a literary analysis in order to discern the individuality of a psalm, seeking to uncover the peculiar features of a psalm rather than what is typical.

the isolation of the formal features of a text, the content and mood also play a role.[4] While in principle drawing conclusions from the process of analyzing both form and content simultaneously is no different, for example, than methods employed for determining which, of two formally identical dramas, is a comedy and which is a tragedy,[5] the result with respect to psalm studies has been less than salutary. Much depends on whether one gives more weight to formal characteristics of the text or its content. Scholars frequently disagree as to which poems, both within and outside of the Psalter, ought be classified as communal laments. A way beyond this impasse has been offered in a significant study by Joseph Murray Haar[6] whose work will be considered below. Haar has carefully analyzed the communal lament genre and, in so doing, has developed a more objective set of criteria for the identification of the *Gattung*.

Prior to discussing the contribution of Haar, however, it remains to articulate a second, related cause for the lack of scholarly consensus. While one might suppose that, by definition, communal laments involve the concerns of a larger group and therefore could be at least initially identified in the Hebrew texts by the use of the first common plural forms, critical scholars writing during this past century have often voiced a contrary opinion. Specifically, not a few scholars, including most notably, H. Birkeland,[7] S. Mowinckel,[8] J.H. Eaton,[9] and S.J.L. Croft,[10] have held the view that a number of Hebrew lamentations, characterized by first common singular pronouns and verbal conjugations, were in fact composed with the full community of faith in view. These so-called "I" psalms, though putatively giving voice to concerns of an individual, are considered by these scholars to be, in fact, communal in character since the individual speaker stands as a representative of the community at large,

---

[4] Gunkel, "The Poetry of the Psalms", p. 125. Although Gunkel here criticizes Mowinckel's attempt to establish a *Gattung* on the basis of "ideas and moods" present in the text, in the next pages he relies on these features for his own classification.

[5] John Barton, "Form Criticism (OT)," *ABD*, p. 840.

[6] Joseph Murray Haar, "The God-Israel Relationship in the Community Lament Psalms" (unpublished Ph.D. dissertation, Union Theological Seminary, 1985).

[7] H. Birkeland, *Die Feinde des Individuums in der israelitischen Psalmenliteratur* (Oslo: Grondahl, 1933); *idem, The Evildoers in the Book of Psalms* (Oslo: J. Dybwad, 1955).

[8] Especially his *The Psalms*.

[9] J.H. Eaton, *Kingship and the Psalms* (2nd ed.; Sheffield: JSOT, 1986).

[10] S.J.L. Croft, *The Identity of the Individual in the Psalms* (Sheffield: JSOT, 1987).

a king or perhaps a priest, and the "enemies" are actually almost all foreigners. For this reason the list of those psalms which ought be considered communal laments should, in this view, be expanded considerably so as to encompass not only those psalms marked by first common plural discourse, but many of those texts which are only superficially laments of the individual as well. Mowinckel, for example, would include Psalms 3; 5; 7; 9/10–12; 17; 22; 25–28; 31; 34–35; 37; 40; 42/43; 51–52; 54–57; 59; 61; 63–64; 69–71; 77; 86; 90; 94; 102; 109; 130; 141–143 among those that are actually communal laments in the "I" form.[11]

Obviously, if those who hold this view are correct, the difficulty in circumscribing constitutive features of the communal laments would be greatly exacerbated. A study of communal laments would need, perforce, to include any formal features and themes characteristic of the "I" psalms and integrate these into the total portrait of Israel's communal laments. On the other hand, if the assumption that the "I" psalms are communal by virtue of their recitation by a representative individual proves erroneous, studies which weld these materials into a composite portrait of communal laments are likely to reach skewed conclusions. If these results are then used as the basis for comparison with the communal lament traditions of other peoples, further distortion can be anticipated.

The recently published volume on the genre of the communal lament by Paul Wayne Ferris provides a case in point. Ferris identifies Psalms 31, 35, 42, 43, 44, 56, 59, 60, 69, 74, 77, 79, 80, 83, 85, 89, 94, 102, 109, 137, and 142, as well as the entire Book of Lamentations, as appropriate objects of study for a larger investigation of the genre of communal lament.[12] How does he come to determine that these materials are communal laments? As Ferris concurs wholeheartedly with Mowinckel's assessment of the royal identity of the speaker in these poems, a number of the "I-form" psalms appear in his list.[13] Beyond this, Ferris identifies those biblical texts which include expressions of the thought and mood of grief and appeal for deliverance of a community as the proper subject of his study. Only those compositions which include penitential statements are omitted since these are classified by him as penitential psalms rather

---

[11] Cf. Mowinckel, *The Psalms*, vol. 1, pp. 225–246.
[12] Ferris, *Genre*, p. 14.
[13] *Ibid.*

than as laments.[14] This means, however, that practically speaking *any* composition may be classified as a communal lament so long as it is without extended penitential portions and its

> verbal content indicates that it was composed to be used by and/ or on behalf of a community to express both complaint, and sorrow and grief over some perceived calamity, physical or cultural, which had befallen or was about to befall them and to appeal to God for deliverance.[15]

Although this definition of communal lament is sufficiently broad to encompass any number of prophetic oracles, Ferris provides neither discussion of these texts nor an explanation for their omission. Instead, of the vast array of materials included in his definition, Ferris discerns that most of these include what he regards as formal factors, namely an invocation, a hymn of praise, expression(s) of confidence and trust, lament, appeals and motivation for response, a protestation of innocence, an expression of confidence and hope, and a vow of praise.[16] Of these features, direct address, the complaint/lament, and the appeal are judged most common, although none of these, he acknowledges, are "inherently communal." This confession, one would suppose, already casts sufficient doubt on the utility of the formal factors he uses for his analysis as to call into question any conclusions drawn by his study. Be that as it may, Ferris's next step is a comparison of these structural elements with those of various types of Mesopotamian lamentations. His approach to the Mesopotamian compositions is equally monolithic. Mesopotamian communal laments, like the Hebrew texts, include any and all "compositions which concern themselves primarily with some issue or event which has caused or is causing grief in the community"[17] including the Sumerian city laments, *balag*s, *eršemma*s, *šuilla*s, *eršaḫunga*s, and various funerary dirges and elegies.

Perhaps not surprisingly, Ferris discovers few points of commonality between Hebrew and Mesopotamian communal laments. Similar structural elements appear in both culture's compositions, but these similarities are judged coincidental, stemming from "those aspects of ancient Near Eastern culture and experience which the

---

14 *Ibid.*, p. 10, n. 32.
15 *Ibid.*
16 *Ibid.*, pp. 89–100.
17 *Ibid.*, p. 109.

two have in common"[18] such as death by natural causes, plagues, famine and war, as well as similarities in their respective views on kingship and the nation. While frequently helpful as a summary of various aspects of the Mesopotamian lament tradition, the work as a whole is fatally flawed by an overly broad definition of that which constitutes communal lamentations in both the Hebrew and the Mesopotamian traditions. Mesopotamian materials find employment in his argument without discrimination, so long as they have as their content something to do with a calamity facing a group. The Hebrew compositions, including the "I-form" laments, find inclusion on the same grounds. The validity of Mowinckel's designation of a large number of these poems as "national psalms of lamentation in the I-form" remains unquestioned throughout the study. The juxtaposition of these sundry materials and their subsequent comparison have predictably negative results; the conclusions derived on these grounds would be little different, one suspects, had Ferris chosen to compare the Hebrew compositions with the written complaints of any literate culture, no matter how far removed or near that culture's temporal and geographic context.

While the numerous problems with Ferris's methodology trouble much of his investigation, that author's unquestioning acceptance of Birkeland's and Mowinckel's assessment of the nature of the "I-form" lament touches most directly on the present discussion. Ferris's silence on the subject notwithstanding, pressing reasons exist for challenging the inclusion of the "I form" laments in the *Gattung* of communal lamentations.[19] One must, of course, acknowledge that at least some of the "I-form" psalms portray the enemies as foreigners and therefore allow the possibility that the speaker is a king or some other representative of the nation.[20] Having noted that, however, it should quickly be added that Birkeland's extreme claim to the effect that all these laments were written for recitation by a king and have foreign enemies in view not only exaggerates the available evidence[21] but confuses the genuinely royal motifs found

---

[18] *Ibid.*, p. 170.

[19] For the following, see especially Day, *Psalms*, pp. 22–23.

[20] E.g., the explicit reference to foreigners in Psalms 9:5,8,15,17,19; 10:16; 56:7; 59:5,8.

[21] J. Day, *Psalms*, p. 23. See the similar assessment of Birkeland's thesis by A.R. Johnson, "The Psalms," in *The Old Testament and Modern Study*, ed. by H.H. Rowley (Oxford: Clarendon, 1951), p. 203.

elsewhere in the Psalter.[22] The mere fact that the psalmists employ stereotypical language with the result that foreign and other kinds of enemies sometimes are portrayed in the same terms does not lead to the inevitable conclusion that all unnamed enemies mentioned in these psalms were therefore foreigners. In Psalms 6, 13, 38, 39, 69, and 88, for example, the psalmist complains of illness; the conclusion that enemies mentioned in these contexts were foreigners can be reached only with great difficulty.

Several other arguments against the view that the enemies are primarily foreigners have been offered by J. Day:[23]

1. In the individual lament psalms the speaker seems not to represent a group but instead stands alone.
2. While a number of psalms do describe the enemies' actions as aggressively warlike, others claim that the abuse is verbal rather than physical and imply that the psalmist's plight has to do with false accusations.[24]
3. Not a few psalms specifically identify the enemies as neighbors and compatriots.[25]
4. Jeremiah's prophecies, which certainly contain a number of passages in the individual lament form,[26] have been shown by W. Baumgartner to be dependent on an original psalm form rather than appearing as the creation of the prophet[27] and thus testify to the use of these materials by private individuals—or at least an association of them with private individuals—and not just the king.

The cumulative weight of these several objections presses against wholesale acceptance of the interpretation of the "I-form" laments offered by Birkeland and others. In particular the clear evidence provided by Jeremiah's confessions to the effect that individual lament psalms were connected with persons other than a representative figure prior to the destruction of Jerusalem in 587 BCE raises the

---

[22] J. David Pleins, *The Psalms: Songs of Tragedy, Hope, and Justice* (Maryknoll, NY: Orbis Books, 1993), p. 194, n. 1.

[23] J. Day, *Psalms*, p. 24–25.

[24] E.g., Pss 64:3; 57:4; 140:3,9.

[25] E.g., Pss 55:12–14; 31:11; 35:11ff.; 69:8,20ff.; 88:8,18.

[26] Jeremiah's so-called "confessions," Jer 11:18–12:6; 15:10–21; 17:14–18; 18:18–23; 20:7–18.

[27] W. Baumgartner, *Die Klagegedicte des Jeremia*, BZAW, Vol. 32 (Giessen: A. Toppelmann, 1917), [Eng. *Jeremiah's Poems of Lament* (Sheffield: Almond, 1988)].

possibility that the derivation of the "I-form" laments, on those few occasions when they do appear to involve foreign enemies and a representative spokesperson, was the reverse of that proposed by Birkeland: originally individual lamentations were later adapted and employed for corporate worship.[28]

Claus Westermann, whose form critical work on the psalms continues profoundly to influence psalm studies, soundly rejects Birkeland's and Mowinckel's analysis of the "I-form" laments.[29] Westermann does, of course, recognize the similarities between structural features of the individual and the communal laments. Specifically, the lament psalms, whether individual or communal, share the structural components of address (and introductory petition), lament, a confession of trust or turning to God, petition, and a vow of praise.[30] Nevertheless, Westermann insists, the communal laments are form critically distinctive on a number of levels. For example, certain thematic elements within the lament portion receive greater emphasis, especially the complaint against God, the lament over personal suffering, and the complaint about the enemy.[31] Moreover, he observes, other significant differences manifest themselves: a section treating the review of God's past help appears regularly in the communal laments but is all but absent in the individual laments.[32] Individual laments, on the other hand, typically witness expressions of confidence and the assurance of being heard in their conclusions; these features almost never occur in the communal laments.[33]

---

[28] Contemporary analogies to this phenomenon abound. The text to the perennially favorite Christian hymn, "Amazing Grace, How Sweet the Sound," for example, was composed by John Newton (1725–1807) in grateful response to God for the salvation which he believed he had received. The hymn alludes to aspects of his own early life (he was a self-described "infidel and libertine, a servant of slaves [slave trader] in Africa") and is composed in the first-person singular throughout. This clergyman's hymn continues to be sung by Christians in corporate worship settings without alteration of the first-person singular pronouns. For details on the life of Newton, which included the award of a Doctor of Divinity degree from the College of New Jersey (now Princeton University), see Marilyn Kay *Hymnal Companion to the Lutheran Book of Worship* (Philadelphia: Fortress, 1981), pp. 333–334.

[29] Claus Westermann, *Praise and Lament*, p. 167.

[30] *Ibid.*, p. 170.

[31] *Ibid.*, pp. 176–181.

[32] The two exceptions are Psalms 22 and 143.

[33] Claus Westermann, *The Psalms: Structure, Content and Message* (Minneapolis: Augsburg Publishing House, 1980), p. 62.

Undergirding Westermann's research are a pair of postulates which, he argues, can be demonstrated by texts from within and outside of the Book of Psalms. First, Westermann assumes that psalm types have a history which is evolutionary in character and which can be discerned. Second, Westermann postulates a more or less pure form for each of the psalm types: the forms emerged in the course of the historical development of their respective types. While tolerating a good deal of individual variation, the psalm types demonstrate a consistency of subject matter and order which is sufficient for form-critical classification and, to a lesser degree, for dating the psalm. Westermann's suggestions for dating a particular psalm are often given in connection with its adherence to or deviation from the pure form: the closer the psalm is to the pure form, the older it is.

On the basis of his pure structure, Westermann can find but six, or possibly seven, laments of the people (Psalms 44; [60]; 74; 79; 80; 83; 89)[34] all of which diverge in one way or another from his ideal type. When Westermann stops to explain these variations he does so on the grounds of his assumptions mentioned above. Communal laments in the Psalter are the result of an evolutionary literary process that can be traced. According to Westermann, communal laments have their origin in primitive complaints found within narrative texts where they appear unadorned by petitions, motivation clauses, or any of the other accoutrements that came to be formally characteristic of the canonical psalms of communal lament and that, in post-biblical writings, were again separated from the lament proper. At some point during this developmental process a "pure" form of communal laments emerged, that is, a lament marked by the first-person plural as well as the aforementioned component parts of address, lament, confession of trust, petition, and vow of praise. As none of the communal laments in the Psalter represent the "pure" form, they must represent a later stage in the

---

[34] *Ibid.*, p. 31. There Westermann also identifies "motifs or reflections" of the communal lament psalms in Psalms 82, 85, 68, 90, 106, and 115. Elsewhere he discovers the communal lament form in Isaiah 63:7–64:12 and Lamentations 5. Cf. his *Praise and Lament*, p. 174; *idem, Isaiah 40–66*, trans. by David M.G. Stalker (Philadelphia: Westminster, 1977), p. 386; *Lamentations*, p. 211. Curiously, Westermann, *Praise and Lament*, p. 174, also lists Habakkuk 1 under the communal laments in spite of the observation on the previous page of that same volume that Habakkuk 1:2ff. is formally a lament of the individual. He explains that within the context of the whole book, only a lament of the people can be in mind (cf. p. 173, n. 22).

literary evolution. He notes of Psalm 83, for example, that since references to the enemy predominate the text including even the petitionary portion and, further, since similar features elsewhere appear only in a group of individual laments, "Ps. 83 probably belongs close to this group [of individual laments] and is for this reason a mixed form. Certainly it is to be considered a postexilian Psalm."[35] As this example illustrates, Westermann grants the communal laments in the Book of Psalms a relative dating based on whether or not their present form is nearer or farther removed from the floruit of the hypothesized early pure form. He is persuaded that the lament of the people, though rarely found in the Psalms, "must have played an important role in Israel during the pre-exilic period, for the laments collected in Lamentations, which with certainty began to appear after 586 BC, *already represent a mixed form which presupposes the pure form of the lament of the people and is possible only after it.*"[36]

While the assumption of a late compositional date does account for the "mixed form" of these psalms, it does not suffice to explain how it is that many of these same texts include images and language that would have been highly unlikely to appear after the destruction of the Temple. One obvious example is Psalm 80:1–3, which refers to God "enthroned upon the cherubim" as well as to what appear to be explicitly northern traditions. The cherub throne as God's seat, an architectural feature of the Solomonic Temple and an image amply evidenced elsewhere in the Hebrew Bible,[37] seems an unlikely subject for a psalmist writing after the destruction of the Temple in 587 BCE. Likewise the references to Ephraim, Benjamin, and Manasseh seem to point to northern traditions—and perhaps to a time even before 722 BCE—for their inspiration. This implies, however, that Psalm 80 would have more likely been composed at some undetermined time prior to 587 BCE, in some period more proximate, presumably, to that period when Westermann's pure *Gattung* existed and the lament of the people played a more important role in Israel's worship. Why then does this psalm not provide a closer representation of the pure communal lament *Gattung* as Westermann conceives of it? That it does not is evidenced by West-

---

35 Westermann, *Praise and Lament*, p. 174.

36 *Ibid.*, p. 173 (emphasis added).

37 E.g., 1 Sam 4:4; 2 Sam 6:2; 2 Kgs 19:15; Isa 37:16; Ps 99:1.

ermann's own shifting evaluation of this psalm. There is a marked contrast in his treatment of verses 8–11 between earlier and more recent publications. Although he earlier identified these verses as comprising the "confession of trust" component of this psalm,[38] he seems subsequently to have recognized that the verses in question do not seem to fit that function. Doubtless this explains why Westermann more recently has spoken of these verses not as a confession of trust but rather as a "review of God's past saving acts" which, when inserted between the lament portions of verses 4–7 and 12–13, serve both to reproach God for the contrast between the glorious past and the difficulties of the present, as well as to influence the course of present history.[39] This means, however, that this psalm also exemplifies the mixed form that, as has already been noted, Westermann believes must be later than the destruction of Jerusalem. But what of the reference to the cherub throne and the epithets in the first verses? Westermann regards these features as an "amplification" of the invocation that mirrors those epochs in Israel's history when Israel did experience God's help. But this, in turn, implies that

> in principle, then, it is not permissible to draw conclusions from the statements in vv 1–2 about the date of the psalm or to claim that it originated in North Israel; at most, one can speak of the adaptation of a Northern tradition.[40]

This statement does not resolve the issues, however, since even if the psalm represents no more than an adaptation of a northern tradition, the explanation for the near exclusive employment of that tradition in a communal lament composed, presumably, long after the fall of Israel and after the fall of Jerusalem, remains unoffered.

Behind the questions about the origin and development of communal laments as conceived by Westermann, however, is the larger question about the feasibility of isolating the communal laments on the basis of observations about their structural units, whether those structural units are considered alone or in combination with considerations of style and theme. The mere fact that scholars often disagree relative to the identification of various parts of the respective

---

[38] Westermann, *Praise and Lament*, p. 54.

[39] Claus Westermann, *The Living Psalms*, trans. by J.R. Porter (Grand Rapids: William B. Eerdmans, 1989), p. 30, 32.

[40] *Ibid.*, p. 28.

psalms, quite apart from the lack of unaminity as to which psalms fall into the *Gattung*, suggests some refinement of the approach is in order. Precisely this problem with the identification of the characteristic features of the communal laments led M. Haar to investigate the matter afresh in his 1985 dissertation "The God-Israel Relationship in the Communal Lament Psalms."

Haar begins by noting that, in spite of many exceptions, scholars have achieved a general consensus about a core group of psalms that can be classified as communal laments.[41] The core consists of Psalms 44, 60, 74, 79, 80, 83, and 89 (see Table 1 above). Are there, Haar wonders, features of these psalms that can be identified so as to confirm the loose consensus about these materials which already exists as well as to adjudicate claims about other biblical texts? Haar answers this question affirmatively, and then convincingly evinces his case by the demonstration that these materials manifest an unusual collocation of certain stylistic, thematic, and structural elements. Table 2 below summarizes the evidence adduced by Haar and augmented by the present writer as it pertains to the "core" group of communal laments in the Psalter.[42] None of these elements, he admits, are in themselves unique to the communal laments. When all these elements appear in combination within a text, however, they serve to identify the *Gattung* and to mark the text specifically as a communal lament. Stylistically these psalms are all marked by both the use of the first-person plural form and the use of the second-person singular possessive suffix, the latter serving to emphasize the close relationship between God and Israel. These psalms also are joined thematically in that they all manifest accusatory statements and/or questions directed primarily at God as well as motivations for God to act. Typically, the motivational portions contrast God's past actions on behalf of Israel with his present silence. Structurally, these psalms all feature imperative petitions exhorting God to act, as well as the striking absence of anything resembling a "certainty of a hearing" or "assurance of being heard" on the part of the psalmist. Perhaps anticipating accusations that the last point is no more than an *argumentum ad silentium*, Haar immediately points out,

---

[41] For the following see Haar, "The God-Israel Relationship," pp. 30–31.

[42] *Ibid.*, pp. 32–46.

Table 2.   Characteristic Features of the Communal Laments

Stylistic elements
  1) Use of first-person plural form:
        Ps 44:2, 6, 8–12, 14–15, 18–21, 23, 25–27
        Ps 60:3, 5, 7, 12–14
        Ps 74:1, 9
        Ps 79:4, 8–9, 13
        Ps 80:3–4, 7–8, 19–20.
        Ps 83:
        Ps 89:18–19
  2) second-person singular suffix used to remind God of God's
     relationship with Israel:
        Ps 44:6, 13
        Ps 60:5, 7
        Ps 74:1, 2, 4, 7, 10, 18–23
        Ps 79:1–2, 10, 13
        Ps 80:5, 18
        Ps 83:3–4
        Ps 89:3, 6, 12, 14–16, 20, 39–40, 50–52
Thematic elements
  1) Accusatory statements and/or questions directed primarily
     at God:
        Ps 44:10–15, 16–17, 18–20, 21–23, 24–26
        Ps 60:3–6, 12
        Ps 74:1, 10–11
        Ps 79:1–4, 5, 10
        Ps 80:5–7, 13–14
        Ps 83:2–6
        Ps 89:39–46, 47–52
  2) Motivations contrasting God's past actions on Israel's behalf with
     God's present silence:
        Ps 44:2–4
        Ps 60:8–10
        Ps 74:(10)11–17,18
        Ps 79:11
        Ps 80:9–12 (contrasted to vv 13–18)
        Ps 83:10–13
        Ps 89:10–14, 20–38 (contrasted with vv 39–46)
Structural elements
  1) Imperative petitions exhorting God to action:
        Ps 44:24, 27
        Ps 60:7, 13

Table 2.   *continued*

Ps 74:2, 3, 18–23
Ps 79:6, 8, 9, 10, 12
Ps 80:3, 4, 8, 15–16, 20
Ps 83:14–19
Ps 89:48, 51
2) anticipated but missing elements:
   a) certainty of being heard—absent in all core psalms
   b) penitential elements, reference to sin/forgiveness

Since a certainty of a hearing is such a constituent part of the psalms of lament, its absence in these psalms is conspicuous. Accordingly, it may be fair to assert that the lack of a certainty of a hearing in a psalm of lament can be understood as a distinct part of the structure of the psalm, i.e., it was omitted for a specific reason.[43]

Later in his work, Haar observes that these laments lack another anticipated structural element, namely, penitential elements, including references to sin and repentance.

This last mentioned feature—the absence of penitential elements and references to sin and repentance—deserves a further brief comment since, of the psalms identified by Haar as genuine communal laments, Psalm 79:8–9 appears to be an exception.[44] The verses in question read.

ʾal tizkor-lānû ʿăwōnōṯ riʾšōnîm
  mahēr yĕqaddĕmûnû raḥmêkā kî dallônû mĕʾôd
ʿozrēnû ʾĕlōhê yišʿēnû ʿal-dĕḇar kĕḇôḏ-šĕmekā
wĕhaṣṣîlēnû wĕkappēr ʿal-ḥaṭṭōʾṯênû lĕmaʿan šĕmekā

Do not remember against us the iniquities of (our) ancestors;
  let your compassion be drawn near us speedily for we are brought very low.
Help us, O God of our salvation, for the sake of the glory of your name,
Deliver us, cover over our sins, for your name's sake.

---

[43] *Ibid.*, p. 31.
[44] *Ibid.*, p. 93. Cf. p. 104, n. 47, where he observes that the single exception is Psalm 79:8–9 where sin is mentioned only in a subordinate manner for "it is not mentioned again nor is it a central structural or theological component in the psalm."

First, it should be noted, it appears that the issue for the author of these verses does not primarily involve a focus on any sin of his own generation or community. Instead, the meaning of the petition *kappēr ʿal-ḥaṭṭōʾṯênû* in verse 9 should be guided by the previous plea of verse 8, wherein God is urged not to remember against the community the ancestors' iniquities (*ʿăwōnōṯ riʾšōnîm*).[45] If the lamenting community experiences 'guilt' and that, in turn, precipitates disaster, the guilt is something passed on by their ancestors and not brought on by their own wrongdoing. In verse 9, therefore, the poet articulates his recognition that the iniquities of the ancestors remain a potential cause for punishment and an explanation for the present disaster.[46] This implies, however, that these verses do not truly represent an exception to Haar's criteria. While using a few words common to the terminology of penitence and sin, their purpose appears to be to articulate further the inequity of the lamenting community's present plight. Supporting this is a second observation, namely, that these two verses seem poorly located in their context. Verses 1–7 and 10–12 describe the destructive activities of the foreign enemy and their consequences for the lamenting community. Verse 7 portrays the overthrow of Jacob and his habitation while verse 10 reports the mocking of alien invaders. The intervening speech about iniquities and sin seems intrusive and, possibly, appears here as a consequence of a later redactional insertion. Whether these verses result from such a late insertion or not, however, it remains the case that the penitential concerns in this psalm are, at best, muted.

Other compositions, of course, have communal lament elements within them, but as they lack the total collocation of the stylistic, structural, and thematic identifiers of the communal laments Haar considers them to be a related but distinct type of corporate prayer for help. To illustrate this distinction Haar examines a plethora of texts, none of which he judges to be representative of the communal lament *Gattung*. Because two of these texts, Lamentations 5 and

---

[45] *Pace* Marvin E. Tate, *Psalms 51–100*, WBC, vol. 20 (Waco, TX: Word Books, 1990), p. 297, n. 8b, where he maintains that the word ought to be understood as an adjective, here "former iniquities." Tate interprets verse 9 in light of verse 8. Against Tate's interpretation are the the similar uses of *riʾšōnîm* as a substantive noun found in Deuteronomy 19:14 and Leviticus 26:45. The latter verse is particularly illuminating: *wēzākartî lāhem bĕrîṯ riʾšōnîm ʾăšer hôṣēʾtî-ʾōṯām mēʾereṣ miṣrayîm*.

[46] So Kraus, *Psalms 60–150*, p. 135.

Isaiah 63:15–64:12, are often regarded as communal laments, it is important to know why and by what principles Haar removes them from that category.

Before turning to those texts, however, it is helpful to illustrate the principles Haar employs for assessing disputed texts, including Lamentations 5 and Isaiah 63:15–64:12, as well as other passages found both within and outside of the Psalter. Haar's treatment of Psalm 85 serves as an useful example. He readily admits that Psalm 85 contains all of the identifying characteristics of a communal lament up through verse 8, but notes that the psalm betrays itself as a "mixed type" by means of the inclusion of the certainty of a hearing in verse 9f. Moreover, where the genuine communal laments associate Israel's misfortunes with the misfortunes of God, Psalm 85 offers no hint of this understanding. Missing too are the usual taunts directed at God, any mention of the enemies, the lament cry "why," or accusatory statements which speak of God not acting responsibly toward God's people. Finally, the cause of Israel's misfortune in this poem appears to be sin, a feature absent from the core group of communal laments.[47] Thus, while there exists a good deal of similarity between the genuine communal laments and Psalm 85, the differences present in the latter indicate it is actually a corporate prayer for help, and its emphasis is different than the communal laments proper.

Haar's investigation of the other disputed psalms within the Psalter lead to the same conclusion. Only Psalms 44, 60, 74, 79, 80, 83, and 89 enjoy the combination of all of the key elements and thus only these psalms represent the unadulterated communal lament form. Interestingly, these are the very psalms which Westermann had earlier identified as genuine communal laments, albeit on different criteria.

But what of texts outside the Psalter? Lamentations 5 has sometimes been likened to a communal lament, although differences between this poem and the core communal laments find general recognition in the secondary literature. Delbert R. Hillers, for example, while recognizing that the fifth chapter in Lamentations follows more closely than the other four the patterns of the laments of the community, nevertheless notes that "Lam 5 is remarkable, however, for the relatively short appeal for help and the correspondingly

---

[47] *Ibid.*, pp. 47–49.

long description of the nation's trouble; in this respect it is closer to other chapters of Lamentations."[48] Similarly, Westermann points to the poem's preoccupation with the plight of God's people and remarks, "Here the balance has been so radically disrupted that we really have to speak of a transformation of the [communal lament] form."[49] Haar also considers this passage as not representative of the communal lament type, although the grounds for his own judgment consist of the absence of the key characteristic features he believes to be constitutive of the *Gattung*. Specifically, both the use of the second-person singular suffix and the contrast with the past motivation are found missing in Lamentations 5. As a result of this lack, Lamentations 5 represents another type of structure and prayer, one which "is more interested in rehearsing the sin and pain of the community, rather than contrasting God's greatness with the present silence."[50] One could quibble with Haar's assessment of Lamentations 5 in at least a single small detail: the element of the motivating contrast with the past does appear, although in a much muted form, in the final words of verse 21, "renew our days as of old." However, the strong presence of the penitential theme (vv 16–17, cf. v 7), coupled with the all-but-absent contrast between the present situation and the past, leads to the conclusion that Haar, Hillers, and Westermann are correct in not regarding the present form of the composition as representative of the communal lament type. Westermann believes it highly possible that one of the preexilic communal laments has been carried over and expanded to fit the historic situation of 587 BCE and, "in the process of adapting the traditional psalm for its new function, parts of the original were lost."[51] As the text now appears, however, it echoes, rather than represents, the communal lament *Gattung*.

Haar's assessment of Isaiah 63:15–64:11 [12] is harder to discern and his views appear to be guided more by the judgment of Westermann than by a strict application of his own criteria. Westermann regards Isaiah 63:7–64:11 as a "community lament in psalm form,"[52]

---

[48] Delbert R. Hillers, *Lamentations*, AB, Vol. 7a (Garden City: Doubleday, 1972), p. 102.

[49] Westermann, *Praise and Lament*, p. 174.

[50] Haar, "The God-Israel Relationship," p. 51.

[51] Westermann, *Lamentations*, p. 219.

[52] Westermann, *Isaiah 40–66*, p. 386.

but one whose overall structure is hard to see.[53] Verses 7–14, which Haar omits from his consideration without explanation, expand the survey of God's earlier saving to such an extent that the verses form, according to Westermann, "almost an independent historical psalm."[54] The lament proper, according to both Haar and Westermann, commences with verse 15 although, as Westermann observes, "The usual sections in a lament do not simply follow upon one another, but are very freely interwoven."[55] Recognizing that all of the distinguishing features of communal laments appear in this poem, Haar seems initially to judge it a representative of the communal lament type.[56] In a subsequent discussion of the passage in the same study, however, he claims it is best described as part of Israel's tradition of corporate prayers for help, a tradition which, again, is similar to but not identical with the communal laments.[57] Of the two opinions expressed about this passage in his study, the latter appears to be more correct. There is a decidedly penitential emphasis in Isaiah 63:5b–7 [4b–6] and 9 [8] which one would not expect, given the absence of this feature in the core communal laments; this feature is more typical of personal laments and of "mixed types." Second, while it is true, as Haar claims, that first-person plural form is present throughout the poem,[58] if Isaiah 63:7–14 is considered as part of the same pericope, the poem as a whole takes on a different tone. Verse 7 makes it clear that the first common plural forms present are uttered by the voice of a single speaker, as one would expect in individual laments, albeit here a representative of the whole people. Verse 15, and the appearance of the first common singular form there, confirms this observation.[59]

The pericope, moreover, displays a number of features which suggest that (1) the composition in its present form should be as-

---

[53] *Ibid.*, p. 392.

[54] *Ibid.*, p. 386.

[55] *Ibid.*, p. 392.

[56] Haar, "The God-Israel Relationship," p. 52.

[57] *Ibid.*, pp. 75–78, 94.

[58] *Ibid.*, p. 77.

[59] The emendation suggested by D. Winton Thomas in the *BHS* notes and followed by John L. McKenzie, *Second Isaiah: Introduction, Translation, and Notes*, AB Vol. 20 (Garden City: Doubleday, 1968), p. 189, n. g-g, would alter the MT ʾēlay hitʾappāqû ("are withheld from me") to ʾal-nāʾ hitʾappāq ("do not restrain"). The change is at once unnecessary and difficult to justify.

signed to a date sometime after 587 BCE, and (2) the psalm represents a genuine example of a "mixed type" of communal lament. These two factors account for the strange admixture of penitential themes and communal lament features.

First, and relative to those features suggesting a compositional date for the poem: Westermann observes that, besides the free interweaving of the usual sections of a communal lament, several concepts appearing in the passage point to a relatively late compositional date. One discovers, for example, two references to God's "holy spirit" (Isa 63:10,11) and a third reference to the spirit of Yahweh (Isa 63:14). Apart from this passage, the concept of the "holy spirit" occurs only in Psalm 51:13 [11], a poem that is generally considered to have originated in exilic or post-exilic period.[60] Moreover, while the use of the term 'spirit' in verses 10 and 14 has the old meaning of power that works miracles, verse 11 has a wider and more general meaning which seems to represent a development in Israel's understanding of 'spirit.'[61] Victor H. Matthews says of this,

> The juxtaposition of *rûaḥ* and *qōdeš* is oxymoronic in that a concept of dynamic power beyond human control, *rûaḥ*, has been combined with a word of static character, *qōdeš*. The combination becomes a technical expression in Christian usage first through the evangelist Luke and in rabbinic literature.[62]

---

[60] Proponents of an exilic or post-exilic date for Psalm 51 include Dahood, *Psalms II: 51–100*, p. 2; Kraus, *Psalms 1–59*, p. 501; Mays, *Psalms*, p. 199; Victor H. Matthews, "Holy Spirit," *ABD*, vol. 3, p. 261; Claus Westermann, "Geist im Alten Testament," *EvT* 41 (1981), 224; cf. A. Caquot, "Purification et expiation selon le psaume LI," *RHR* 169 (1966), 133–154. Nevertheless, there are a few scholars who would place the psalm's composition in the preexilic period. Dalglish, *Psalm Fifty-One*, 201–208, believes the psalm is best located in the time of Josiah (640–609 BCE); J.H. Eaton, *Kingship and the Psalms* (2nd ed.; Sheffield: JSOT, 1986), pp. 71–72, 177–181, believes possession of the 'holy spirit' was a particular perogative of the king and, therefore, that the psalm originated prior to 587 BCE (so too Daglish, p. 228). More persuasive is L. Neve, "Realized Eschatology in Ps 51," *ExpT* 80 (1968), 264–268, who rejects Dalglish's notion of the 'holy spirit' as the permanent possession of the Davidides; he argues, as does Kraus, *Psalms 1–59*, p. 501, that the concept was more likely dependent upon prophetic promises for the future such as are found in Jeremiah 24:7; 31:33; 32:39; and Ezekiel 36:25–27. Moreover, Kraus points out, verses 18–19 suggest the knowledge of prophetic protests against the sacrificial system (Amos 5:22; Isa 1:11; Jer 6:20). Kraus concludes that the psalm is to be dated later than Ezekiel 36 but, because of the final two verses, not after the time of Nehemiah.

[61] Westermann, *Isaiah 40–66*, p. 389.

[62] Matthews, "Holy Spirit," p. 261. Cf. Westermann, "Geist," 224.

That is, the terminology employed in this passage suggests a development in the concept of God's 'holy spirit' which leads toward the use of 'Spirit' in relation to God "in which each and all of his acts can be attributed to his Spirit or to God's Holy Spirit."[63] That development, coupled with the use of the term in the late Psalm 51, points toward a post-exilic compositional setting for this passage.

Another expression, *ʿam-qodšekā* in Isaiah 63:18, points toward a later compositional setting.[64] Although the concept of the holiness of God's people is not confined to Deuteronomy, besides the present verse the noun *ʿam* appears in construct with *qādôš* only in passages found in that book,[65] in the unquestionably late Daniel 12:7 (*ʿam-qādôš*), and in Isaiah 62:12 (*ʿam-haqqōdeš*).

The association of this passage with Deuteronomy goes beyond the connection made with the last-mentioned expression. The theological perspective of the piece points to another connection which, again, leads toward the conclusion that this poem's compositional setting is later than 587 BCE and, further, that the poem represents a 'mixed' type of communal lament. Westermann has noted that a historical survey, such as is found in verses 7–14, followed by a confession of guilt, is characteristic of the theological thought and literature of the Deuteronomistic history.[66] Indeed, Westermann discerns a structural affinity between Isaiah 63:7–14 and the Deuteronomistic history which he outlines as follows:

---

[63] Westermann, *Isaiah 40–66*, p. 389.

[64] The suggestion of McKenzie, *Second Isaiah*, p. 189, n. h-h, to emend the MT's *lammisʿar yārēšûʿam* ("for a little while [your holy people] possessed") to *lammāh ṣā ʿādû rešāʿim* ("why have the wicked trodden [on your holy place]") seems improbable as it involves supplying a consonant, changing one, and omitting another. The text is not unintelligible as it stands. Within the context of the lament, the complaint is that God's holy people took possession (of the land) for only a little while, but now their adversaries have trampled down God's sanctuary. Besides the absence of a single textual warrant for emending the verse, the use of the verb *yrš* to describe, specifically, God's people 'taking possession' is characteristic of its employment elsewhere in Isaiah 40–66. That is, whenever this verb is used in these chapters (Isa 54:3; 57:13; 60:21; 61:7; 65:9), the subjects of the verb are the "chosen," the "people of Jerusalem," and so forth. This contrast markedly, for example, with the use put to the verb the three times it appears in Isaiah 1–39 (Isaiah 14:21, 34:11, and 34:17). Moreover, the rare verb McKenzie would have us read in its place, *ṣʿd*, does not appear in the Isaianic corpus or, indeed, in any of the prophetic literature except Jeremiah 10:5 and Habakkuk 3:12.

[65] Deut. 7:6; 14:2,21; 26:19 (*ʿam qādôš*).

[66] Westermann, *Isaiah 40–66*, p. 386.

7a   Introduction: I will remember the gracious deeds of Yahweh. . .
7b-9   God, deliverer and preserver of his chosen people.
10b   Israel turns against God, whereupon God turns against Israel.
11-14   In their extremity they thought about God's deed in the
            past.[67]

This structure anticipates the confession of guilt which in fact follows in 63:5b-7 [4b-6] and 9 [8]. Westermann sees this overall structure as a reflection of a developing pattern:

> Looking at the history of the psalms of lamentation, we notice that from the exile onward the charge brought against God falls more and more into the background until in the end it completely disappears from the prayer. As a result, greater and greater importance is given to the confession of sin. Isaiah 63f. are a good illustration of this transition.[68]

The accuracy of this observation is not diminished by the fact that Westermann does not appear to apply it to his interpretation of the development of those communal laments in the Psalter which lack any confession of sin. As it is, however, the pronounced confessional and penitential aspects of this lament—coupled with those features already identified as constitutive of the genre—all indicate that in this instance Westermann is correct in seeing the present poem as a representative of a late stage in the lament tradition. The poem's terminology, structure, and theological orientation all seem to suggest that, whatever aspects of the text originally antedate 587 BCE, the composition presently reflects the influence of that strain of theological thinking that likewise stood behind the Deuteronomistic history. Whether further evidence toward the confirmation of that suggestion can be gathered or not, however, the presence of penitential motifs and the heavier use of the first-person singular forms point to the conclusion that Isaiah 63:7–64:11 [12] represents, at best, a mixed form of communal lament and is better considered a part of Israel's tradition of corporate prayers for help.

Haar's investigation of other key corporate prayers for help—Exodus 32:11–14, 33:12–17, Deuteronomy 9:25–29, Daniel 9:4–20, and Nehemiah 1:4–11—leads to the same conclusions as the examination of Isaiah 63:15–64:12.[69] These texts contain the same com-

---

67 *Ibid.*, p. 387.
68 *Ibid.*, p. 396.
69 Haar, "The God-Israel Relationship," pp. 65–94.

bination of essential elements identified in the community lament psalms and likewise omit a certainty of hearing. And yet the communal lament psalms remain distinguishable from the corporate prayers for help: some are not as elaborate and others contain lengthy confessions of sin, absent in the community psalms. Haar concludes from this that, while not exactly the same, the corporate prayers for help and the seven communal lament psalms identified above are parts of Israel's larger tradition of corporate prayer for help.[70] Nevertheless Psalms 44, 60, 74, 79, 80, 83, and 89 remain distinctive exemplars of the communal lament *Gattung*. Accordingly, these seven psalms will provide the basis for the following typological description of the communal laments.

A TYPOLOGY OF ISRAEL'S COMMUNAL LAMENTS

Haar's successful isolation of the communal lament psalms makes it possible to refine further the structure, content, and themes of these materials in an effort to isolate, beyond their formal features, those aspects of these psalms which are characteristic of Israel's communal laments. As the larger goal of the present investigation remains to compare the communal laments with suspected similar materials from Mesopotamia, the exposition of those typical features, when possible, will echo the order provided for the typology of the *balag/eršemma* compositions in the previous chapter. For the most part, however, explicit comparison of the two cultures' lamentation will be delayed until the following chapter.

General Structure

As noted above, Westermann's work, built on the foundations established by Gunkel, has shown that the seven psalms under consideration do appear to share a common corpus of structural elements. The five elements he believes are basic to the form of the communal lament are well known:[71]

I. The address and introductory cry for help,
II. A lament in which the enemies, the plight of the psalmist's community, or God is the subject

---

[70] *Ibid.*, pp. 94–98.
[71] Westermann, *Praise and Lament*, pp. 52–54.

III. A confession of trust
IV. A petition for God to rescue Israel which is often coupled
     with the wish that God might simultaneously punish the
     enemies, and
V. A vow of praise

Recognizing that the content of the communal laments often exceeds these five sections, Westermann proposes that the psalms were lately expanded to include the following additional elements:[72]

A. At the beginning, praise of God by way of introduction,
B. In the middle and after the petition, an expression of the
   certainty of being heard and "expansions of a reflective
   nature," and
C. At the end, a concluding petition or praise of God.

Reference has already been made to the evolutionary assumptions undergirding Westermann's analysis. The so-called expansions, inasmuch as they represent a deviation from the "pure" form as Westermann imagines it, must be late additions and not a part of the proto-typical communal lament. This explanation serves to account not only for materials regarded by Westermann as extraneous to the components of a "pure" communal lament, but it also serves to explain why no "pure" examples of that genre are to be found in the Psalter; what communal laments remain represent late examples of the genre only after it has been "mixed" with other forms. Thus, for example, Psalm 89:5–18 consists of a descriptive psalm of praise which has found its way into the composition through an expansion of the pure communal lament *Gattung*.[73]

No reason exists, however, to assume that the hymn contained in Psalm 89:5–18 was a late expansion of either the original *Gattung* or of that particular composition. To the contrary, the hymnic section stands as an integral part of the lament as a whole and, from all appearances, was so at the time of its composition. Verses 1–4 praise God's steadfast love and covenant loyalty to David. This is followed by the hymn in verses 5–18 wherein Yahweh is celebrated as the cosmogonic divine warrior who rules over the divine assembly (vv 5–7), defeats the chaos monsters and thereby creates both

---

[72] *Ibid.*, p. 52.
[73] *Ibid.*, p. 122.

the heavens and the earth (vv 9–13), and rules forever over Israel as king (vv 14–18). This hymn is matched by a recitation of God's establishment of the monarchy (vv 19–37), describing the divine determination of the Davidide in terms that reflect perfectly what has just been said about God's own rule. As God's regent, David will reign over God's people (vv 19–21); his reign will, like God's own, be characterized by the defeat of his enemies and even cosmogonic victory over the sea (vv 22–25); God will cause David and his line to rule perpetually (vv 26–37). The tone of the psalm takes a decided turn in verses 38–52 where the psalmist takes up, seemingly for the first time, the themes of lament. Evidently there has been a reversal in the fortunes of the Davidide: God has rejected the chosen king, destroyed his strongholds, allowed him to suffer defeat at the hands of his enemies, and removed the scepter from his hand (vv 38–45). The lament themes continue throughout verses 46–51 wherein God is specifically reminded of the divine reputation for steadfast love as well as of God's oath to David:

> Lord, where is your steadfast love of old, which by your faithfulness you swore to David? (v 49).

Besides forming an *inclusio* with the opening four verses of the psalm, the question of verse 49 makes clear that the hymnic portion of verses 5–18 stands as an integral component of the lament as a whole. God, whose steadfast love and choice of David is lauded (vv 1–4), whose rule and power are without rival (vv 5–18), and whose promise to David and his line is irrevocable (vv 19–37), is left, as it were, without excuse for the troubles which have befallen the monarchy. That is, since God has the unquestioned power to alter the course of events and God has sworn an irrevocable promise to David, God simply ought to have done more to protect and preserve the monarch from disaster. Thus the explicit language of lament, which only appears to begin with the complaint of verse 38, in fact includes the extended hymn of praise which appear before it; the hymn of praise emerges as the psalmist's stratagem by which God will be constrained to act on Israel's behalf.

The presence of the hymn as an integral part of the lament strategy and the psalm's structure indicates, minimally, that this psalm does not easily correspond to Westermann's five-fold analysis of the communal lament. For this reason Westermann assumes the hymn represents a characteristic later expansion. If so, however, it must be understood as an expansion of the conception of the communal lament *Gattung* and of those elements which comprise it, for the section of the psalm containing the more obvious lament language clearly presupposes the hymnic material which precedes it. That is, for this communal lament, the lengthy hymn of praise (and the recitation of God's elevation of David) is a critical structural component of the entire lament.[74]

Nor does Psalm 89 serve as the only example of a communal lament which integrates an intrinsical hymn. Of the other six communal laments, hymns or hymnic elements are present in Psalms 44:2–9, 74:12–17, and 80:1,9–12. In each instance, like Psalm 89, praise appears to be a crucial aspect of the overall lament structure. The psalmist employs hymns in order to motivate God to action on Israel's behalf. Judgment as to whether or not this use of a hymn within the lament is, in fact, a later expansion of the formal aspects of the *Gattung*, as Westermann maintains, will be delayed until later in this study. At this juncture, however, it is important simply to note that of the seven communal laments present in the Psalter, four contain significant sections of praise as constitutive elements of their overall structure.

In addition to hymnic material these laments naturally also include references to some disaster or distress suffered by the community as well as various importunities or pleas which summon God to redeem Israel. These elements correspond to Westermann's points II and IV above. The latter element, the petition or plea to God, appears as the most constant of all the parts and is, indeed, never missing.[75] By contrast, Westermann's fifth element, the vow of praise, turns out to be a rarer feature of the communal laments. In the psalms under consideration, Psalms 79:13, 44:9, 80:19 appear to

---

[74] Nor is Psalm 89 the sole exemplar of a lament psalm which includes Westermann's "expansionary" elements as integral parts of the poetic and narrative strategy. See especially the "total interpretation" method of Meier Weiss, *The Bible From Within: The Method of Total Interpretation* (Jerusalem: Magnes, 1984), as well as his earlier articles, "Wege der neuen Dichtungswissenschaft in ihrer Anwendung auf die Psalmenforschung," *Bib*, 42 (1961), 255–302, and "Die Methode der 'Total-Interpretation'" *VTSup*, 22 (1972), 88–112. The latter study gives special attention to Psalm 74 as does a subsequent investigation by Pierre Auffret, "Essai sur la structure littéraire du Psaume LXXIV," *VT*, 33 (1983), 129–148. Auffret likewise demonstrates the poetic and narrative coherence of Psalm 44 in his article, "'Pourquoi dors-tu, Seigneur?' Etude structurelle du psaume 44," *JANES*, 21 (1992), 13–33.

[75] Westermann, *Praise and Lament*, p. 55.

include this element, but all three are peculiar. Psalm 44:9, only formally a vow of praise, appears at the end of the hymnic portion of the psalm (vv 2–9) rather than after any petition. Calling God's attention to the cultic community's indebtedness to Yahweh for praise and thanksgiving in verse 9 turns out to be important, for in verses 18ff., subsequent to the description of distress, attention is turned to Israel's faithfulness and constancy in worship life.[76] Structurally and thematically, therefore, Psalm 44:9 seems to support the protestation of innocence appearing in verses 18–22; it is certainly not the response of the community to any explicit or implicit oracle of salvation. Likewise Psalms 79:13 and 80:19 appear not to be associated with any oracle of salvation or certainty of a hearing. Instead they actually connect the "vow of praise" with the concluding petitions, thereby including future praise as yet another factor which ought to motivate God to act.

In sum, the various components that Westermann insists are definitive of the communal lament turn out to be not entirely descriptive of the genre. The psalms often contain units of praise that are intrinsic to the structure of the poems as a whole. They also, of course, include descriptions of the distress and various segments that give voice to the pleadings of the community, a fact to which Westermann readily gives assent. They do not, however, betray any hint that a cultic oracle of salvation has been given nor that a hearing is assured; the putative "vows of praise" are instead part of the motivation undergirding the pleas of the community.

Subject and Mood

The communal laments of the Psalter concern themselves with describing and lamenting a national disaster: defeat at the hands of a foreign army.[77] The consequences of such a defeat were, of course, dire. Foreign victory included the capture of the capital city and its destruction.[78] The psalmist's community became the object of foreign scorn and derision,[79] and was forcibly enslaved and exiled by its captors.[80] Worst of all, enemy victory included the spoilation and

---

[76] Kraus, *Psalms 1–59*, p. 447.

[77] Pss 44:9–17,22,25; 60:10–11; 79:1–3.

[78] Pss 79:1; 89:41.

[79] Pss 44:15; 74:18; 79:4,10.

[80] Ps 44:12–13.

destruction of the sacred precincts and Temple.[81] In the face of this calamity the psalmist and his community complain bitterly before God. The mood of these psalms, therefore, is mournful and somber.

Poetic Techniques and Devices

The various poetic techniques and devices present in these laments appear commonly in Hebrew poetry, including the sundry devices of parallelism and refrains repeated at intervals.

The shift of speakers within these texts also appears commonly in other types of poetry. The authorial point of view within the laments, for the most part, is that of the united voice of the community speaking in complaint or praise. Other voices can be heard, however, as the authorial point of view shifts. An unnamed speaker praises God in Psalm 44:5–7. The spiteful sayings of the enemy are quoted in Psalms 74:8, 79:10, and 83:5,13. Psalm 60:8–10 records God's own speech; in context it appears to be a recitation of an oracle of salvation given sometime in the past which now has been called into question by the defeat of Israel's armies.[82] The various voices in these psalms and the change in narrative perspective that they signal serve to build pathos in the reader/listener by the articulation of the praise and lament of the various *dramatis personae*.

One notable characteristic is the appearance of three lists in these seven psalms. The divine oracle of Psalm 60:8–10 contains a recitation of the various countries that God previously promised to master and defeat. Psalm 83:7–9 lists those nations that have conspired against Israel, while verses 10–12 of that same psalm recall a list of persons and places in Israel's past involving God's actions on the people's behalf. Lists are, of course, not unknown in Hebrew narrative literature,[83] although they are less common in poetic texts. The presence of lists in these psalms seems somewhat remarkable, therefore, particularly when it is remembered that similar lists are characteristic of the *balag/eršemma* materials.

---

[81] Pss 74:3–9; 79:1.

[82] Sabourin, *The Psalms*, pp. 300–301.

[83] Cf. Norman Gottwald, *The Hebrew Bible—A Socio-Literary Introduction* (Philadelphia: Fortress, 1985), p. 100, who notes the lists of persons and groups in Genesis 10; Numbers 1:26; 2 Samuel 8:16–18; 20:23–26; Ezra 2; Nehemiah 3, and the list of places in Numbers 33:1–49; Joshua 15–19; Micah 1:10–16. To the latter, one should add the list included in Jeremiah 25:18–26, a text that will become important later in this investigation.

The Weeping Goddess Motif

The weeping goddess motif, ubiquitous in the Mesopotamian laments, does not appear in the seven Hebrew communal lament psalms. A full discussion of this subject will be delayed until
the next chapter when the *balag/eršemma* laments and those communal lamentations of Israel are directly compared. For now, however, it suffices to call to mind what has already been suggested in
the previous chapter, namely, that Ezekiel 8 provides solid evidence
for Israel's familiarity with the motif prior to the Exile. On the other
hand, the fact that the weeping goddess does not appear in the
canonical lamentations of Israel can hardly be considered surprising given the henotheistic (and later monotheistic) orientation of
Israel's religion and particularly of its canonical literature. The absence of this motif, therefore, does not necessarily disprove that the
psalmists were familiar with the Mesopotamian tradition. Gwaltney's comment about the Book of Lamentations and its potential
relationship to the Mesopotamian tradition is equally *apropos* in
connection to these psalms: "Because of the polytheistic theology
underlying the Mesopotamian laments and their ritual observance,
they could not be taken over without thorough modification in theology and language."[84] Indeed, Dobbs-Allsopp has made a strong
case for understanding the personified Jerusalem who speaks
in Lamentations, as a modification of the tradition received directly
from Mesopotamia.[85] If Dobbs-Allsopp is proven correct, the presence of a modified version of the motif in Lamentations provides
strong circumstantial evidence that the Mesopotamian lament tradition exercised some influence on the practice of public laments in
Israel, even if that influence is missing from the small sampling of
communal laments that remain extant.

The Destruction

The Hebrew communal laments generally concern themselves
with the destruction of the capital city and the Temple. As with the
previous chapter, the specific content of these lamentations and
their description of the devastation can be considered conveniently
under three headings: (1) the agents of destruction, (2) the assign-

---

[84] Gwaltney, "The Biblical Book of Lamentations in the Context of Near Eastern
Lament Literature," p. 211.
[85] Dobbs-Allsopp, *Weep, O Daughter of Zion*, pp. 75–90, and especially p. 85.

ment of responsibility for the destruction, and (3) the description of the destruction.

The Agents of Destruction

The primary destructive agent in the Hebrew communal laments is the foreign invader. The activity of the enemies has already been described.[86] The enemies are not, however, specifically identified, a fact that accounts for the continued debate about the date of these psalms or of the historical events that, many suppose, stand behind them. Only Psalm 83:7–9 provides a list naming the enemies. Although there seems no end to the suggestions made by commentators for locating the "historical situation" behind this list,[87] the basic question remaining is whether one may assume any specific historical situation at all. Kraus notes that the text does not mention an approaching alliance of foreign forces, but rather that these peoples merely conspire to annihilate Israel. Partially for this reason Kraus concurs with F. Nötscher who believes that, in all likelihood, the enumeration of nations was "poetically and freely composed."[88] The fact that there are ten nations named suggests that the listing is stereotypical[89] and, in any event, "a large coalition of nations in alliance against Israel is both unknown and improbable."[90] The explicit mention of Assyria does suggest a preexilic time frame, and the preeminence of southern nations (except Tyre) may suggest a Judean provenience for the composition.[91] Historical specificity beyond that remains speculative.

---

[86] See the previous discussion in the subsection, "Subject and Mood."

[87] Kraus, *Psalms 61–150*, p. 161, summarizes several proposals for the historical setting of this psalm: R. Kittel asserted that Psalm 83 "almost certainly" is to be equated with the events reported in 1 Maccabees 5; H. Ewald and C.A. Briggs identify the setting during the time of Nehemiah; H. Gunkel thinks of some otherwise unknown event between the time of Ezra and Alexander the Great; H. Schmidt takes the reference to Assyria in verse 8 as an indication of the preexilic provenance of the psalm.

[88] *Ibid.*

[89] Cf. Dan 7:7, 20, 24.

[90] Marvin E. Tate, *Psalms 51–100*, p. 345.

[91] Kraus, *Psalms 60–150*, p. 161–162. Cf. Tate, *Psalms 51–100*, p. 345, who claims, on grammatical grounds, that the psalm is post-exilic and the reference to Assyria is given by the psalmist only as an example of one of the great world powers allied with the smaller states around Israel. Tate's grammatical argument is, however, unconvincing as the direct object marker in verse 13 and the relative pronoun 'šr in 13a are insufficient for claiming a late compositional date of the entire poem. It is true, as Tate

The list of nations in Psalm 83 nevertheless proves significant for another reason. This psalm is the single example among
the seven communal laments that does name specific foreign enemies. Since, however, it appears extremely unlikely that a specific
historical situation was in mind for this psalm, one can reasonably
infer that actual historical incursion or invasions were not pre-
requisite to this or the other communal lamentations' composition.
That is, while these psalms provide what appears to be detailed
and graphic historical reminiscences of actual foreign invasions
and of destruction subsequent to those attacks, there is no inherent reason to suppose that a specific historical event stood behind
the descriptions.[92] Indeed, given a nearly identical phenomena in the
Mesopotamian laments, one is led toward the conclusion that the
references to foreign invaders had a cultic rather than an historical
significance. This possibility will be explored further in the next
chapter of this study.

The destructive power of the word of the deity, ubiquitous in the
balag/eršemma lamentations, is not attested in the communal lament
psalms. Psalm 83:2, however, presents a variation of this theme.
There, God's silence and the absence of God's powerful word is the
source of the complaint:

> O God, do not keep silence;
> do not hold your peace or be still, O God!.

The verse implies that God's word, if uttered, would bring about
disastrous consequences not for Israel but for Israel's enemies.

Likewise the destructive power of the storm of God is a theme
not altogether absent from the Hebrew communal laments. Psalm 83
associates the destructive activity of God with a "tempest" (*sa'ăreká*)

---

notes, that Assyria does become a stereotyped reference to foreign power in biblical
and extra-biblical literature (e.g., Ezra 6:22, 1 QM 1.2; 18.2; 19.10), but he exaggerates
the evidence and, moreover, does not give an adequate explanation for what he acknowledges as the strange lack of mention of Egypt and Babylon.

[92] In this connection it is interesting to note the observation of Othmar Keel, *The
Symbolism of the Biblical World: Ancient Near Eastern Iconography and the Book of Psalms*,
trans by. Timothy J. Hallett (New York: Crossroad, 1987), p. 101: "The national
laments portray catastrophe as having already struck. Nowhere, for example, is there
evidence of a state of siege. . . . Humiliating circumstances generally appear to have
prevailed for some time (Ps 74:9–11). Only the beginning and then (above all) the
result of the catastrophe are described." Keel does not explain this curious omission
although he is persuaded that the psalms are based on historical circumstances.

and "storm-wind" (*sûpātĕkā*). Both terms include the second masculine singular suffix, clarifying that it is indeed God's own storm. In this instance, however, the psalmist prays that the storm of God might fall upon Israel's enemies:

> O my God, make them like whirling dust
>   like chaff before the wind.
> As fire consumes the forest, as the flame sets the mountains ablaze
>   so pursue them with your tempest and terrify them with your
>   storm-wind. (vv 15–17)

The presence of storm imagery and the concept of the storm of God in this passage assumes more significance than might first be supposed. The nouns occur somewhat infrequently: *s'r* or *s'rh* appears twenty-three times in the Hebrew Scriptures, although the homophonic *ś'r/ś'rh* raises the total to twenty-seven; *sûpāh* occurs only sixteen times. Apart from this psalm, however, the two nouns occur in parallelism—or indeed in the same context—only in two other passages, Amos 1:14 and Isaiah 29:6. In addition, Nahum 1:3 has *bĕsûpāh ûbis'ārāh*, bringing the total to three occurrences. Like Psalm 83, Amos and Nahum understand the storm of God to be directed against Israel's enemies, the Ammonites and the Assyrians, respectively. In Isaiah 29:6, however, Yahweh's tempest and storm-wind are marshalled against Jerusalem and her inhabitants:

> You will be visited by YHWH Sabaoth,
>   with thunder and earthquake and great noise,
>   with storm-wind and tempest,
>   and the flame of a devouring fire.

The enemies are associated with, but not identical to, the storm: the enemies are likened to the discomfiting dust and flying chaff driven on ahead of the tempest (v 5). But it is Yahweh's tempest and storm-wind, accompanied by the theophanic signs of thunder, earthquake and fire, that will prove to be the true destructive agent of Jerusalem. Isaiah's prophetic utterance, therefore, provides important evidence that Israel was familiar with the concept of the storm of Yahweh as a destructive agent that could be marshalled against God's own city, and not just against Israel's enemies. The use of the rare word-pair in Isaiah and Psalm 83 links the two passages. Moreover, all three prophetic texts in which the word-pair appears are preexilic, a fact that *may* be seen to support Israel's familiarity with an important feature of the Mesopotamian lament tradition prior to the destruction of Jerusalem in 587 BCE and, hence, prior to those events which putatively served as the inspiration for a number of the communal laments.

The Assignment of Responsibility

While foreign enemies are identified as the primary destructive agents in the Hebrew communal lamentations, the psalmists were disinclined to grant these enemies autonomous authority. Behind the enemies' destructive activities stands God who, according to the psalmists, is ultimately charged with the responsibility for destruction and who gives the enemies leave to carry out their hostile plans. That the power of the enemy is understood as a reflection of the power and inscrutable will of God finds verification not only in those places where God is accused of giving the enemies their victory,[93] but also in occasional references associating the enemies' destructive activity with divinely wrought cosmic turmoil. In Psalm 60, for example, God is charged with having forsaken Israel's armies on the battlefield (v 12), an action associated with a ground-rending earthquake sent by God (v 3). Nevertheless, a tension permeates this attribution of foreign oppression to Yahweh. While recognizing that even foreign armies stand under the purview of the divine authority and responsibility, the psalmists are also eager to remind God both that the enemies of Israel remain God's enemies and that the divine well-being includes the safety of God's faithful community.[94]

The enemies' victories find partial explanation in the failure of the divine warrior to advance ahead of Israel's armies,[95] a sign of God's rejection of Israel as a whole.[96] But the reasons for the apparent divine rejection remained mysterious to the psalmist. Divine inattention,[97] and the notion that God simply had not adequately considered the plight of God's people[98] are suggested as explanations. That Israel's sin may have precipitated God's disfavor was,

---

[93] Pss 44:10–11; 60:12; 74:19; 79:4–5; 80:5,11; 89:39–42.

[94] Ps 83:3–4; cf. 74:18; 79:10; 80:18.

[95] Pss 44:8; 60:12.

[96] Pss 44:10; 60:3,12; 74:1; 89:39–40.

[97] Pss 44:24–25; 74:23; 89:49.

[98] Ps 79:11.

however, a consideration all but ignored; rather the psalmists were inclined to protest the people's innocence.[99]

If the psalmists were uncertain about God's motives in bringing disaster, they perceived with perfect clarity the fact that national calamity jeopardized the elemental beliefs upon which they understood Israel's relationship with God to rest. National disaster, wrought by God's active direction of foreign invaders or by God's passive toleration of their misdeeds, challenged the fundamental faith in God's power and in God's covenant relationship with Israel. Indeed, the assault on these beliefs, more than the physical devastation caused by the enemy, accounts for the excruciating anxiety evident in all of these poem prayers.

Craig C. Broyles's recent study, *The Conflict of Faith and Experience in the Psalms,*[100] explores this aspect of Israel's lament tradition as it occurs in both the individual and the communal lamentations. As the title of his work suggests, the dissonance between the expectations of faith and the experience of distress emerges in each of what he calls the "God-complaints," that is, laments that are directed against God.[101] Broyles's primary concern is to uncover

---

[99] Pss 44:18–19, 21–22.

[100] Craig C. Broyles, *The Conflict of Faith and Experience in the Psalms: a Form-Critical and Theological Study,* JSOTSup, Vol. 52 (Sheffield: JSOT, 1988).

[101] Broyles believes it important to make distinctions among various types of lament psalms. True laments are those whose complaint is directed not against some situation but against God. These he would call "God-laments" or "complaint psalms," and distinguishes them from "laments" or "plea" type psalms. The latter category, in his terminology, includes the I/We- and foe-laments, and those God-laments that do not connote complaint against God. Broyles, p. 40, summarizes the distinction he seeks to establish:

> Lament can be addressed to anyone; complaint must be addressed to the one responsible. A lament focuses on a situation; a complaint focuses on the one responsible. A lament simply bemoans the state of things; a complaint contains a note of blame and rebuke. In sum, most God-laments are expressions of complaint regarding God's disposition or action, which the psalmists in their distresses interpret as being indifferent or hostile.

J. Day, *Psalms,* p. 20–21, properly remarks that Broyles's "terminology is not wholly felicitous, however, since almost all the lament psalms contain complaints (even if not directly against Yahweh) as well as pleas." Day questions whether or not the psalms can be neatly divided into two categories as Broyles does, noting that Broyles "plea" psalms (Pss 27, 69, 143) all contain a request to Yahweh not to hide his face; there is "surely only a fine line between this and some of Broyles's complaint psalms which declare that Yahweh is hiding his face from the psalmist (Pss 13:1; 88:14)." So too

the specifics of the psalmists' complaint about God's disposition or (in)action. Toward this end, he divides the "God-complaints" into those of the individual and those of the community, seeking to discern in the respective types, first, the source of the psalmists' distress and, second, the religious beliefs and traditions of the psalmists which seem threatened by his situation.

In the opinion of the present writer, Broyles's analysis falters at this point. The basis for his distinction between the individual and communal laments is left unsaid and at times he further confuses matters by leveling individual laments (or individual "God-complaints") with the "God-complaints" of the community.[102] In spite of this flaw, however, the results of his study are generally fruitful. The source of the psalmist's distress in the individual God-complaints revolves around the impending threat of the psalmist's own death.[103] God-complaints of the community, on the other hand, are rooted in the community's experience of national disaster and, specifically, the defeat of Israel's armies, the consequent destruction and plunder of Jerusalem and the Temple, and the exile of the people.[104] The latter experiences, Broyles points out, jeopardize specific theological presuppositions of the psalmists which he identifies

---

Psalm 102 (a complaint according to Broyles, based on verses 11 and 24), and Psalm 38:1 and 69:26 clearly hold God responsible but are, according to Broyles, "plea psalms." Cf. also the review by Patrick D. Miller, "Review of *The Conflict of Faith and Experience in the Psalms: A Form-Critical and Theological Study* by Craig C. Broyles," *CBQ* 53 (1991), 459–460.

[102] See, for example, pp. 96–97, where he includes Psalms 10, 55, 94, and 109 under the subheading "The Laments of the Community," even though only Ps 9/10 is elsewhere identified by Broyles, without explanation, as a communal lament.

[103] *Ibid.*, pp. 84–95.

[104] In addition Broyles, pp. 96–98, believes the nation suffered from a general plunder of its cities, "murderous social violence," and "an absence of current saving deeds" which resulted in "the nation in dearth." He adduces, however, no conclusive evidence for these claims. He believes that Psalm 80:12–13 and 17 speak of the general plunder of the nation's towns, but the metaphor used there, though ambiguous, seems more naturally to refer to the decimation of the population, especially given the verse's affinity with Exodus 15:17 (on which, see below). Explicit evidence for "murderous social violence" is lacking in the communal laments, as is the "absence of current saving deeds," for which he cites only Psalm 77, an individual lament. Nor do Psalms 85 and 126, which do not fully correspond to the communal lament, serve to support the claim that the nation experienced dearth. Although all of these last themes might be logically inferred from the capture and plunder of Jerusalem, they are simply not present in the communal laments.

as (1) the divine warrior tradition (Pss 44 and 60), (2) the Royal Zion tradition (Pss 74, 79, and 89), and (3) the exodus/conquest tradition (Ps 80).[105] Although Broyles neither considers Psalm 83. nor explains its omission from his discussion, the psalm is clearly a communal lament evoking the exodus/conquest tradition. Against the supposition that the divine warrior was to lead the fight on Israel's behalf stood the army's defeat, a sure sign that Yahweh had not in fact preceded them (Pss 44:10, 60:12). The promises of perpetual lineage and rule to David and the divine protection extended over Zion have been thwarted, it seemed, in light of the conquest of Jerusalem and the deposition of the monarch (Pss 74:2,20; 79:1; 89:39–46). God's election and gift of the land likewise appear terminated by the decimation of the population and the conquest by foreigners (Pss 80:9, 13–14; 83:10–13).

While Broyles is perfectly correct in noting that national disaster threatens a variety of sacred traditions, it remains a striking fact that, whatever other traditions are evoked, six of the seven psalms under consideration explicitly extol the power of God as a cosmogonic divine warrior.[106] As noted, the motif dominates Psalms 44 and 60. But the cosmogonic divine warrior is also the subject of the central hymns in Psalm 74:12–17 and 89:6–19 where the power of God is placed in deliberate juxtaposition to the plight of God's people.[107] Likewise in Psalm 83, the summons for God to defend Israel against the hostile nations surrounding it, coupled with storm imagery, implies that God's preeminence (v 19) is achieved through the power of a divine warrior. In addition, Psalm 83 evokes the divine warrior tradition by means of the explicit shepherd imagery of verse 13 where the psalmist attributes the role of shepherd to God

---

[105] *Ibid.*, pp. 135–139, 150–154, 157–164, 168–173, and the summarizing chart on pp. 214–215.

[106] Cf. Keel, *Symbolism*, pp. 100–101, 106–107. Psalm 79 appears not to include explicit references to the cosmogonic divine warrior. God's dominion over the affairs of the world is, however, assumed in this text. Moreover, note the comments on the enemies' taunts in Chapter 5, below.

[107] Bernhard W. Anderson, "Introduction: Mythopoeic and Theological Dimensions of Biblical Creation Faith," in *Creation in the Old Testament*, IRT, No. 6 (Philadelphia: Fortress, 1984), p. 9, notes the use of parallel creation and redemption verbs in Psalm 74:2 (*qānâ* and *gāʾal*). This verse, like the creation hymn in Psalm 89, associates God's creative activity with the Royal Zion tradition: the restoration of order and stability would, in the psalmists' view, correspond to the cosmic creation.

as the enemies conspire to take possession of God's pastures (*nᵓwt*).[108] The image of God as shepherd, frequently associated with the Exodus,[109] is also linked with the divine warrior both within the Hebrew Scriptures and in the ancient Near East. The god Enlil, for example, is explicitly referred to as the "faithful Shepherd, master of all countries" in a *gala balag* ritual;[110] elsewhere Marduk and Utu/ Šamaš are similarly addressed.[111] While not explicitly addressing Yahweh as a shepherd, Exodus 15:13 is nevertheless particularly interesting in that the text refers to Yahweh's *nĕwê qodšékā,* interpreted by Cross[112] as a twelfth-century reference to an Israelite tent-shrine but associated with a pastoral abode. An alternative construct form of this noun, *nĕwat* (perhaps a corruption of *nĕwê*?) appears in Job 8:6. Psalm 83:13 appears to be unrelated until one realizes that the construct plural form of *nāwāh*, *nĕᵓôt*, translated in the NRSV (following BDB) as "pastures," also is attested as *nwt* in Zephaniah 2:6 where it is pointed as *nĕwōt*. The fact that the root radicals for these related nouns are identical, coupled with the confusion between the construct forms, suggests that *nĕᵓôt ᵓelōhîm* in Ps 83:13 may have been confused for *nĕwat/nĕwê ᵓelōhîm*, the "tent-shrine" or "encampment" of God. The possibility that the text originally read *nĕwat/nĕwê ᵓelōhîm* is further strengthened by evidence drawn from the LXX which translates the noun in the psalm as *hagiastērion*, a word elsewhere used only to signify a holy place or sanctuary.[113] If so, the context of the psalm may suggest an intentional hearkening to Exodus 15:13 where the shepherding activity of God is linked to the mythological activity of the cosmogonic divine warrior. In any case, the association between the divine shepherd and the divine warrior intensifies in Psalm 79:13, with its reference to Israel as God's flock, and in Psalm 80:2, with the explicit epithet "Shepherd of Israel." Indeed, Psalm 80:9–12 echoes much of the thought of Exodus 15:17, a verse that follows fast upon a recitation of the saving activity of God where God finds portrayal as the cosmogonic divine warrior. Both texts refer to God's deliverance of the people from

---

[108] *Pace* Dahood, *Psalms II: 51–100*, p. 276, who reads *ᵓĕlōhîm* here as a superlative.

[109] Exod 15:13,17; Ps 78:51–54,69–72; cf. Jer 23:1–8; 31:8–4; Isa 40:11; 49:9–13.

[110] *ANET*³, p. 337.

[111] Jack W. Vancil, "Sheep, Shepherd," *ABD*, Vol. 5, p. 1188.

[112] Cross, *CMHE*, p. 243, n. 101; cf. p. 125, n. 41 and the bibliography cited there.

[113] E.g. Lev 12:4; Ps 72[73]:17; 73[74]:7.

Egypt, to God's bringing them into a land, and to God's "planting" the people. Mountain imagery likewise appears in both texts. J.P. Hyatt concludes that the first phrase in Exodus 15:17, "the mountain of your own possession," likely refers to the hill-country of Palestine or to the whole land of which the hill-country was a prominent part,[114] which is, of course, precisely the context of Psalm 80:10–12.

The Description of Destruction

The portrayal of destruction within the seven communal lament psalms includes descriptions of violence done to the land surrounding the city, the people and, especially, to the Temple. The earth quakes, causing fissures in the ground.[115] Fortifications crumble.[116] Deep darkness prevails throughout the land,[117] resulting in wasted human habitations.[118] Dwellings are transformed into the abodes of wild animals.[119] The defenseless population is indiscriminately slaughtered,[120] and their bodies left as food for scavenging beasts.[121] Those who do survive are captured and exiled,[122] all the while suffering the ignominy of the enemies' taunts.[123] Although these psalms do not specifically describe the social upheaval that doubtless was considered a consequence of this destruction, the psalmists seem to allude to it in Psalm 60:5: "You have made your people suffer hard things; you have given us wine to drink that made us reel."

Most traumatic of all, however, was the plunder and destruction of the Temple's sanctuary. The enemies' defilement of the sacred precincts serves as the primary subject of Psalms 74 and 79. The psalmists complain that the enemies have not been content to enter

---

114 J.P. Hyatt, *Exodus* (Grand Rapids: Wm. B. Eerdmans, 1971), p. 168. Hyatt holds that the references to the "place" God made for an abode and the sanctuary established by God's hands are likely references to Solomon's Temple. See also Cross, *CMHE*, p. 97, n. 24, who concludes that this archaic text uses *šébet* to refer to the earthly shrine of Yahweh.

115 Ps 60:3–4.
116 Pss 80:13; 89:39.
117 Ps 44:20.
118 Pss 79:7,20; 80:17.
119 Pss 44:20; 74:20; 80:13.
120 Pss 44:23,26; 79:10.
121 Pss 74:19; 79:2–4.
122 Pss 44:12–13; 79:11.
123 Pss 44:15; 74:21–22; 79:4,10,12.

the sanctuary but have hacked it with their axes, burned it with fire, and defiled it by establishing their own emblems in the ruins.[124] Moreover, the psalmists take pains, through the use of the second-person suffix, to emphasize that God ought be concerned about this sacrilege. God's Temple has been defiled and, as a result, cultic activity honoring God has been disrupted:

> They set your sanctuary on fire; they desecrated the dwelling place
> of your name, bringing it to the ground.
> They said to themselves, "We will utterly subdue them"; they
> burned all the meeting places of God in the land.
> We do not see our emblems; there is no longer any prophet, and
> there is no one among us who knows how long. (Psalm 74:7–9).

Because the cessation of cultic activity provides an obvious bridge to the Mesopotamian laments, it is fitting to note that the meaning of Psalm 74:9 has been the subject of no little interpretive debate. The absence of prophets and signs has led some to conclude that this psalm must have been composed in the Maccabean period when such things had ceased in the life of the cult.[125] Other, more likely possibilities suggest themselves. ʾôṭōṭēynû, translated above as "our emblems," connotes omens or signs which indicate future events.[126] The text may therefore be simply reporting that various omens, as well as those who read them, have been removed and possibly replaced with alien rites (cf. v 4) by the invading foe. Similarly, J.J.M. Roberts has shown that "signs not seen" can be understood in relation to ancient Israelite oracular practice. 'Signs' refer here, he believes, to unrealized signs which the prophets promised as confirmation of their oracles of salvation. Correspondingly, he explains the complaint about the lack of prophets or anyone knowing 'how long?' not as a literal cessation of prophecy but rather as a collapse of public confidence in the prophetic institution and in the prophet's ability to set a limit to the period of divine wrath. Thus, he concludes, "the verse, far from suggesting a later date, actually

---

[124] Ps 74:3–9.

[125] Cf. Kraus, *Psalms 60–150*, p. 96f. and the bibliography cited there as well as J.J.M. Roberts, "Of Signs, Prophets, and Time Limits: A Note on Psalm 74:9," *CBQ* 39 (1979), 474–475.

[126] Ludwig Koehler and Walter Baumgartner, *Lexicon in Veteris Testamenti Libros* (Leiden: E.J. Brill, 1985), p. 23. Similar meanings for this word can be found in Genesis 1:14; 1 Samuel 14:10; 2 Kings 20:8,9, etc.

supports a date for the psalm in the early exilic period."[127] Roberts apparently believes that the verse has to do with an historical event and associates it with the destruction of the Temple in 587 BCE. If that proves not to be the case, however, Roberts's conclusion can be modulated: there is no reason to suppose that the *terminus ante quem* for the crisis described in 74:9 is the Babylonian destruction of Jerusalem or, for that matter, that it relies upon any actual catastrophic destruction of Temple and city. Given the cultural contact between Mesopotamia and Israel, it appears possible that the motif of a disruption in prophetic activity and priestly ritual was one long available to Israel through the Mesopotamian lament tradition and, like the latter traditions, may not have had a historical destruction in mind.

Importunities

A final characteristic of the Hebrew communal lamentations finds expression in the array of importunities addressed to God. The importunity, or petition, emerges as the most consistent aspect of the communal lament; it is never missing.[128] Primarily, the psalmists urged God to action in such a way as to relieve the distress. God is summoned to "awaken" from slumber and to "rise up":

> Rouse yourself! Why do you sleep, O Lord? Awake, do not cast us off forever . . .
>
> Rise up, come to our help. Redeem us for the sake of your steadfast love. (Psalm 44:24,26; cf. Ps. 74:22)

Likewise God is summoned to "grant help" against the foe,[129] to "remember" the plight of God's people,[130] and to redeem, deliver, and restore the faithful.[131] In several instances the psalmist utters imprecations against the enemies, calling upon God to avenge the people's suffering, as well as the slight to God's own reputation, with violence. This subject occupies most of Psalm 83,[132] for example, but also appears in Psalm 79:10–12 where the Lord is en-

---

127 Roberts, "Of Signs, Prophets, and Time Limits," 481.
128 Westermann, *Praise and Lament*, p. 55.
129 Ps 60:13.
130 Ps 74:2,18; 89:48; cf. Ps 79:14.
131 Ps 44:27; 74:19; 79:9; 80:4,8,19–20.
132 Cf. vv 10–18.

couraged to wreak sevenfold vengeance upon those who have taunted God.

Psalm 79 also assumes that God has abandoned both the sanctuary and Mt. Zion and must, therefore, be informed of the fate that has befallen the Temple, Jerusalem, and God's servants there:

> O God, the nations have come into your inheritance; they
> have defiled your holy temple; they have laid Jerusalem
> in ruins.
> They have given the bodies of your servants to the birds of the air
> for food, the flesh of your faithful to the wild animals of the
> earth. (vv 1–2)

This theme emerges unmistakably in Psalm 74 as well. Although Zion is God's proper dwelling (v 2), God has clearly abandoned the Temple and must be summoned to return to it in order that God might see the destruction of his abode:

> Direct your steps to the perpetual ruins; the enemy has destroyed
> everything in the sanctuary.
> Your foes have roared within your holy place; they set up their
> emblems there. (vv 3–4)

God has indeed abandoned the Temple and, in so doing, left the Temple vulnerable to attack. The divine abandonment is further signaled in these psalms by the various allusions to God having failed to go forth with Israel's armies and by God turning and hiding God's face.[133] Restoration and deliverance can only come when God's face shines once more.[134]

Related to the importunities, and often interspersed with them, are the woe cries "How long?" and other mournful questions born of the psalmists' distress. The following are representative:

> How long, O LORD? Will you be angry forever? (Ps 79:5)[135]

> Why do you hide your face? Why do you forget our affliction
> and oppression? (Ps 44:25)

> O God, why do you cast us off forever? Why does your anger
> smoke against the sheep of your congregation? (Ps 74:1)

---

[133] Cf. Ps 44:25.
[134] Ps 79:19.
[135] Cf. Pss 74:10; 80:5; 89:47.

The cry "how long" and the other inquiries imply a request that God might consider the circumstances of God's city, Temple, and people, and that God might be moved thereby quickly to alleviate the distress. The psalmist prays that the enemy might be subdued, the people delivered, and order restored.

SUMMARY

The discussion above outlines those aspects of the Hebrew communal lamentations that are characteristic of that genre. Following Haar, Psalms 44, 60, 74, 79, 80, 83, and 89 were identified as communal laments based on their unique combination of stylistic, thematic, and structural elements. In addition, however, a number of consistent features were seen to appear throughout these psalms including the following:

1. Structure and content
   A. Sections of explicit praise in which God is described as a cosmogonic divine warrior
      (1) As the divine warrior who brooks no equal, God is held responsible for the calamity which has befallen Israel
   B. Descriptions of the disaster in which
      (1) God, responsible for the course of historical events, nevertheless permits foes, the chief destructive agents, to attack and prevail over Israel
      (2) the armies of Israel suffer defeat because God has abandoned them; the foes taunt
      (3) Jerusalem and its environs are destroyed by earthquake, fire, and enemy assaults; the city is transformed into a habitat fit only for wild beasts
      (4) God's people are indiscriminately slaughtered or driven into exile
      (5) the Temple is plundered and destroyed as a consequence of divine abandonment with a resulting cessation of cultic activities
   C. Importunities that disaster might end and order be restored, including
      (1) petitions that God awaken and rise up
      (2) petitions that God might look upon the disaster

    (3) petitions that God might return to the Temple
    (4) various woe cries and questions directed to God,
       including "How long?"
  2. Various poetic devices, the most notable being
    A. A shift in speakers; various *dramatis personae* are given
      voice
    B. Lists
  3. The absence of either an assurance of being heard or
    penitential motifs

That God might be moved to act, granting the various importunities, is the ostensive purpose of the communal lament psalms.
Firmly persuaded that the cosmogonic God of creation who fashioned the people Israel had the power and responsibility to act concretely in history on Israel's behalf, the psalmists address God as
though in the throes of a historical calamity from which deliverance
was anticipated—or at least hoped for. The psalms are elusive with
respect to the specifics of the historical situations they describe, a
fact which, it is almost universally supposed, can be attributed to
the metaphorical character of the poetic form as well as to the adaptation of the psalm for ongoing use in the cult. And yet there seems
little doubt on the part of biblical scholars that these psalms owe
their inspiration to some event in Israel's history, whether that be a
defeat of Israel's armies in the preexilic or Maccabean era, a destruction of the Temple by the Babylonians or by Antiochus IV, or some
other historical location. Granting, for the time being, the validity
of that supposition, a question immediately surfaces: if the communal laments are rooted in a historical event for their inspiration
and composition, what accounts for the adaption and preservation
in the cult? Haar surveys, and severely criticizes, the widespread
belief that the communal lament psalms survived and found continued use through various penitential ceremonies in Jerusalem's
post-exilic cult.[136] With the single exception of Psalm 79:8–9 the Psalter's communal lamentations are curiously silent on the subject of

---

[136] Haar, "The God-Israel Relationship," pp. 11–14. Included among those scholars
who stress the penitential aspects of the communal lament's *Sitz im Leben* are Mowinckel, *The Psalms*, vol. 1, p. 193; Weiser, *The Psalms*, p. 68; Kraus, *Psalms 1–59*, p. 51;
Sabourin, *The Psalms*, p. 295; E. Lipinski, *La liturgie pénitentielle dans la Bible*, Lectio
Divina, No. 52 (Paris: Éditions du Cerf, 1969), pp. 43–81.

sin and penitence. Even in that psalm it remains unclear that the psalmist confesses his own generation's sins so much as recognizes that the iniquities of the ancestors remain a potential cause for punishment and an explanation for the present disaster. Otherwise, one searches as vainly for penitential themes in these materials as in the Mesopotamian lamentations.

Haar believes it is precisely the absence of both penitential themes and sections indicating the assurance of being heard that proves significant for the interpretation of the communal laments as well as for the interpretation of the related corporate prayers for help. He vigorously denies that the central concern of genuine communal laments is the issue of sin, arguing instead that

> the primary goal of community lament prayers appears to be to move Yahweh to act on Israel's behalf commensurate with his relationship to his people. God is not so much asked to forgive or pardon Israel, though that element is present at times. Rather he is urged to recognize that his relationship to Israel is greater than any sin that might have been committed. . . . The critical issue was not the forgiveness of sins but rather the fidelity of Yahweh to his people even in the midst of sin.[137]

The fidelity of Yahweh and the divinely established relationship between Israel and God were, in Haar's view, the *raison d'être* for the composition of the communal laments. In times of distress, whatever the cause, corporate Israel called upon Yahweh to recall this relationship and to deliver salvation on account of it.[138]

The preliminary evidence adduced thus far, however, suggests that Haar, though correct about the absence of a penitential motif in these materials, stands on less solid ground when he asserts that the communal lament psalms functioned precisely as corporate prayers

---

137 *Ibid.*, p. 92–93.

138 *Ibid.*, p. 93–95. Haar develops this interpretation at some length by means of an exposition of eight theological assumptions of the community lament psalms: (1) God is the creator of Israel, (2) the faithfulness of God is a problem for Israel, (3) when Israel is in pain, God is obligated to act on her behalf, (4) the fate of Israel and the fate of God are bound together, (5) the importance of the reputation of God should impel Yahweh to act on Israel's behalf, (6) God can be affected by prayer; God needs to be reminded of former promises, and such reminders can influence God and/or motivate God to act, (7) the issue of Israel's sin is always secondary to the importance of the God-Israel relationship, and (8) God is expected to act concretely in history on behalf of Israel. Cf. pp. 159–175.

for help. First of all, as he acknowledges, the two genres are similar, but not quite the same. Frequently, the difference involves the inclusion of penitential motifs in the corporate prayers for help, or an assurance of being heard, two of the characteristics that distinguish the communal laments. Secondly, the extremely occasional circumstances under which these psalms would be used hardly account for their preservation at a time when the boundaries of the Hebrew canon were by no means certain. Haar proposes that the psalms would have been recited "whenever the nation was threatened or had undergone a terrible hardship."[139] Even considering the turbulent history of Israel, does not this proposal assume that the psalms found little or no cultic use during the relatively long periods of peace? If so, how does one account for their preservation? A clue may be had in a further comparison of the Sumero-Akkadian *balag*s and *eršemma*s, toward which this study now turns.

---

[139] *Ibid.*, p. 93.

CHAPTER 5

COMMUNAL LAMENTS IN MESOPOTAMIA AND ISRAEL: COMPARISONS AND CONTRASTS

In 1952 Folker Willesen published an essay in which he maintained that Psalms 74 and 79, traditionally associated by scholars either with the desecration and destruction of the Jerusalem Temple in 587 under the Babylonians or that which took place in the Maccabean period, actually bore no relation whatsoever to any historical occurrence but rather were completely cultic in character.[1] Willesen tried to demonstrate the existence of a ritual destruction and re-establishment of the Temple by relating a hypothesized profanation ritual (i.e., the destruction) and a death of the god cult, thus tying the lament over the destruction of the Temple to the lament for a fallen deity. This correspondence seemed to him to be likely since, he argued, in the Semitic world the cultic profanation of the temple and the ritual death of the god are bound in such a way that the cultic lamentation accompanying the god's descent to the netherworld would have integrated aspects of the temple profanation as well. As this was the case, Willesen stated, "the determination of their type as 'national psalms of lamentation' must fall, and it will come out that originally they were ritual laments with a fixed position in the cult drama."[2]

Willesen's article proved to be the whipping boy of many a psalm commentator who criticized him both for creating a false

---

[1] Folker Willesen, "The Cultic Situation of Psalm LXXIV," *VT* 11 (1952), 289–306.
[2] *Ibid.*, 289.

distinction between mythic and historical language in the psalms.[3] as well as for the implication contained in his argument, namely that these laments were uttered in Israel as laments for a dead god.[4] Even if his basic thesis proved unconvincing, however, Willesen nevertheless can be credited with having marshalled an impressive array of parallels between East and West Semitic texts and Psalms 74 and 79, parallels which in turn suggest that these psalms, at least, do enjoy some kind of relationship to other cultures' communal laments. In the following pages, an effort is made to focus the contours of that relationship and to suggest the possible cultic use not only of these psalms but of the other Hebrew communal laments as well. Specifically the Hebrew communal lament psalms will be compared and contrasted with the *balag/eršemma* lamentations. The comparison, moreover, will be guided by the criteria of cultural contact and comparability discussed in Chapter 2, as well as the principles of adoptability and adaptability. A preliminary step, however, involves closer scrutiny of Willesen's argument.

WILLESEN'S HYPOTHESIS

Willesen's attempt to establish the purely cultic origins of Psalms 74 and 79 originate in his perception of a temple ideology, common throughout the ancient Near East, whereby the establishment of a temple was necessary to secure the existence of the gods

---

[3] Mitchell Dahood, *Psalms II: 51–100*, p. 205, commenting on Psalm 74 remarks: "This copious use of mythological motifs does not, however, warrant the conclusion of Folker Willesen . . . that this psalm has no relation whatever to any historical occurrence, but is completely cultic. . . . Willesen unfortunately overlooks those historical psalms, such as Ps 1xxxix, which intersperse the description of historical occurrences with mythological motifs." So too Kraus, *Psalms 60–150*, p. 96: "Willesen takes a few parallels to Babylonian and Canaanite laments for the dying god-king as warrant for a wholesale transposition of the song to the sphere of the mythical; basic insights for determining the category of the psalm are thereby ruled out." Cf. Sabourin, *The Psalms*, pp. 303–304. Note however, that Willesen has found some supporters, most notably Karl Heinz Bernhardt, *Das Problem der altorientalischen Königsideologie im alten Testament, unter besonderer Berücksichtigung der Geschichte der Psalmenexegese dargestellt und kritisch gewürdigt*, VTSup, Vol. 8 (Leiden: E. J. Brill, 1961), p. 217f., and Helmer Ringgren, "Die Funktion des Schöpfungsmythus in Jes. 51," in *Schalom: Studien zu Glaube und Geschichte Israels*, ed. by Karl Heinz Bernhardt (Stuttgart: Calwer, 1971), p. 39.

[4] Weiser, *The Psalms*, p. 518, n. 1.

and their work as well as to guarantee the peace and happiness of a
newly enthroned king. Drawing particularly upon the *Enuma Eliš*
(tablet vi, 35–54), he points out that the creation of Esagila "stood
as the keystone of Marduk's creative efforts, and at the same time
as the guarantee of the maintenance of the work" since the temple
was needed by the gods in order to maintain life and to undertake the determination of the destinies.[5] A similar concept emerges
in the West Semitic world as well where there seemed to be a connection between the establishment of a new sanctuary and the well-
being and success of a new king; hence, says Willesen, we have
Solomon's immediate start of such a construction project upon his
accession, Jeroboam's building of shrines, and the many instances
in the Old Testament where the concept of covenant or renewal of
covenant is associated with the idea of the temple.[6] Nor is the connection between the establishment of the temple and world order
absent in the Old Testament. Willesen writes:

> In ch. vii 19–22 of the same book [2 Chron.] the relation between
> Cosmos-temple and Chaos-profanation is exposed; here Jahwe is
> promising the king that the Temple will be destroyed and blas-
> phemed, if or when the nation is ruined. The specific Israelitic
> form of the primeval creation, the liberation from Egypt, is here
> set against "all this misery" (v. 22). In Ex. xxv ff. the Tabernacle is
> one of the signs of the Covenant, and the first one even ordered by
> Jahwe.[7]

But it is in the Ugaritic materials that Willesen believes the connection between the temple ideology and cultic drama emerge
with particular clarity and, accordingly, he devotes several pages of
his essay to the link between the fall of a temple and the debase-
ment/death of the deities Ba'al, 'Anat, etc.[8] His assertion that the
conflict myths associate the failure to establish a house/temple for
the deity "like unto the gods" with the lamentation accompanying
that deity's descent into the nether-world, is a point well taken and
the evidence drawn from III AB C 16–20 in this connection can

---

[5] Willesen, "Cultic Situation," 290.

[6] *Ibid.*, 291–292. Willesen cites as examples 2 Samuel 7, Ezekiel ch. 40ff., 1 Kings
8:14ff. (and parallels), the Book of Haggai, and more.

[7] *Ibid.*, 292.

[8] *Ibid.*, 293–296.

hardly be gainsaid.[9] He does not, however, demonstrate his further
contention, namely that these texts have strictly to do with a cultic
drama enacted in the sanctuary and that "this passage thus is an
ascertainment of the ritual profanation of the temple, one of the features of the Semitic New Year Festival."[10] Having made that claim,
however, Willesen can proceed little further as he fails to produce
solid evidence or argument either for the existence of a ritual of profanation of the temple or for its association with a Semitic New Year
festival. Indeed Willesen is finally forced to admit, "It is true that
a profanation ceremony is nowhere directly asserted, but it cannot
be denied that it is postulated by the rituals."[11] Nevertheless, and in
this connection, he makes reference to the Akkadian *akîtu* festival
which, again, he deduces must have had a profanation ritual as a
part of the initial ceremony. Willesen's supposition on this point
may have more merit than he could have realized when he made
this suggestion. Although Willesen was evidently unaware of it,
the Uruk Ritual for the *akîtu* festival of the seventh month, *Tašrītu*,
includes instructions for the recitation of several known *balag*s
on days ten and eleven of the ceremony.[12] Given that the primary
significance of the *Tašrītu akîtu* festival seems to have been the cele-
bration the deity's grandiose entry into the city from whence he had
been removed to the *akîtu* house on the first day,[13] the use of *balag*s

---

9 *Ibid.*, 295; cf. J.C.L. Gibson, *Canaanite Myths and Legends* (Edinburgh: T. & T.
Clark, 1977), p. 38: I iii 16–20. However, Willesen supposes that Ba'al is the complain-
ing deity in this passage rather than—as the context would suggest—the deity Attar
[cf. I iii 12, 24].

10 Willesen, "Cultic Situation," 293.

11 *Ibid.*, 297.

12 Cf. AO 6459 and AO 6465 (= *Textes cunéiformes du Louvre* 6 39 and 40); Thureau-
Dangin, *Rituels accadiens*, p. 89ff.; Cohen, *The Cultic Calendars of the Ancient Near East*,
pp. 431–433, where the texts appear in translation. Specifically the Uruk rubrics specify that on day ten the Sumerian lamentation *umun še-er-ma-al-la-an-ki-a* ("Lord,
Respected One of Heaven and Earth," = *balag* 21) should be recited to Anu and *an-na
e-lum-e* ("The Honored One of Heaven" = *balag* 9) is spoken to all the gods. On day
eleven *balag* 6, *am-e am aš-a-na*, and *balag* 7, *e-lum di-da-ra*, are to be recited to Anu and
"all the gods" respectively.

13 Cohen, *Cultic Calendars*, p. 404. Cohen discusses the origin and practice of the
akîtu festivals at some length on pp. 400–453. Cf. Svend Aage Pallis, *The Babylonian
Akîtu Festival* (København: Bianco Lunos Bogtrykkeri, 1926); J.A. Black, "The New
Year Ceremonies in Ancient Babylon: 'Taking Bel by the Hand' and a Cultic Picnic,"
Religion 11 (1981), 39–59. The purpose of the *Tašrītu akîtu* festival seems to have been
other than a second annual *akîtu* that took place in *Nisan*. In a recent article Karel van
der Toorn, "The Babylonian New Year Festival: New Insights from the Cuneiform

which ritually lament divine abandonment and the destruction of the temple appear to be well suited to the context. The texts in question, however, are from the late first millennium and, unfortunately, little more is known about the exact significance of the placement of these compositions in the *akîtu* festival. Consequently Willesen's suggestion that a profanation ceremony played a part in the larger *akîtu* observances remains suggestive but unproven.[14]

More intriguing is the connection Willesen draws between Akkadian temple lamentation rituals performed by the *gala* (= *kalû*) priests as a part of a ceremony to restore a ruined or desecrated sanctuary. In particular he notes the remarkable correspondence between the an *eršemma*-composition, K. 4608,[15] and Psalm 79:[16]

K.4608	Psalm 79 (NRSV)
Obv.	
7. Into Eulmas thy sanctuary the foe entered	1. O God, the nations have come into your inheritance;
9. Thy holy chamber he defiled	they have defiled your holy temple; (Ps 74:3b–4)
11. In thy holy place he set his foot	They have laid Jerusalem in ruins.
13. Thy far-famed dwelling he destroyed	(Ps 74:5–7)

Texts and Their Bearing on Old Testament Study," VTSup 43 (1991), 331–343, focuses on the latter *akîtu* festival. Rather than celebrating the dying and rising of Marduk or a "cultic battle" between Marduk and Tiamat, van der Toorn believes that the festival served to renew the civil authority of the king and the religious *status quo.* "This renewal," he writes, "takes the form of a ritual process in which the old order is momentarily jeopardized, emerges intact, and is reaffirmed," and its purpose was to celebrate "the undiminished validity of both the political and the religious order" (339). Van der Toorn does not treat the *Tašrītu akîtu* in his study.

[14] In this connection it is also worth noting that several leading scholars including W. von Soden, "Gibt es ein Zeugnis, daß die Babylonier an Marduks Wiederauferstehung glaubten?" ZA 55 (1952–1955), 130–166, and W.G. Lambert, "The Great Battle of the Mesopotamian Religious Year: The Conflict in the Akitu House (A Summary)," *Iraq* 25 (1963), 189–190; *idem*, "Myth and Ritual as Conceived by the Babylonians," *JSS* 13 (1968), 104–112; Karel van der Toorn, "The Babylonian New Year Festival," 337, deny, *pace* Pallis (and by inference, Willesen), that the *akîtu* festival had any connection with the dying and rising god motif. On dying gods cf. Cohen's chapter "Festivals for the Netherworld," in *Cultic Calendars,* pp. 454–481, and especially p. 465ff.

[15] Cf. S. Langdon, *OECT,* VI, p. 37. The translation following is that of Langdon.

[16] Strangely, however, Willesen does not note the several places where the imagery of K. 4608 corresponds more closely to Psalm 74. In what follows the references within parentheses mark what the present writer regards as parallels.

K.4608 (*continued*)	Psalm 79 (NRSV) (*continued*)
15. Thy precious rituals he[17]	4. We have become a taunt to our neighbors, mocked and derided by those around us. (Ps 74:9)

Rev.

1. How long, O my lady, has the mighty foe plundered thy sanctuary?	5a. How long, O Lord? Will you be angry forever? (Ps 74:10)
2. In thy city Erech lamentation is raised	(Ps 74:2)
5. In Eulmas, the house of thy counsel, blood like water was sacrificed.	3. They have poured out their blood like water all around Jerusalem, and there was no one to bury them
7. In all thy lands fire he cast and heaped them like roasted grain	5b. Will your jealous wrath burn like fire? (Ps 74:7–8)

Of these two texts Willesen remarks:

> The congruity of these two psalms might indicate that psalm lxxix forms part of the general Semitic pattern in its description of the temple profanation. Of course, both poems might be understood as depicting a historic disaster, but the congruity of all such psalms is an indication that they have been built up according to the same schema all over the Semitic world, and to my mind this favors a ritual interpretation.[18]

As this quote indicates, Willesen's thesis finally includes two parts: (a) an insistence on a divorce between ritual and history and (b) a pan-Semitic profanation ceremony which, elsewhere in his essay, he couples with an emphasis on the role played by the dying god motif. In retrospect one can readily see why Willesen earned the criticism he received. Above all, his detailed reconstruction of the details of an Israelite cult drama strain credulity,[19] and Willesen's identifica-

---

[17] Willesen thinks the broken portion of the tablet must have included taunts against the worshipers and therefore sees a correspondence with Psalm 79:4 (296). An argument based on this kind of lacuna in the texts is problematic, particularly when the plain meaning of the preserved portion would, as in other *eršemma* materials, seem to indicate that the rituals of the cult had been violated or brought to an end.

[18] Willesen, "Cultic Situation," 292.

[19] E.g., *Ibid.*, 305: "After the introduction follow the rites representing the conquest of the sanctuary by the Chaos powers, viz. the roaring, the bringing in of signs fol-

tion of the origin of that cultic connection is unsatisfactory, as many commentators have pointed out.

Flawed as Willesen's evidence may be, however, scholars have been too quick to dismiss Willesen's two-part thesis. In the first place, if the details he provides for a pan-Semitic profanation ceremony are fanciful and not convincingly evinced from Ugaritic sources, the fact remains that the practitioners of at least one Semitic religion, the *gala* priesthood of Mesopotamia, did conduct ahistoric rituals, the texts of which focused on descriptions of the temple's destruction and included specific references to profanation or desecration. The texts used for these rituals were, of course, the *balag/eršemma* materials toward which Willesen points. In this connection it is noteworthy that many of the descriptions of the alleged destruction of the city and temple in other *balag/eršemma*s are every bit as graphic as those found in the psalms. For example, one reads concerning a temple:

> Its crenelated wall has been destroyed. Its dove hovers about.
> Its door-frame has been torn down.[20] What was once a place of
>   marvel is no more.
> Its rafters lie exposed to the sun like a man felled by a disease.
> Its jutting brickwork is crouching in tears like a mother in
>   mourning.
> Its reed eaves are lying on the ground like plucked hairs.
> . . .
> In closing (the door), its doorposts have fallen. . . [21]

Nor, as will be shown below, are the corresponding themes, motifs, and images restricted to descriptions of the temple's destruction.

---

lowed by burning and complete ritual destruction. One of the rites, the disposition of the hostile signs, is explained by verses 5–6: the performing persons take the axes, Ba'al's insignia, into the sacred house after having removed Jahwe's signs, and this act is described further by an allusion to a—no doubt well-known—mythic idea: it has to look like the behavior of Ba'al when felling Jahwe's forest, i.e., that the actors are cutting, hewing, and hammering with their tools on the wooden furniture destined for this purpose. After this casual flash on the sacred acts generally forgotten long ago the cultic text proceeds with the next picture, the burning of the ruined building. . . . How this was done we do not know—perhaps the broken bits were burned."

[20] The reference here and in line 26 to the destroyed door-frame and door posts is especially interesting in light of the LXX and ʹ rendering of Psalm 74:6: there for MT's *pittûḥeyhā* (its wood carvings) the LXX and ʹ translate *tas thuras autēs*, presumably reading *pĕtāḥeyhā* (its doors). Similarly the Syriac seems to have seen *pĕtāḥîm*.

[21] *balag* 3:19–26; cf. *balag* 4:140–150, a nearly identical description of the destroyed temple.

Second, if Willesen is guilty of an overemphasis on the dying god motif, Westermann is too severe when, besides faulting Willesen with the erroneous conclusion that these laments in Israel were spoken as laments for a dead god, he adds:

> Moreover, in making this identification there is a blending of the lament of the dead and the lament of distress which in any case cannot be the original one for Israel.[22]

While the blending of the lament of the dead and the lament of distress may not be an *original* one for Israel, the presence of the Tammuz/Dumuzi cult, which by Ezekiel's account flourished in Judah prior to 587 BCE, suggests that the link between the lament of the dead and the lament of distress was known in Israel, if only through the imported cult. Moreover, it seems more than coincidental that a number of the *balag* laments of distress specifically treat the Tammuz/Dumuzi myth, lamenting the dead deity. Ezekiel certifies that Israel was familiar with the Tammuz/Dumuzi myth. Was Israel likewise familiar with the only known literature that links the destruction of the temple with the dying/rising God motif? Willesen does not pursue the question, nor indeed does he fully note the significance of the *balag/eršemma* materials for his own thesis. Nevertheless, his article does serve to highlight at least one important dimension of these psalms: the apparent affinity of these poems with texts having to do with the establishment and well-being of the temple and, specifically, with those laments associated with the rituals of the Akkadian *gala* priests such as the *eršemma* K. 4608. Again, the question is whether or not Israel could have been sufficiently familiar with the *balag/eršemma* lamentations for them to have materially affected the composition of Israel's own communal laments.

THE CRITERIA OF CULTURAL CONTACT AND COMPARABILITY

The question of Israel's possible familiarity with the *balag/eršemma* compositions once more brings the criterion of cultural contact to the foreground and, in particular, the factors of temporal and geographic proximity discussed earlier in this study.[23] To re-

---

[22] Claus Westermann, *The Praise of God in the Psalms*, trans. by Keith R. Crim (Richmond: John Knox, 1965), p. 175, n. 24.

[23] Cf. Chapter 2, "The Criterion of Cultural Contact."

view quickly the case to this point: (1) Cultural contact between
Israel and the various successive Mesopotamian states hardly needs
be argued for the first millennium based on the abundant witness of
both the Hebrew scriptures and cuneiform artifacts. (2) The *balag/
eršemma* lamentations represent a living religious tradition; the
materials were copied and used by the *gala* priests from the Old
Babylonian era down to the close of the first millennium. The Mesopotamian lamentations were temporally proximate to the psalms
of Israel. (3) Strong evidence exists to suggest that scribal schools
in which various types of literature were copied operated in Hazor,
Megiddo, and Aphek until at least the end of the Late Bronze period.[24] Inscriptional cuneiform evidence from this period in Canaan
remains sparse, and none of it pertains to *balag/eršemma* compositions. Nevertheless the presence of scribal schools in this earlier
period provides one means by which the *balag/eršemma* lament tradition could have formally found its way into Israelite territories of
the Iron I period. The intercourse between the Israelite kingdoms
and those of Mesopotamia during the first millennium, including
trade, various diplomatic exchanges, and even the experience of the
northern exiles, provides other possibilities for Israelite familiarity
with the Sumero-Akkadian rites and texts. In short, the circumstantial evidence strongly suggests that the two lament traditions also
shared geographic proximity.

Besides satisfying the criterion of cultural contact, the caution of
the criterion of comparability is also met in the alignment of the
balag/eršemma lamentations and those of Israel. Both genres represent corporate laments, used ritually in connection with temples.
Both genres find general correspondence in terms of subject matter,
mood, and content. In addition, both traditions share a number of
other significant features that point toward an affirmative answer to
the question as to whether or not Israel could have been sufficiently
familiar with the *balag/eršemma* lamentations for those writings to
have materially affected the composition of Israel's own communal
laments.

POINTS OF CORRESPONDENCE

When comparing the typological characteristics of the b*alag/
eršemma* lamentations and the Hebrew communal laments, a num-

---

[24] See Chapter 2, n. 45.

ber of rather obvious points of correspondence emerge. No one of these similar features stands as singularly conclusive. The combined evidence, however, indicates these are not mere surface similarities: Israel's communal laments were composed by persons familiar with the Mesopotamian traditions. The primary points of correspondence include structure and content, poetic devices, and the general absence of penitential motifs.

Communal laments of both Mesopotamia and Israel characteristically contain sections of praise in which the deity is most often described as a powerful cosmogonic divine warrior. Allusions to the creation myths are ubiquitous in both traditions and appear even in those psalms that incorporate the *heilsgeschichtliche* traditions of Israel. In both traditions the chief deity struggles against sundry monsters that are more often than not connected with the theme of watery chaos. Long ago Gunkel suggested that the appearance in the Hebrew scriptures of cosmogonic motifs involving water could only have been borrowed from Mesopotamia since Palestine lacks the requisite geographic and meteorological features for the mythology to have arisen there.[25] Since Gunkel's day, of course, the discovery of the Ugaritic texts has done much to reshape scholarly opinion about the origin of Israel's mythological views, views that clearly were influenced by Canaanite traditions. One finds, for example, references to Anat or Baal's triumph over the serpentine sea monster *ltn*, also described as "Shalyat of the seven heads,"[26] a beast linked by J.A. Emerton to the biblical Leviathan.[27] Nevertheless, it is interesting to note an older Mesopotamian text likewise describes one of the monsters against which An struggled as a seven-headed snake.[28] The mythological view betrayed by the latter text, like the references in the Ugaritic materials, seems likely also to correspond

---

[25] Hermann Gunkel, "The Influence of Babylonian Mythology upon the Biblical Creation Story," trans. by Charles A. Muenchow, in *Creation in the Old Testament*, ed. by Bernhard W. Anderson, IRT, No. 6 (Philadelphia: Fortress, 1984), pp. 31–32.

[26] Cf. H.L. Ginsberg, "Poems about Baal and Anath, *ANET*, 137, D:34–39 (= *UT*, ʿnt III:34–39; *KTU*, 1.3.III.37–42); *ANET*, 138 (= *UT*, 67:I:1–3; *KTU*, 1.5.I.1–3).

[27] J.A. Emerton, "Leviathan and *ltn*: The Vocalization of the Ugaritic Word for Dragon," *VT* 32 (1982), 327–331. Rather than the usual vocalization of *ltn* as Lotan Emerton suggests an original *liwyatanu > liyatanu > litanu*. Cf. John Day, "Leviathan," *ABD*, Vol. 4, 295–296; James B. Pritchard, *ANEP*, 670–671, 691; the bibliography cited in *HALAT*, "לִוְיָתָן."

[28] Cf. *balag* 29:d+151.

to the biblical Leviathan, a creature described in Psalm 74:14–15 as having many heads and, in Isaiah 27:1, as "Leviathan the twisted serpent" (*liwyātān nāḥāš ʿăqallātôn*). The possible influence of Mesopotamian motifs on Israel, therefore, whether direct or mediated through the Canaanite traditions, need not be discarded.

In the Mesopotamian lamentations the chief deity—normally Enlil or An—was held accountable for the destruction while lesser deities stood by helpless to prevent the superior's actions. Israel's theology, of course, did not recognize members of the divine assembly as deities. Yahweh is described as incomparably superior to all others in the divine assembly and as "a God dreaded (*naʿărāṣ*) in the council (*sôḏ*) of the holy ones, greatly terrible above all that are round about him."[29] Consequently, Yahweh was considered solely responsible for the calamities described in the psalms. That is, Israel understood the members of the divine assembly to be as incapable of altering Yahweh's decisions and as impotent before God as were the lesser deities of Mesopotamia.

Narrative descriptions of the disasters said to befall the nation are likewise similar. In the *balag/eršemma* materials, the chief deity, responsible for the fate of the city and temple, sends destructive agents that wreak havoc, described mainly as a cosmic storm, a divine word, or as alien invaders. The reasons for the god's decision to unleash these forces remained mysterious to the Mesopotamian poets. Israel likewise looked to Yahweh as ultimately responsible for the fate of the city and the temple owing to God's covenantal promises. Nevertheless Yahweh, like Enlil, also unaccountably unleashes destructive agents against God's own habitation. Although Israel most often described these agents of destruction as alien foes, traces of the destructive power of the divine word and the divine storm also appear. Both traditions include references to enemy victory that has come about because the deity has not gone forth with the nation's armies. In both traditions the results of the destructive activity are the same: the city and its environs are decimated by earthquake, fire, and enemy assaults. The city itself becomes an abandoned tell, a habitation fit only for wild beasts of the desert. The city's population is indiscriminately slaughtered or driven into captive exile. Both traditions describe the temple of the deity as defiled, plundered and destroyed, either as a consequence of or lead-

---

[29] Ps. 89:8; cf. v 7.

ing to divine abandonment on the part of the god. A further result of all of this, again common to both traditions, is the cessation of cultic activities honoring the deity.

The intolerable situation leads to various importunities in both lament traditions, voiced in terms that, again, are strikingly alike. The deity, be it Enlil or Yahweh, is summoned to awaken from his slumber, to rise up, and to gaze upon the disaster. The god is called upon to return to the abandoned temple. In order to motivate the deity's response, the laments include various woe cries and questions including the query "how long?" Israel's laments, of course, do not include petitions to lesser deities to intercede with the chief god on behalf of the population; the exclusiveness of Yahwism precluded such a possibility.

A comparison of most of the various poetic devices employed by the poets of the respective traditions yields inconclusive results. The presence of a shift in speakers and lists in both traditions, however, appears to be somewhat more significant. Obviously the fact that various *dramatis personae* are given voice in the respective compositions points toward a cultic setting of some sort.[30] Indeed the shift in speakers suggests some sort of cultic drama that may have included a monarch or priest as representative of the people speaking some of the parts, although this cannot be demonstrated conclusively for either tradition. The presence of lists, though not solely sufficient to link the two traditions, provides yet another point of convergence between the two culture's lamentations, especially given the relative paucity of such lists in the psalms.

Finally, however, it is the conspicuous absence of penitential motifs and, one should add, of any elements of the assurance of being heard, which links the two traditions. Poets in both cultures were demonstrably familiar with the concept of a causal linkage between human sin and divine punishment,[31] yet neither evoked this concept when composing their respective communal laments. In the case of the *balag/eršemma* materials, the reasons for this omission are clear: the cultic setting had nothing to do with penitence but instead focused on averting divine wrath and, consequently, calamity. The poems were recited earlier on those occasions when temples were partially demolished in order to be renovated and, later, as a part of

---

[30] *Pace* Haar, "The God-Israel Relationship," p. 93.
[31] E.g. Pss 51:2,9; 19:12; 25:11,18 and Chapter 3 above.

the routine cultic calendar. The fact that Israel's psalms also lacked penitential features minimally implies, as Haar has already noted, that penitential motives did not undergird the cultic setting for the Hebrew lamentations. But in the case of Israel's lamentations, the absence of penitential features presents a problem, particularly if one assumes that the communal laments are properly located in some period after 587 BCE, that is, in a period roughly concomitant with the compositional activity of the Deuteronomistic Historian, not to mention Ezekiel and Jeremiah. Given the pronounced emphasis on reward and retribution in those materials as well as the clearly articulated understanding that at least the Northern Kingdom's demise came about as a consequence of Jeroboam and his successors' sin, the absence both of penitential motifs and of the idea that covenant disloyalty might have precipitated the destruction of Jerusalem and the Temple, is, at the very least, surprising. How could it be, assuming that the communal lamentations were composed subsequent to the Temple's destruction and in an era that otherwise did not hesitate to draw a connection between that destruction and a human breach in the covenant, that these features are absent from the psalms? Granted, this is an *argumentum ad silentium*, but in this instance the silence is a *silentium altum*. If the Hebrew communal laments were predicated on the historical events of 587 BCE and owe their inspiration to those events, one would expect some reflection of a theological motif that plays such a prominent role in other literature of that period similar, perhaps, to what one finds in Isaiah 63:7–64:12 [11]. Instead there is the absence of penitential motifs in both the Hebrew and Mesopotamian traditions, a fact that, when coupled with the other points of correspondence noted above, suggests already that these psalms originally found employment in Israel's cult for like reasons and similar situations as their kindred compositions of Mesopotamia. Before that suggestion can be seriously entertained, however, it is necessary to recognize that, in spite of their great many similarities, the respective compositions also manifest important differences.

POINTS OF CONTRAST

As impressive as the just noted parallels may be, they are not yet sufficient proof of literary influence between the older *balag/eršemma* compositions and the Hebrew laments. Indeed critics contend that the similarities prove nothing more than the existence of a common repository of themes, motifs, and images within the context of communal suffering in the ancient Near East,[32] or that Israel at most simply borrowed the "idea" of a lament over the destruction of a city or temple from her Mesopotamian neighbors.[33] This latter view is bolstered by an argument, *e silentio*, that the absence in the Hebrew corpus of themes and motifs typical of the Mesopotamian laments is proof that literary influence is lacking. But this sword of silence cuts in two directions: the relative paucity of Hebrew temple/city lament materials cautions against a hasty judgment on the question of literary influence based on themes not present. Nevertheless, it must be acknowledged that some themes important to the *balag/eršemma* compositions are absent from the Hebrew communal lamentations and, vice-versa, the Hebrew laments contain elements not present in the Sumero-Akkadian texts.

---

[32] This seems to be the major criticism of Ferris, *Genre*. However, Ferris is too severe when he remarks:

> regardless of how one isolates and identifies what appear to be the structural components of the lament—either Sumero-Akkadian or Hebrew—the structural grid cannot be forced upon the individual laments. They will not fit. These structural observations are helpful as heuristic devices. But it must be noted that the elements do not appear to get an equal amount of attention. (264; cf. 275)

Ferris's objection is a methodological one: form and structure are not, he believes, very reliable criteria by which to determine a literary influence, especially when, as in the Sumero-Akkadian and Hebrew laments, a fluidity or flexibility marks the structure of the materials under scrutiny. However, if *exact* structural correspondence is made the criteria by which one makes form critical judgments, it is difficult to see how *any* form critical decisions can be made, including the decision to place any given psalm under the rubric of "communal laments." Ferris is quite willing to grant that form-critical designation to a plethora of psalms as well as other texts, and that in spite of their distinctive content and structure, but is unwilling to grant that these unique compositions were influenced by demonstrably older texts whose outline corresponds to these psalms both in terms of general units (i.e., sections of complaint, appeal, and praise) and, frequently, in terms of the order of specific images and themes. Such correspondences do exist; it simply strains credulity to think they could have arisen apart from literary influence.

[33] Thomas F. McDaniel, "The Alleged Sumerian Influence Upon Lamentations," *VT* 18 (1968), 198–209, voices just this objection against those who view the Book of Lamentations as dependent upon the Sumerian city-laments. Gwaltney, "The Biblical Book of Lamentations in the Context of Near Eastern Lament Literature," pp. 205–211, responds directly and effectively to McDaniel.

Specifically, the *balag/eršemma* materials have, as characteristic features, both the heart pacification unit as well as the weeping goddess motif, neither of which appears to be present in the Hebrew texts. On the other hand, the Hebrew psalms accent the activity of the enemies and, specifically the taunts of the enemies, in ways not evidenced in the Sumero-Akkadian texts. Some of these differences can, however, readily be understood by means of the principles of adoptability and adaptability discussed in Chapter 2.

The Heart-Pacification Unit

Israel's laments do not include the "heart pacification" unit characteristic of many of the *eršemma*s. Not all of the *eršemma*s, of course, contain the heart pacification unit,[34] and one could argue that the absence of the heart pacification unit in the few extant communal laments of Israel is not, therefore, proof that these materials were unfamiliar with such a structural component. On the other hand, there may be another explanation for the absence of these units in the Hebrew writings: an appeal to God's heart and liver did not translate well into the conceptual idiom of Israel. In the course of creative adoption of the Mesopotamian traditions, the Hebrew poets adjusted such appeals to their own theological and anthropological understanding, focusing on God's face rather than God's heart and liver.

To begin with, when "heart" appears in the Hebrew scriptures it refers almost exclusively to the human heart (814 times) as compared to much less frequent references to "God's heart" (26 times) and the "heart of the sea" (11 times).[35] Moreover, as Hans Walter Wolff has shown, "the heart of God is most often mentioned as the organ of God's distinct will, against which man is judged."[36] Rather than being immediately associated with God's compassion, God's heart is conceptually linked to the deity's plans and decsions. Psalm 33:11, for example, finds the thoughts of God's heart (*maḥšĕbôṯ libbô*) set in poetic parallelism with God's counsel (*'aṣaṯ yhwh*). Wolff

---

[34] Cf. Chapter 3, "General Structure."

[35] Douglas R. Edwards, "Heart," *HBC*, p. 377. Cf. Heinz-Josef Fabry, "lēḇ," *TDOT*, VII, 399–437.

[36] Hans Walter Wolff, *Anthropology of the Old Testament*, trans. by Margaret Kohl (Philadelphia: Fortress Press, 1974), p. 55. Cf. Fabry, "lēḇ," pp. 434–435.

has demonstrated that even passages such as Hosea 11:8f., which appear to relate God's heart to God's compassion, have more to do with the overthrow of God's deliberate decision to act in judgment.[37] By contrast, in Akkadian anthropology *libbu* was evidently understood as the locus of the emotions that are subject to the will such as desire, love, mercy, and friendship,[38] and only rarely does a text mention the *libbu* of a deity with reference to the deity's desire, pleasure, plan, or decree.[39] Israelite poets, therefore, would find appeals to God's heart as a specific organ of compassion inappropriate. Likewise, the Hebrew scriptures omit any references to the "liver" of God; the only references to liver occur in passages describing the details of sacrificial rites[40] and, once, in connection with foreign heptascopic practices.[41]

Instead of references to the "heart" or "liver" of God, the psalmists petition God to turn or direct God's face toward them. In the communal laments under discussion, references to God's face appear in Psalms 44:24 and 80:3,7,19. Here, as elsewhere in the Hebrew scriptures, *pānîm* serves not only to express a broad range of emotions but also, in those passages where God is said to turn God's face, signals God's presence, God's attention, and usually God's positive response to the petitions of God's people.[42] Reference to the "face" of God turning in compassion toward God's people, therefore, would be an appropriate cultural translation of the sentiment expressed by the heart pacification unit and an example of the principle of adoptability. In short, the absence of a heart pacification section in the Hebrew psalms can be explained and does

---

[37] Wolff, *Anthropology*, p. 57. Obviously the compassionate and gracious character of Israel's God means that the decision of God's heart, that is, God's plans and intentions, are congruent with God's steadfast love. The point here being made is simply that the heart, as an anthropological term applied to God, refers primarily to acts of will or decisions rather than to feeling or sentiment, however much God's will may be bound to God's compassionate nature.

[38] Fabry, "lēb," p. 403. Fabry further reports that volatile, blind passions, were associated with the liver (*kabbattu*) rather than with the heart. Cf. C. Dohmen, "kābēd," *TDOT,* VII, p. 15, for a similar comment.

[39] *Ibid.,* p. 404.

[40] Exod 29:13,22; Lev 3:4,10,15; 4:9; 7:4; 8:16,25; 9:10,19.

[41] Ezek 21:26 [Eng. v 21]. P. Stenmans, "kābēd," *TDOT,* VII, 21, suggests that Israelite hostility to foreign heptascopic practices helps explain why the Old Testament rarely speaks of the liver.

[42] Joel F. Drinkard, Jr., "Face," *ABD,* Vol. 2, pp. 743–744.

not in any case serve as proof that Israel's poets were unfamiliar with the Mesopotamian lament tradition.

The Weeping Goddess Motif

The one motif ubiquitous among the *balag/eršemma* materials as well as in the antecedent Sumerian city-laments is that of the weeping goddess who bemoans the fate of her temple, city, and people. Gwaltney's claim that vestiges of this motif remain in the feminine personification of the city such as we find in Lamentations[43] has not convinced his critics, doubtless because another explanation of the origin of this motif has long been regarded as established dogma by scholars who query after the meaning of the image of cities personified as women. Crucial in the formation of this critical consensus are the views of Aloysius Fitzgerald, F.S.C., forwarded over twenty years ago in a pair of seminal articles.[44]

Fitzgerald attempts to locate the origin of the motif of the feminine personification of cities in the West Semitic religious sphere. Fitzgerald does not justify this embarkation point; it appears rather to be predicated on the assumption that, because the feminine personification of cities in Hebrew literature antedates the Exile and contact with the East was presumably limited, the motif must stem from West Semitic sources. In any event, no consideration is given to the possible East Semitic origins of the motif. Instead Fitzgerald, building on the observations of Julius Lewy,[45] argues that the Hebrew personification of cities as women stemmed from a specifically West Semitic idea that capital cities were understood to be goddesses who were married to the patron god of their respective cities. Fitzgerald draws his primary evidence for his thesis from Phoenician coins of the Hellenistic period which portray a woman wearing a walled or turreted crown, positing that this image, the *tychē poleōs*, or deified Fortune, represents the personified and deified city.[46] In addition, Fitzgerald proposes that the city was the

---

[43] Gwaltney, "Lamentations," p. 208.

[44] Aloysius Fitzgerald, "The Mythological Background for the Presentation of Jerusalem as a Queen and False Worship as Adultery in the Old Testament," *CBQ* 4 (1972), 403–416; "BTWLT and BT as Titles for Capital Cities," *CBQ* 37 (1975), 167–183.

[45] Julius Lewy, "The Old West Semitic Sun-god Ḥammu," *HUCA* 18 (1943–44), 436–443.

[46] Fitzgerald, "Jerusalem as Queen," 406–407.

deified wife of the local chief god, an assertion he believes is shown by the association of various titles with both goddesses and capital cities[47] and the evidence that city names were derived from divine names.[48]

Although a few scholars view the phenomenon of female personified cities as Israel's adaptation of language and concepts drawn from elsewhere in the ancient Near East,[49] the majority have simply adopted Fitzgerald's thesis as the starting point for their own investigations, assuming that the motif originated in a West Semitic conceptualization of a deified city.[50] Recently, however, Peggy L. Day has re-examined the evidence marshalled by Fitzgerald and has come to the conclusion that that scholar simply did not establish a convincing case for a West Semitic origin of the motif.[51] Day shows that, when scrutinized, Fitzgerald's thesis lacks substantiation and is founded upon a series of flawed assumptions. For example, where Fitzgerald supposes that coins whose inscriptions include references to cities as "mothers" also meant that the city was a goddess, Day points out that the coins nowhere refer to the same cities as

---

[47] *Ibid.*, 407–410. Fitzgerald believs that *rbt, btwlt/bt, ʾm and qdš* are titles used of both capital cities and goddesses.

[48] *Ibid.*, 410–412.

[49] Dobbs-Allsopp, *Weep, O Daughter of Zion,* pp. 75–90; Tikva Frymer-Kensky, *In the Wake of the Goddesses: Women, Culture, and the Biblical Transformation of Pagan Myth* (New York: Free Press, 1992), p. 170.

[50] Mark E. Biddle, "The Figure of Lady Jerusalem: Identification, Deification and Personification of Cities in the Ancient Near East," in *The Biblical Canon in Comparative Perspective: Scripture in Context IV,* ed. by K. Lawson Younger, William W. Hallo, and Bernard F. Batto, ANETS, Vol. 11 (Lewiston: Edwin Mellon, 1991), pp. 179–181; Daniel Bourguet, *Métaphores de Jérémie,* Études Bibliques, NS 9 (Paris: J. Gabalda, 1987), pp. 481–484; Mary Callaway, *Sing, O Barren One: A Study in Comparative Midrash,* SBLDS, No. 91 (Atlanta: Scholars, 1986), p. 65; Karen Engelken, *Frauen im Alten Israel: eine begriffsgeschichtliche und sozialrechtliche Studie zur Stellung der Frau im Alten Testament* (Stuttgart: W. Kohlhammer, 1990), p. 43; Julie Galambush, *Jerusalem in the Book of Ezekiel: The City as Yahweh's Wife,* SBLDS, No. 131 (Atlanta: Scholars Press, 1992), p. 20; J.J. Schmitt, "The Motherhood of God and Zion as Mother," *RB* 92 (1985), 568; O.H. Steck, "Zion als Gelände und Gestalt: Überlegungen zur Wahrnehmung Jerusalems als Stadt und Frau im Alten Testament," *ZThK* 86 (1989), 275.

[51] Peggy L. Day, "The Personification of Cities as Female in the Hebrew Bible: The Thesis of Aloysius Fitzgerald, F.S.C.," in *Social Location and Biblical Interpretation in Global Perspective,* Vol. 2 of *Reading from This Place: Social Location and Biblical Interpretation,* ed. by Fernando F. Segovia and Mary Ann Tolbert (Minneapolis: Fortress, 1995), pp. 283–302. I am grateful to Dr. Day for sharing her work with me in advance of publication.

both mother and goddess. Again, where Fitzgerald avers that "mother" was meant and understood literally by the Phoenicians and that these "mother" goddesses had intercourse with a divine sexual partner who was the sole male patron god of the city from whence the coin came, Day counters that the inscriptional evidence from Phoenicia supports neither the idea of a sole or dominant male patron god partnered with a female deity or that these two engaged in either marriage or intercourse. Fitzgerald's evidence drawn from divine titles and city names fares no better: Day demonstrates that a number of the "titles" he sees as applied to the goddess are not, in fact, titles and therefore do not serve to substantiate Fitzgerald's proposal.[52] Furthermore, Day uncovers the nebulous character of Fitzgerald's argument about the significance of pairing male and female divine names. Fitzgerald assumes, but cannot find evidence to prove, that this pairing points to (1) a marriage relationship between a god and goddess and (2) to the conclusion that the concept of the city as goddess came into being when cities were named after male deities (by adding a grammatically feminine *-t* ending). Thus a city such as Anat is, according to Fitzgerald, "a feminine formation from the name of the patron deity."[53] Day comments on this:

> It should be noted that Fitzgerald makes this proposal in spite of acknowledging that An was not an important deity in any West Semitic pantheon known to him. His response to this problem is to assert that pantheons differed according to era and area and so "if what has been suggested up to this point is correct, it just has to be assumed" that when the town of Anat was named, An was an important West Semitic deity. Once again the argument retreats into the impenetrable mists of prehistory.

Fitzgerald evidently intends his readers to believe that goddesses themselves "came into being" when cities, named after male deities by adding a grammatically feminine *-t* ending, were themselves deified. This reconstruction, Day observes, stems from Fitzgerald's evident acceptance of a modern type of mythology, which believes

---

[52] Day cites, as one example, Fitzgerald's (mis)use of the proper name *ʾm ʿštrt* ("Astarte is [my] mother") as an example of "mother" as a title applied to the goddess and *lṣr ʾm ṣdnm* ("belonging to Tyre, mother of Sidonians") as an example applying to a city.

[53] Fitzgerald, "Jerusalem as Queen," 411, n. 42.

in the priority of males and the derivativeness of females. "Much like the myth of Eve born from Adam, Fitzgerald's goddesses are born from their eventual spouses."

Day's systematic dismantling of Fitzgerald's thesis re-opens the question of the origin of the personification of cities as women. Although Day offers no positive proposal of her own, she has shown that at least the evidence adduced by Fitzgerald will not serve to prove a West Semitic origin for the feminine personification of cities in the Hebrew scriptures. But if the motif did not stem from West Semitic notions of a city goddess, where did the idea originate? Whence, for example, comes the feminine voice of personified Jerusalem in Lamentations? As no other West Semitic precursors beyond those offered by Fitzgerald have been proposed (or indeed seem likely), one is constrained to re-evaluate Gwaltney's suggestion: this motif was introduced into Israelite literature from the East Semitic world, where the continuous presence of a weeping goddess, both identified with and speaking laments on behalf of her city, can be documented for the entirety of the second and first millennia.[54] Vestiges of the weeping goddess persist in Israel's feminine personification of cities.

Evidence drawn from another quarter goes far to confirm this suggestion. In a recent article J.J.M. Roberts demonstrates that within Jeremiah's oracles one hears not only the lament of the personified city (Jer 10:19–21) but the lament of the weeping God as well.[55] Specifically, Jeremiah 8:18–9:3, 14:17–18, and 4:19–21— three passages which Roberts points out can be regarded as the *vox* Jeremiah only by exegetical contortion or by resorting to textual emendation—record the weeping anguish of God over the fate of God's people.[56] Moreover, the motif of the weeping God in Jere-

---

[54] Cf. Chapter 3, n. 96.

[55] J.J.M. Roberts, "The Motif of the Weeping God in Jeremiah and Its Background in the Lament Tradition of the Ancient Near East," *Old Testament Essays* 5 (1992), 361–374.

[56] Mark S. Smith, "Jeremiah IX 9—A Divine Lament," *VT* 37 (1987), 97–99, has made a similar argument for Jeremiah 9:9, although Smith seeks to support his case by reference to CTA 5 (KTU 1.5). VI. 25 - CAT 6 (KTU 1.6). I.7. There Anat seeks Baal and discovers him on the "steppe"(*dbr*), which Smith associates with *midbār* in Jer 9:9. Similarly he views the search of the goddess to "every mountain" (*kl ǵr*) and "every hill" (*kl gbᶜ*) as corresponding to "mountains" Jer 9:9. These geographical references need not, however, have been drawn from Ugaritic sources. The weeping goddess also searches the mountains and steppe in search of Damu, e.g, *balag* 49:c+68–69, d+122–123.

miah's oracles, as in the *balag/eršemma* materials and the Sumerian city-laments before them, is coupled with the idea that the deity has no choice but to abandon his house and city in spite of God's love for God's people (cf. Jer 12:7–13). Yet another connection with the Mesopotamian lamentation traditions emerges in the observation that the lament over the capture and death of Dumuzi, one of seven mythological themes recurring in the *eršemmas*, was known and practiced in Jerusalem in Jeremiah's time (cf. Ezek 8:14). Roberts comments: "The presence of similar motifs and the indication that Israel was familiar with the Tammuz mythology suggests that the Mesopotamian lament tradition exercised some influence on the practice of public laments in Israel." To that comment can be added the observation that the startling character of the weeping God image applied to Yahweh makes it difficult to dismiss this motif as yet another similarity between these materials which can be explained on the basis of a general similarity of subject matter.

If, however, one assumes that the weeping Yahweh in Jeremiah is a reflection of Israel's adaptation of the Mesopotamian weeping goddess motif, one is further constrained to query as to how such a transformation might have been possible. Is it likely, after all, that aspects of a weeping goddess tradition could be absorbed in Israel's conception of Yahweh? This question seemingly was anticipated by Patrick D. Miller in his essay "The Absence of the Goddess in Israelite Religion."[57] Building on a proposal by Paul Riemann, Miller employs biblical and inscriptional evidence to successfully show that centralization of divine reality and power in Yahweh included an absorption of the feminine dimension of deity. Because the characteristics of goddesses in the ancient Near East are shared (except for child-bearing) by male deities, the feminine dimension of deity consequently disappeared as a separately identifiable dimension. In the case of Israel's Yahwism, Miller states, "The feminine dimension of deity is absorbed or absent from the beginning."[58] Nevertheless, Miller discovers evidence that the feminine dimension of the deity does not disappear altogether in (1) a large number of female figurines discovered in Israel and the evident figurative association of these with known goddesses of Syria-Palestine, (2) the inscriptional references to *yhwh šmrn wlʾšrth* from Kuntillet Ajrud and *yhwh* . . .

---

[57] Patrick D. Miller, "The Absence of the Goddess in Israelite Religion," *HAR* 10 (1986), 239–248.

[58] *Ibid.*, 245.

lᵊšrty from Khirbet el Qôm, (3) the late biblical hypostatization of ḥokmāh/wisdom and šĕkînāh/presence, and (4) in those occasional feminine characteristics and images applied to Yahweh in the Hebrew scriptures (e.g., Ps 90:2; Deut 32:18; Isa 49:15; Num 11:12; Isa 66:13).[59]

It appears that the absorption of the weeping goddess into Jeremiah's weeping Yahweh can be added to the list of those feminine dimensions of the deity that did not disappear altogether into Israel's deity, Yahweh. Moreover the motif of the weeping goddess, when adapted to Yahwism, seems likely to have been adapted in a second way, namely, and as Gwaltney proposed, as the feminine personification of cities. Indeed, Gwaltney's proposal has recently found confirmation in a study by F.W. Dobbs-Allsopp.[60] Dobbs-Allsopp convincingly demonstrates that Hebrew *bat* followed by a geographical name (GN) is best understood as a divine epithet with the GN analyzed grammatically as a genitive of location. This conclusion is based in part on the close resemblance of the Hebrew phrase with the Akkadian divine title *mārat* GN as well as the occurence of *bat* GN as a designation of the personified city in what he terms "modulated" city lament passages in the Hebrew Bible. In the Hebrew literature, however, *bat* GN ceases to function as a divine epithet. Instead the biblical writers, by employing divine titles and features characteristic of city goddesses in the Mesopotamian laments, create the literary metaphor of the personified city. Thus, not a few Hebrew texts demonstrate a familiarity with this aspect of the Mesopotamian lament tradition, including the Book of Lamentations as well as in a number of prophetic oracles,[61] many of the latter including, significantly, pronouncements made prior to the invasion of Babylon in 587 BCE. The presence of this

---

[59] *Ibid.*, 245–246. Mary Wakeman, "Sacred Marriage," *JSOT* 22 (1982), 21–31, reconstructs a similar phenomenon in Sumer where, she claims, the goddess Innana was the original patron of the city and was accompanied by a male consort. Innana was gradually transformed into a consort-goddess, a process that was completed with the Assyrian takeover; at that point the mortal king began to participate in the divine marriage ceremony as the representative of the god, thus sacralizing the hegemony of the male god and his representative over the goddess.

[60] F.W. Dobbs-Allsopp, "The Syntagma of *bat* Followed by a Geographical Name in the Hebrew Bible: A Reconsideration of Its Meaning and Grammar," *CBQ* 57/3 (1995), 451–471.

[61] E.g., Amos 5:1–2; Isa 1:21; Jer 18:13.

feature in other texts reduces the significance of the absence of an explicit reference to the motif in the few Hebrew communal laments available. Again, vestiges of the East Semitic weeping goddess tradition, applied by Jeremiah to Yahweh, serve as sufficient proof that the Mesopotamian tradition did influence this aspect of Israel's laments. Given the relatively few communal laments available for study, the absence of the motif may indicate no more than the vagaries involved in the process of the preservation and subsequent canonization of the psalms. More likely, the weeping goddess motif, which clearly needed to be and was adapted in various ways in order to correspond to Israel's exclusive worship of Yahweh, may simply not have seemed as crucial to the Hebrew poets as they adapted the Mesopotamian lamentations into their own conceptual and religious idioms.

The Taunting Enemies

One aspect of the Hebrew laments that does not find a corresponding reflex in the Sumero-Akkadian compositions is the prominent complaint about the humiliation Israel suffers as a consquence to the taunts and jeers of the foreign foes. One reads, for example,

> You have made us the taunt of our neighbors, the derision and
> scorn of those around us.
> You have made us a byword among the nations, a laughingstock
> among the peoples. (Ps 44:14–15)

> Remember this, O Lord, how the enemy scoffs, and an impious
> people reviles your name (Ps 74:18)[62]

Because the taunts of the enemies are so pronounced a characteristic of the Hebrew compositions, the motif may potentially manifest a telling distinction between the Sumero-Akkadian laments which, in turn, could be construed as evidence that the two traditions enjoyed only a generic relationship. Once again, however, a feature of the Hebrew lamentations may be more indicative of the Hebrew poets' own peculiar contribution to the adaptation of the older laments. Two factors must be borne in mind. First, and

---

[62] Cf. Pss 74:8a; 79:10; 80:7; 89:43,51; cf. 83:3.

as already noted, like the *balag/eršemma*s, nothing in the Hebrew communal laments points toward an identifiable historical situation for these psalms. Indeed, Psalm 83, the one psalm in the collection which lists historical nemeses and articulates their joint schemes, seems not to stem from any such actual historical alliance. The taunts of the enemies are stereotypical expressions of those who would destroy the nation, humiliating God and God's people. Second, and again like the Mesopotamian laments, the attack by foreign foes is perceived by the Hebrew poets as an aspect of a disaster with cosmic proportions. The success of the enemies signals the triumph of chaos with which the alien invaders are aligned. Both the destructive activities of the foes and their taunts are in several instances explicitly coordinated with the manifestations of the primordial chaotic forces such as the raging sea monster, fire, and earthquake.

The latter point provides an indication of why the foes' taunts play such a prominent role in these psalms. As a cosmogonic divine warrior, God engages in mortal combat with the chaos dragon as a means of establishing divine control of the world.[63] But the forces of chaos are not exhausted by their ancient defeat. In Israel's human foes the ancient dragon finds allies. Note, for example, Psalm 89:11:

> *ʾattāh dikkiʾtā kehālāl rāhab*
> *bizrôaʿ ʿuzzĕkā pizzartā ʾôyĕbêkā*
>
> You crushed Rahab like a carcass;
> you scattered your enemies with your mighty arm.

Here "enemies" should likely be interpreted as chaotic forces aligned with Rahab. Tellingly, however, these ancient allies of chaos reappear in verse 43, now identified as those who oppose and prevail over the monarch. One should therefore understand references to the foreign enemies and their destructive activities as a reemergence of the threat posed in the mythological past by the chaos dragon. Just as Rahab, supported by other foes of God once threatened the stability and divine rule of the world, so the foreign invaders challenge the authority of God anew.

The link between the activities of the chaos monster and the enemies is borne out in another respect: the primary attribute char-

---

[63] Pss 89:10–11; 74:13–15.

acteristic of the chaos dragon is its arrogance.[64] It claims dominion over the streams, over the seas, and over dry land; in short over
the whole of creation.[65] Against the chaos dragon's boast of creative
potency[66] Israel's poets set the counter claim that the dragon was a
creature of God's creation.[67] Nevertheless, the dragon's arrogance
continues to find human expression in the activities of Israel's enemies who are identified with the chaos monster both in their claim
for earthly dominion and their antagonism to God.[68] If the dragon
is arrogant, the human foes likewise both scoff at God and revile
God's name.[69] They "raise their heads," a sign of haughtiness.[70] Their
noisy clamor reaches the heavens.[71] Like the ancient chaos monster,
the challenge posed by Israel's stereotypically portrayed enemies
threatens the sovereignty of God. Both the dragon and its allies fail
to recognize their status as creatures and discount the power and
authority of God over their activities.[72] Thus, in the voice of their
enemies Israel heard the roar of the ancient foe of God who, though
conquered "from of old,"[73] now renews its challenge through its
human agents. In ways that are more direct and immediate than
their Mesopotamian predecessor compositions, the communal laments of Israel link the activities of human foes to the forces of
chaos. This in turn helps explain the prominence of the enemies'

---

[64] Hermann Gunkel, "The Influence of Babylonian Mythology," 38.

[65] Cf. Job 41:26 [34]; Ps 89:10 (the waves rise in revolt against God); Ezek 29:3; Pss Sol 2:(25–)29. The last example demonstrates the tenacity of the theme. The first century BCE document, which evidently concerns itself with the invasion of Jerusalem by Pompey, identifies that Roman as an arrogant dragon (v 25) who boasts of himself, "I shall be lord of land and sea." Cf. R.B. Wright, "Psalms of Solomon," in *The Old Testament Pseudepigrapha: Expansions of the "Old Testament" and Legends, Wisdom and Philosophical Literature, Prayers, Psalms, and Odes, Fragments of Lost Judeo-Hellenistic Works*, ed. by James H. Charlesworth (Garden City: Doubleday, 1985), pp. 640–641, 653 and nn. a2–c2.

[66] Ezek 29:3, "I made it [the Nile] for myself"; cf. 32:2.

[67] Job 40:15–19; Ps 104:26.

[68] E.g., Ps 74:18,23.

[69] Ps 74:18 (*ḥērēp, niʾăṣû*); cf. Pss Sol 2:32–33.

[70] Ps 83:3. The noun is singular, i.e., *nāśěʾû rōʾš* and indicates a collective. On the association of pride with "raising the head" and, conversely, of the inability to raise one's head in humility and defeat, see Judg 8:28; Ps 24:7,9; Job 10:15; Zech 2:4. Cf. Tate, *Psalms 51–100*, p. 343, n. 3c.

[71] Ps 74:23.

[72] Ps 79:10.

[73] Ps 74:12; cf. Isa 51:9.

taunts and boasts in these psalms: their very boasts represent the threat of chaos renewed and the victory of chaos. Israel's poets, whose interest in the traditional destructive agents of the Sumero-Akkadian laments focused more on human foreign invaders, expressed the gravity of the threat of chaos through an emphasis on the enemies' taunts. Once again, therefore, the distinction between the Hebrew communal laments and those of Mesopotamia is a difference of Israel's own peculiar interest and accents rather than a distinction of kind.

ADDITIONAL CORROBORATING EVIDENCE

In addition to the parallel themes and motifs already mentioned, there exist three additional pieces of corroborating evidence that lead toward the determination of the literary influence of the older *balag/eršemma* texts upon the Hebrew psalms. The first is an observation concerning the possible correspondence between the colophons of the *balag/eršemma*s and a feature of the biblical psalms. The second involves additional internal indications from the psalms themselves. The third piece of corroborating evidence is provided by a pre-exilic prophecy of Jeremiah.

Colophons

First the observation about the colophons: *eršemma*s and *balag*s are characteristically concluded with a genitive construction, "an *eršemma* of DN," and "It is a *balag* of DN." These appended designations presumably signify that the respective texts were used in the cult of the named deity.[74] The assumption that the Hebrew Psalter lacked any corresponding phenomena has been vigorously challenged in a recent article by Bruce Waltke.[75] Through an investigation of various biblical materials and Qumran texts, Waltke argues that in a received superscripted "title" to a psalm the expression *lamnaṣṣēaḥ* plus the optional prepositional phrase was originally a postscript of the preceding psalm and the rest of its material introduced the genuine superscript of the following psalm. Moreover, Waltke claims, the original postscript probably includes technical terms for the psalm's performance while the genuine superscription contains matters about the psalm's composition.

---

[74] Cohen, *SH,* p. 20.
[75] Bruce K. Waltke, "Superscripts, Postscripts, or Both," *JBL* 110/4 (1991), 583–596.

Bringing this observation to bear first on Psalm 79, one discovers that the heading of the succeeding Psalm 80 does begin with precisely the formula Waltke identifies, *lamnaṣṣēaḥ* plus the prepositional phrase *ʿal šōšannîm ʿēdût*.[76] This enigmatic expression occurs in three other psalm superscriptions, those of Psalm 45 (a prayer for a royal wedding), Psalm 60 (a communal lament), and Psalm 69 (a lament). With the inclusion of Psalm 80, three of the four supposed superscriptions have to do with laments, while the fourth, Psalm 45, is unaccountably associated with the presumably joyful occasion of a royal wedding. The situation is altered somewhat, though not yet definitively, if the superscripts are understood to be post-scripts to the preceding psalms: Psalms 44 and 79 are communal laments, Psalm 59 appears to be an individual's lament, while Psalm 68 eludes form critical classification. Although not strictly a lament, Psalm 68 *may* still be understood to have been linked to the lament tradition in a way analogous to those *eršemma*s in which praise of the deity's power and conquest predominate. The *eršemma* to Enlil known by the incipit *enzu samarmar*.[77] provides an example. Even if that possibility is not conceded, however, the elusive form and character of Psalm 68 and the more certain lament classification of the other psalms just mentioned suggest the possibility that the expression *lamnaṣṣēaḥ ʿal šōšannîm ʿēdût* signals some connection with lament.

Equally intriguing is the superscription of Psalm 75. The heading appearing on this psalm of national thanksgiving, *lamnaṣṣēaḥ ʾal-tašḥēt* ("do not destroy"), elsewhere heads only Psalms 57, 58, and 59, all psalms of lament. However, if the expression is read as a subscript to the preceding psalms a more uniform result is obtained: Psalms 56, 57, 58, and 74 are all laments and all appended with the rubric "do not destroy."

The point of these observations is not to suggest the meaning of these two putative superscriptional phrases but, rather, to illustrate the presence of a scribal tradition corresponding to that evidenced in the *balag* and *eršemma* subscripts. Waltke's study at least raises the possibility that Israel's scribes, like their neighbors, identified and classified laments by their form, content, or cultic use by means of

---

[76] That MT *ʾel* should read *ʿal* is attested by the appearance of the identical expression in the "superscriptions" of Pss 60 and 69; cf. Ps 45.

[77] Cf. *SH, eršemma* 163.1, pp. 121–124.

an appended colophon. This observation swells in significance when one recalls that the *balag* evidently derived its name from the fact it was chanted to the accompaniment of a musical instrument called the *balag*[78] and, similarly, the *eršemma* appears to mean "the wail of the *šem* drum."[79] If, as it has been proposed, *šôšannîm* turns out to be related to Akkadian *šuššu* and mean "six-sided" or "six stringed,"[80] we may have a reference to some particular sort of musical instrument in a subscript just as in the *balag*s and *eršemma*s.[81]

Indicators from Psalms 74 and 79

Of the seven psalms under consideration, Psalms 74 and 79 are especially worthy of closer scrutiny since, it is believed, the dates of these psalms are relatively secure: based largely on their content and, specifically, on references to an alien invasion of the Temple, they are almost universally considered to have been composed subsequent to the destruction of Jerusalem in 587 BCE. If, however, indicators within these two psalms can be discerned which point to either a Mesopotamian literary milieu or a compositional date prior to the Babylonian invasion, there would be grounds to challenge the scholarly consensus not only with respect to the compositional date of these psalms but their cultic function as well.

To begin with, it should be noted that the dispute in the secondary literature revolves not around *whether* these two psalms reflect the destruction of the city and Temple but rather *how far removed* the composition might be from the actual historical circumstances that inspired it. Critical debate about the setting of both of these psalms has oscillated between those who relate the references to the destruction of the Temple with the events of 587 BCE and

---

[78] H. Hartmann, "Die Musik der sumerischen Kultur," (Inaugural dissertation; Universität Frankfurt am Main, 1960), pp. 52–67, 210–211.

[79] *Ibid.*, pp. 216–219.

[80] Cf. Glaser, *Zeitschrift für Semitistik* 8 (1932), 195 and Kraus, *Psalms 1–59*, p. 30. The meaning of this word is, however, much debated. Cf. Koehler/Baumgartner, *Lexicon in Veteris Testamenti Libros*, p. 1350, and the bibliography cited there.

[81] Another possibility, suggested to me by Professor C.L. Seow, is that the root in question here is the geminate *šnn*, of which *šĕnînāh* (sharp [cutting] word, taunt) is attested in Deut 28:37, 1 Kgs 9:7 (= 2 Chron 7:20); Jer 24:9. The initial reduplicated *š* would correspond to similar phenomena in geminates such as Hebrew *kbb* > *kôkābîm*, or Akkadian *qdd* > *qaqqadum*.

those who associate both the destruction and the psalms' composition with events of the Maccabean period.[82] The argument has persisted in large measure because of what is *not* contained in the psalms, namely, calibrating historical references such as mention of the exile or the dedication of the Temple to an alien deity.

Coloring the conversation on both sides of the debate is the supposition that references to the Temple's destruction pertain to *some* historical destruction of Jerusalem, the *terminus ante quem* of which is 587 BCE. If, however, the literary precursors of these psalms were the *balag/eršemma* materials one would not necessarily anticipate an allusion to a particular historical destruction of Jerusalem. At least three internal features of Psalm 74 indicate that the search for reference to a specific destruction is misdirected and that, in fact, the psalms are related to their *balag/eršemma* precursors. In addition the explicit citation of Psalm 79 in Jeremiah suggests that that psalm is not dependent upon the destruction of the Temple for its inspiration.

First, there are linguistic hints within Psalm 74 that seem curiously archaic for an exilic or post-exilic composition. Specifically, one notes the appearance of the relative pronoun *zeh* in verse 2 and the first attestation of *ḥayyat* in verse 19, to be read as *ḥayyāt*, representing a feminine absolute noun ending in -*āt*.[83] The appearance of these features are difficult to explain in a post-587 BCE composition, even were one to suppose that they represent an intentional effort to archaize the text. The presence of these antique grammatical features, therefore, suggests a compositional period before the destruction of Jerusalem under the Babylonians and places the notion that 587 BCE represents a *terminus ante quem* for these psalms under no small amount of suspicion.

Second, a specific link to the Mesopotamian milieu is forged by the *hapax legomenon kêlappōṯ* (v 6). This word has been shown by Harold Cohen[84], to be a loan word from Akkadian *kalappu/kalabbu*,

---

[82] Cf. Kraus, *Psalms 60–150*, pp. 96f., 133f. and the bibliography cited there. For an extreme position on the Maccabean dating not only for these psalms but the entire Psalter see the recent publication by Marco Treves Marco, *The Dates of the Psalms: History and Poetry in Ancient Israel* (Pisa: Giardini, 1988), who finds virtually no psalms outside of the Maccabean era.

[83] Kraus, *Psalms 60–150*, p. 71. So too Dahood, *Psalms II: 51–100*, p. 207.

[84] Harold R. (Chaim) Cohen, *Biblical Hapax Legomena in the Light of Akkadian and Ugaritic*, SBLDS, No. 37 (Missoula: Scholars Press, 1978), pp. 49–50.

axe. In Assur-nasir-pal's annals the word appears several times in parallel to *akullu* (hatchet), and describes the tools of that monarch's conquests.[85] Cohen sees the pair "hatchets and axes" in verse 6 as a corresponding parallel to the Akkadian *kalappu//akullu*.[86] The present author is admittedly unaware of any corresponding pairing of "ax" and "hatchet" in *balag* or *eršemma* texts. It is, however, interesting to note the statement from *eršemma* 35.2:28, "My city cried out (like the whir) of an ax,"[87] and, from the *Lament over the Destruction of Sumer and Ur*, "In Ur, the large axes *wreak havoc* before them."[88] Although the match is inexact, the association of 74:6 with the description of the activities and tools of a conqueror serves to illuminate a possible Mesopotamian connection with this psalm.

Third, there is the statement recorded in Psalm 74:8b: *śārĕpû ḳol mô'ădê 'ēl bā'āreṣ*, "they burned all the meeting places of God in the land."[89] The reference to the "meeting places" (plural!) presents an interpretive problem if one assumes the psalm was composed subsequent to 587 and therefore after the Josianic reforms of the late seventh century. "Meeting places" cannot refer to non-Yahwistic sanctuaries throughout the world; it does not at all fit the context of this passage. The proposal that the plural of *mô'ēd* refers to the Temple precincts, ignores the collocation of the phrase with *kol* and *bā'āreṣ* as A. Gelston, in his thorough review of the problem, notes.[90] However, Gelston's own proposal, that the text refers to non-sacrificial sites of Yahwistic worship established in the wake

---

[85] W. King, ed., *Annals of the Kings of Assyria* (London: British Museum, 1902), p. 322:76–77: "Lara, the treacherous mountain which was not suitable for the passage of chariots and troops, I cut up with iron axes (*kalabbate*) and broke up with bronze hatchets (*akkul[li]*), and then had the chariots and troops pass through." Cf. *AKA* 230:11–13 and 330–31:95–96.

[86] Cohen, *Biblical Hapax Legomena*, p. 50, comments, "The pair כשיל וכילפות 'hatchets and axes' is matched perfectly by the corresponding parallel in the above Akkadian passage [AKA 332:76–77] *kalabbāte//akulli* 'axes//hatchets.' In light of these equivalences, the meaning of Hebrew כילפות should be considered as established."

[87] See a similar statement in *balag* 2:28.

[88] *ANET*[3], p. 618. However, Michalowski, *The Lamentation*, p. 61, reads the line "Large axes were sharpened in front of Ur." That is, Michalowski believes that the meaning of u[3/4]-sar . . . ak is "to sharpen." Cf. Cooper, *Agade*, 245–246.

[89] For the meaning of *mô'ēd* in a local sense of "meeting place" cf. Lam 2:6a where *mô'ădô* is paralleled with *śukkô* in a context suggesting the identification of both terms with the Temple. Cf. A. Gelston, "A Note on Psalm 74:8," *VT* 34 (1984), 83.

[90] Gelston, "A Note on Psalm 74:8," 82–87.

of the Josianic reform, is equally problematic. Gelston attempts to substantiate his claim by reference to 1 Maccabees 3:46, a passage which refers to there having been formerly a "place of prayer" (*topos proseuchēs*) at Mizpah. From this slender thread hangs a rather weighty supposition: Gelston first associates this "former" time with the period of the fall of Jerusalem (based on its possible identification as the site of Gedaliah's administration) and suggests that this "place of prayer" served as a prototype to the synagogue, i.e., a building where non-sacrificial aspects of the cult could be practiced. "If so," he extrapolates, "there may well have been other similar 'meeting places of God in the land' at the time of the fall of Jerusalem, though the psalmist's lament that they had 'all' been burnt should probably be regarded as hyperbole."[91] These meeting places, he believes, were likely the former "high places," adapted for non-sacrificial Yahwistic worship after Josiah's reforms.

One major problem with this interpretation is that it depends on an uncertain reference to Mizpah as Israel's "former" place of prayer in 1 Maccabees 3:46. There is, however, no reason to assume that the author of Maccabees intended "former" to indicate the early sixth century. In fact the reference more easily points to another period in Israel's history during which, as with the Maccabeans, Israel suffered under foreign oppression. 1 Samuel 7:5–11 reports that Israel drew together at Mizpah in response to the Philistine threat. In both instances mention is made of a gathering for the purposes of prayer, fasting, and repentance (cf. 1 Macc 3:47 and 1 Sam 7:6). It seems to be more likely that the author of 1 Maccabees mentions Mizpah as a 'former place of prayer' precisely because he intends thereby to evoke the memory of Israel's successful rout of the Philistines which was inaugurated from that place. If this reading of the reference in 1 Maccabees 3:46 is correct, Gelston's suggestion loses its force altogether as the linkage he attempts to establish between the phrase *śārĕpû ḳol môʿădê ʾel bāʾāreṣ* and the destruction of proposed non-sacrificial sites of Yahwistic worship established in the wake of the Josianic reform dissolves.

The problems posed by Psalm 74:8b beggar a solution if one insists on attempting to reconcile the psalm to the historical circumstances surrounding the time of the Babylonian destruction of Jerusalem or thereafter. In the wake of Josiah's reform, reference to

---

[91] *Ibid.*, 86.

the multiple "meeting places of God in all the land" makes little sense. On the other hand, if one were to attribute the psalm to the Maccabean era, assuming multiple meeting places of God for that period, the difficulties posed by both the archaic grammatical features and the *hapax legomenon kêlappōt* resurface. Indeed, if a historical nexus is to be sought, the three factors in combination more naturally point toward some period prior to Josiah's reform.

It may not, however, be necessary to isolate a specific historical occasion for the phrase. As the psalmist who composed Psalm 83 seemed not to have any actual historical alliance of enemies in mind when the list of conspiratorial nations was named, so too the author of Psalm 74 may be drawing upon not a historical but a compositional tradition. In this regard it is instructive to note that within the *balag/eršemma* materials, the "destruction" of "all" the meeting places of deity in the land constitutes the major complaint of the deity as he or she recites, often in dull detail, the names of all temples and cities which have been "destroyed." One reads, for example:

> On account of the destruction of the Kiur, the great place,
> . . . of the great mother Ninlil cries out all day long.
> On account of the destruction of the palace of Kesh, the Ekisiga,
> the . . . of the great mother Ninlil cries out all day long.
> On account of the destruction of the Emah of Adab,
> . . . cries out all day long.
> On account of the destruction of the brickwork of Adab. . .,
> the great god, the mother of Adab . . . cries out all day long.
> On account of the destruction of the Ekisiga,
> the faithful princess, Sud, princely child of the Apsu, cries out all day
>   long.
> On account of the destruction of the brickwork of Isin,
> the lady, the land registrar of heaven cries out all day long.
> On account of the destruction of the brickwork of Uruk,
> the hierodule, Inanna, cries out all day long.
> On account of the destruction of the shrine of Eanna,
> 'she who causes the heavens to rumble,' Inanna, cries out all day long.
> On account of the destruction of the . . . of Kulaba,
> the great . . ., mother . . . cries out all day long.
> On account of the destruction of holy Akkil,
> the faithful . . ., . . ., cries out all day long.
> On account of the destruction of the Esiguzda,
> the lady of the place Zabalam cries out all day long.

On account of the destruction of Akshak, the Urshaba,
the faithful princess, the lady . . ., cries out all day long.
On account of the destruction of her city, Girsu,
Baba, the wife of the lord, cries out all day long.
On account of the destruction of . . . Ur,
. . ., the woman of Ur, cries out all day long.
On account of the destruction of the house of Uruku,
the princess, the one in charge of the shrine of Baba, cries out all day
  long.
On account of the destruction of the . . . of the Etarsirsir,
Lama, the lady of the Etarsirsir, cries out all day long.
On account of the destruction of the back steppe of Lagash,
the old lady, Gatumdug, cries out all day long.
On account of the destruction of the Egalgasu,
Nab, the foremost child of heaven, cries out all day long.
On account of the destruction of the Maguenna,
the lofty princess of the Guenna cries out all day long.
On account of the destruction of the residence of Nina,
my lady, the great lady, the lady of Nina, cries out all day long.
On account of the destruction of the brickwork of Sirara,
the princess, Nanshe, over the brickwork of Sirara, cries out all day
  long.
On account of the destruction of the . . . of the Esukuda,
the brickwork . . . cries out all day long.
On account of the destruction of the chamber, the bedroom of the
  Urshaba, (or the chamber of Kinirsha),
the lament of the small city cries out all day long.
On account of the destruction of the shrine of Guabba,
Ninmar, over the shrine of Guabba, cries out all day long.
On account of the destruction of the Dumusagubba,
my mother, Nanâ, cries out all day long.
On account of the destruction of the brickwork of Sippar,
Aya, the beautiful woman, cries out all day long.
On account of the destruction of the Tintir, (the city) of might,
the lofty princess, the holy one, the lady of Tintir, cries out all day
  long.
On account of the destruction of the brickwork of Borsippa,
the lady of the Edimanki cries out all day long.
She cries out all day long.
All of them perform the gestures of mourning. She cries out all day
  long.[92]

---

[92] *balag* 43:a+58–115. Cf. g+345–356; *balag*s 7:13–22; 10:c+360–383; 25:e+79–97;
26:120–167; 27:a+80–101; 29:b+14–39; 33:a+14–25, *et passim.*

Once again, the enumeration of these various locales and the lament over their destruction apparently had nothing to do with a historical event. Likewise, the search for a historical context for the reference to "all the meeting places of God in the land" may well be misdirected if the expression is an Israelite reflex of this aspect of the *balag/eršemma* materials.

Finally, the independence of these psalms, and especially Psalm 79, from the Babylonian invasion of Judah may be indicated by the quotation of Psalm 79:6–7 in Jeremiah 10:25. The two passages are almost, but not quite, identical. The differences, however, prove minor. Jeremiah 10:25 reads *mišpāḥôt* ("tribes") for the corresponding *mamlākôt* ("kingdoms") in Psalm 79:6. A few Hebrew manuscripts, along with the LXX (*basileias*) and the Targum, substitute *mamlākôt* in Jeremiah. John Bright, perhaps unable to discern a preferable reading, translates the term with the more ambiguous "realms."[93] William L. Holladay, on the other hand, claims that *mišpāḥôt* is "doubtless more original" though he does not explain the rationale for this preference.[94] In the absence of further evidence one should perhaps assume (with Holladay?) that *difficilior lectio potior*. A second difference is the inclusion of *waʾaḵālūhû wayḵallūhû* in Jeremiah, a feature which Holladay, doubtless correctly, believes is a conflate text.[95]

The complex redactional and textual history of Jeremiah makes tenuous the assignation of a date to a good deal of the book, Jeremiah 10:25 not excepted.[96] Nevertheless, while many scholars regard Jeremiah 10:17–25 as a miscellaneous collection of sayings and verse 25 as a later addition,[97] William Holladay argues for the coherence of the passage and the originality of verse 25.[98] Holladay notes that not

---

[93] John Bright, *Jeremiah*, AB, Vol. 21 (Garden City: Doubleday, 1965), p. 71.

[94] William L. Holladay, *Jeremiah 1: A Commentary on the Book of the Prophet Jeremiah, Chapters 1–25*, (Philadelphia: Fortress, 1986), p. 338, n. 25a.

[95] *Ibid.*, p. 339, n. b. Note, however that Mitchell Dahood, "The Word-pair *ʾākal//kālāh* in Jeremiah xxx 16," *VT* 27 (1977), 482, n. 2., treats the word pair as part of an original tricolon.

[96] Cf. Robert P. Carroll, *Jeremiah* (Philadelphia: Westminster, 1986), pp. 38–55, for a convenient summary of the history of Jeremiah research since Duhm as well as a description of the textual difficulties posed by the Greek version.

[97] E.g., Bright, *Jeremiah*, p. 73f., who views Jeremiah 10:17–25 as a continuation of the thought of chapters 8 and 9; Carroll, *Jeremiah*, pp. 259–265, who regards 10:17–18, 19–21, 22, and 23–25 as independent units. Both scholars agree that verse 25 is an exilic addition.

[98] Holladay, *Jeremiah 1*, p. 339.

only verse 25, but also verses 23 and 24 cohere in that all three verses either cite or expand upon scripture.[99] All three verses, he believes, represent the response of the people to Jeremiah's speech in verse 21 and Yahweh's speech in verse 22. These three voices are likewise represented in the previous verses: the prophet speaks in verse 17, Yahweh in 18, and the people in 19–20. The unity of the passage, according to Holladay, consists of a pair of cycles wherein Jeremiah, Yahweh, and the people each speak in turn. Verses 23–25 represent traditional cultic expressions, here parroted by Jeremiah, which are misapplied by the people to justify their own irresponsibility. Based on its affinities with the "basic stratum" of material added by Jeremiah in the second scroll, and particularly on the catchword *'sp* ("gather") which occurs in 8:13, 9:21, and 10:17, Holladay believes the passage to be authentically that of Jeremiah.[100] Moreover, since in this passage the city is envisaged to be under siege (v 17), although the invading army is not yet quite in view (v 22), he maintains that the oracle should be dated after 8:4–13 (*circa* 601 BCE) and before 11:1f. (*circa* 594 B.C.E), that is, to a setting just before the siege of Jerusalem in December, 598 BCE.[101]

Holladay's view of the unity of Jeremiah 10:17–25 is unnecessarily complex and, in any event, ignores the feminine voice of the personified city who speaks at least in verses 19–21[102] if not all the way through to verse 25. The feminine singular imperative of verse 17 is followed by a divine announcement concerning the inhabitants of the land in verse 18. Then the city takes up the lament in verses 19–21:

> Woe is me because of my hurt! My wound is severe.
> But I said, "Truly this is my punishment, and I must bear it."
> My tent is destroyed, and all my cords are broken;
> my children have gone from me, and they are no more;
> there is no one to spread my tent again, and to set up my curtains
> for the shepherds are stupid, and do not inquire of the Lord;
> therefore they have not prospered, and all their flock is scattered.

---

[99] *Ibid.* Cf. pp. 343–344. Holladay sees verse 23 as adapted from Proverbs 16:9 and 20:24 while verse 24 expands Psalm 6:2 and verse 25 quotes Psalm 79:6–7.

[100] *Ibid.*, p. 340.

[101] *Ibid.* Cf. William L. Holladay, *Jeremiah: A Fresh Reading* (New York: Pilgrim, 1990), pp. 101–102.

[102] Roberts, "The Motif of the Weeping God in Jeremiah," 362.

It remains difficult to identify the speaker in verse 22, although the passive description of the approaching tumult contrasts sharply with the speech of Yahweh in verse 18. The speaker may therefore be the city or Jeremiah, but a continued speech by the city seems more likely given the location of this verse between two first-person singular declarations (vv 19–20, 23–24). In any event, there is no need to assume with Holladay that the speaker of verses 23–25 is the collective voice of the people, given in the first-person, and as quoted by the prophet. To the contrary, the presence of the first singular in verses 23 and 24 suggests that the speaker is none other than the feminine personified city who has already spoken in verses 19–21. In other words, the lament which begins in verse 19 continues through verse 25; verses 23–25 (and likely verse 22 as well) represent a continuation of the feminine city's response to the impending invasion.[103] What Holladay views as an abuse of traditional words by the people takes on an altogether different tone when these words are understood to be uttered by the lamenting city whose fate, and that of her children, looms in view. In this context the besieged personified city protests the helplessness of her inhabitants and begs Yahweh to alter his intentions by paraphrasing scripture and by directly quoting Psalm 79, a communal lament.

If the above reading of the feminine city's lament in verses 19–25 is correct, however, the significance of this passage begins to exceed the obvious link to the Mesopotamian weeping goddess tradition discussed previously. For if in fact verses 19–25 in their present form represent a coherent unit, one is also constrained to deal with the fact that the passage seems to anticipate rather than reflect back on the Babylonian invasion. Holladay's observations about the impending character of the invasion in verses 17 and 22, noted above, are not without force.[104] Plausible too is his suggested dating for this passage as a whole, notwithstanding the claims of those who, assuming *a principio* an exilic or post-exilic date for the psalm, discount the possibility that Jeremiah could have been quoting a text already long familiar to his audience.[105] John Bright for example,

---

[103] Carroll, *Jeremiah*, p. 263, regards the speaker of verses 23–25 as the community or city lamenting its fate although he regards all three verses as stemming from a time after the fall of Jerusalem.

[104] Cf. Bright, *Jeremiah*, p. 73, who regards verses 17–21 as original to Jeremiah and as a message uttered just prior to the Babylonian siege of 598/7 BCE.

[105] E.g. Carroll, *Jeremiah*, pp. 262, 264, generally less sanguine than Holladay about scholarly ability to affix a date to material in this book, assigns verses 22–25 to some

comments that "since this psalm is of Exilic date, it is probable (unless one assumes that the psalmist quoted Jeremiah) that the verse is a later addition."[106] But verse 25 need not be understood as an isolated addition, and, indeed, the scriptural expansions in the previous two verses argue against such an interpretation of a third citation in this verse. This fact, especially coupled with the observations above about the unity of verses 19–25 as a whole, leads toward the conclusion that verse 25 was likewise a part of Jeremiah's original speech in this passage.

The likelihood of this conclusion finds negative support in the inability of commentators otherwise satisfactorily to explain the insertion of the Psalm verse at this point. Carroll, for example, regards verse 22 as well as verses 23–25 as discrete units later inserted into the passage. Although verse 22 clearly anticipates the coming destruction, Carroll assigns it to a period after the devastation of the land and, he writes, it "is attached here to indicate the extent to which the policies of the leadership have not prospered." However Carroll's only evidence for this assertion is the putative agglutinative character of the verse, various units of which he believes appear elsewhere in Jeremiah.[107] Even if the agglutinative character of the verse is granted, his treatment hardly explains why such a later writing would be composed as through the devastation had not yet come about. Similarly unpersuasive is his treatment of verses 23–25 and the claim that they should be associated with some time after the fall of Jerusalem. Evidently reading verse 24b quite literally, Carroll relates verses 23 and 24 with the post-exilic problem of population which, presumably, was low enough to jeopardize the nation's survival. But, Carroll continues, as the subject matter of the verse is an obvious appeal to God's justice (not mercy), a connecting conceptual link must be discovered between God's justice and a concern with population level. This Carroll discerns in the similarities between a plea for justice and the "hoped for consequences to oracular expressions of Yahweh's will to increase the nation (29.6; 30.19)."[108] Carroll's point suffers considerably, however, as neither of the two passages he cites seem to be

---

time after 587 BCE. Cf. pp. 43–44 for Carroll's evaluation of Holladay's thesis relative to the septennial reading of Deuteronomy and his biographical approach to the interpretation of the book.

[106] Bright, *Jeremiah,* p. 74.

[107] Carroll, *Jeremiah,* p. 262.

[108] *Ibid.,* p. 264f.

coordinated in the slightest degree to the idea of God's justice. Nevertheless, secure in this interpretation, Carroll proceeds next to treat the addition of verse 25, a redactional insertion which, like Psalm 79, is likewise regarded by him as assuredly from exilic or post-exilic times. The later addition of the psalm quotation in verse 25, he holds, creates an "unintentional irony" since the request for justice for the community is now dangerously juxtaposed with a plea that divine anger be poured out upon the nations.[109] But, he assures his readers, "that irony only arises out of the redaction of the text here and need not be laid at the door of the speaker of v. 24."[110] Presumably the later redactor who inserted verse 25 was unable to see the "unintentional irony" of this insertion. In any event, Carroll does not explain what the later redactor may have intended by including the psalm quotation, and the question posed by the very presence of the quotation in verse 25 remains unanswered. Instead, Carroll simply concludes his discussion of the passage with the suggestion that verses 23–24 represent the community of a later period expressing its piety while "the quotation from Ps. 79.6–7 would then conclude the cycle with an expression of animosity against the nations."[111]

The exegetical tension present in the effort to link Jeremiah 10:25 to verses 23 and 24 or, for that matter, in understanding verses 23–25 in relation to verses 19–22, finds ease if one is willing to dispense with the *a principio* assumption that verse 25 is an exilic or post-exilic insertion based on a psalm which could only have been composed after the events of 587 BCE. As noted above, the structure of verses 19–25 as a whole—as well as the scriptural expansions which appear in the two verses previous to the present quotation in verse 25—argues for the unity of this text. The fact that these verses seem to anticipate rather than reflect back upon the Babylonian invasion can best be explained not as *post eventum* projection but rather as the situation in which they were originally uttered. This in turn points toward the conclusion that this passage, including verse 25, was a part of Jeremiah's original speech. Did the psalmist then simply quote Jeremiah? This prospect seems unlikely given the integral relationship of verse 6 to verses 9 and 10 within

---

[109] *Ibid.*, p. 264.

[110] *Ibid.*, p. 264.

[111] *Ibid.*, p. 265.

Psalm 79 itself. Here key vocabulary knits the verse into its psalmic context: nations and kingdoms do not call upon God's name (*běšimkā*, v 6); God is urged to rescue for the sake of Yahweh's name (*šemēkā*, v 9a, 9b). Likewise the psalmist urges God to pour out (*šěpōk*) God's wrath upon the nations (*haggôyim*) who do not know God (*yědā'ûkā*) in verse 6; in verse 10 God is urged to act in such a way that among the nations (*baggōyyim*) it might be known (*yiwwāda'*) that the outpoured blood (*haššāpûk*, cf. v 3) of God's servants is avenged. It is not impossible, of course, that a later poet structured the psalm on the basis of a single utterance of Jeremiah, but, given the context of the verse in Jeremiah 10:23–25, that hardly seems probable. Instead, one is driven to another conclusion, albeit an unexpected one: not only that Psalm 79 was quoted by Jeremiah but also that the composition of the psalm sufficiently antedated Jeremiah's use of it so as to render its utterance by the prophet meaningful to his auditors. That is to say, if, as the evidence suggests, the quotation of Psalm 79 is authentic to Jeremiah, we have evidence that the psalm was composed and almost certainly used in cultic worship prior to the destruction of 587 BCE.

Evidence from Jeremiah 25:30–38

Another passage from Jeremiah, Jeremiah 25:30–38, likewise commends itself as evidence that the features specifically characteristic of the Mesopotamian communal lamentations were familiar to Judean citizens prior to 587 BCE. The passage is a judgment oracle rather than a lament and, consequently, not all the features which one might anticipate in a communal lament appear or can be expected. Nevertheless, significant aspects of this passage do correspond to the Mesopotamian lament tradition, and the composer's familiarity with that tradition is thereby betrayed.

Once again the opinions of the major commentators divide relative to both the unity of the passage and the judgment as to whether or not the poem represents an authentic utterance of Jeremiah. Carroll, for example, thinks verse 33 is a late prose expansion,[112] and indicators within the poem as a whole "point to redactional influences rather than indicate authentic Jeremiah speeches."[113] Bright,

---

[112] Carroll, *Jeremiah*, p. 505.
[113] *Ibid.*, p. 506.

who also regards verse 33 as an expansion,[114] judges the whole piece as "certainly not later than ca. the mid-sixth century" and some of the poem, such as verses 32, 34–38 "though it cannot be proved to come from Jeremiah, is at least worthy of him."[115] Holladay on the other hand, while acknowledging that "many of the phrases are reminiscent of phrases elsewhere either in Jrm's poetry or in the poetry of other prophets, so that there is uncertainty how much is authentic to Jrm here,"[116] nevertheless goes on to point out that the judgment that the passage is authentic to the prophet is not without merit. In particular Holladay notes that if, as seems to be the case, the reference to "his sheepfold" in verse 30 refers to Judah or Jerusalem, the poem manifests a unity and progressive development, since the movement of the passage is from Judah outward to all the nations of the earth: the effects of Yahweh's "roar" (v 30) and his lawsuit accusation against the nations (verse 31) are extended in the sentence Yahweh passes on the nations (v 32) and continued in a description of the effect of Yahweh's action (vv 33–34).[117] Holladay further observes that the progressive development of the poem's content is matched by its poetic structure. Although verse 33 is often regarded as a prose expansion (e.g., Bright, Carroll), Holladay disputes that claim. He notes first that the phrase "on that day" overloads the verse and is surely a gloss.[118] Secondly, if the expression "lamented nor" is understood as an expansion, the passage can easily be viewed as a poetic tetracolon.[119] Thus corrected, the poetic verse falls nicely between the four cola of verses 32 and 34 which in turn are bracketed by the five cola verses 30–31 and 36–37. Holladay regards verses 36–37 as the conclusion to the poem. Verse 38, in his view, represents a late adaptation of diction from Jeremiah 4:7. However, Holladay's decision relative to this last verse is flawed in the view of the present author, and evidence will be adduced shortly that points to the opposite conclusion.

As to the passage's authenticity, similarity in the present material to other utterances of Jeremiah[120] and its affinity to the thought

---

114 Bright, *Jeremiah*, p. 162.

115 *Ibid.*, p. 164.

116 Holladay, *Jeremiah 1*, p. 678.

117 *Ibid.*, pp. 678–679.

118 *Ibid.*, p. 677.

119 *Ibid.* Cf. pp. 679, 681.

120 E.g., verse 32b, 6:22 and 10:22; 33b and 16:4. Cf. *Ibid.*, p. 679.

pattern of verses 15–29 whereby the activity of Yahweh spreads from Jerusalem or Judah outward to surrounding nations suggests that these verses are original to the prophet. Holladay proposes that, like those texts which this poem resembles, these verses too should be located prior to the final destruction of 587 BCE and in particular to 594 BCE.[121]

If Holladay's analysis of the coherence, authenticity, and date of this passage is correct, then these verses present themselves as possible further evidence of Israel's familiarity with the *balag/eršemma* lamentations. First, one sees here a number of the motifs that appear in the corresponding cuneiform writings. The agents of destruction described in the text are explicitly the tempest (*sa'ar*) of Yahweh and the roar of his voice. Verse 30 describes the roar as originating from the heavens and as directed first against his own sheepfold and secondly against the nations of the earth (v 31). The image of God's articulated roar is coordinated with Yahweh's tempest in verse 32: both are directed (or spread) to the nations, both reach the ends of the earth, and both wreak havoc (vv 31, 32). One is reminded of the frequently manifested feature of the *balag/eršemma* whereby the word of the deity and his storm are equated, as in the previously cited *balag* 5:14.[122] While the Jeremiah passage does not explicitly relate Yahweh's roaring (*šā'ag*) to Yahweh's word,[123] this may be an intentional aesthetic choice on the part of the prophet. The verb *šā'ag* connotes not only the sound of a lion, but frequently finds employment as a figurative description of invaders and other foes as well. The "roar" of the enemies in Psalm 74:4 provides a case in point.[124] Doubtless by the use of this word the prophet intended to evoke a double image: Yahweh as a roaring lion (cf. v 38) and the image of the roaring adversaries. If so, the third of the chief agents of destruction in Mesopotamian lamentations, the invading foe, is brought into the contextual orbit of this passage. In any event, however, it is clear that, like the *balag/eršemma* texts, the roaring of Yahweh itself and its effects are indistinguishable from those of the raging storm.

---

[121] *Ibid.*, p. 679.

[122] Cf. Chapter 3, n. 105, above, for further examples.

[123] Cf., however, the standard introductory formula in verse 30: *tinnābē' 'ălêhem 'ēt kol haddĕbārîm hā'ēlleh.* The prophet word of Yahweh is the substance of his roar.

[124] Other examples include Jer 2:15; Ps 22:14; cf. Isa 5:29; Jer 51:38.

Likewise, it is apparent that the responsibility for the impending destruction is assigned to Yahweh, the reasons for whose activity remain mysterious. Within the larger context of this passage and Jeremiah's message, of course, divine judgment comes and disaster strikes as a consequence of sin. If that is the concept undergirding the present passage, however, it remains strangely muted. Verse 31 reports that Yahweh has an indictment (*rîb*) against the nations, but the nature of the offense of the "guilty" remains unclear. Indeed, in the present verse *hārĕšā'îm* appears to be one of many places where the offense of guilt is simply hostility of God or God's people.[125] They are "wicked enemies," the precise nature of whose sin remains unexpressed. In any event, there seems to be nothing in this passage apart from this colon that suggests an explanation for the approaching storm and which associates the calamity with human indiscretion or sin. Also, in this respect, the present verses correspond to the *balag/eršemma* materials, which likewise do not mention sin or repentance and, further, feature an absence of any causal link between sin and the imminent calamitous storm.

The actual effects of the storm are little described. Destruction of both the shepherds and their sheepfolds is implied. Not insignificantly, however, verse 33—which as noted above appears to belong to the original poem—does include a description of the bodies of the slain, which lie, unburied, from one end of the earth to the other. The storm of Enlil has similar consequences as the bodies of its victims are piled in heaps.[126]

Importunities such as are found in the communal lamentations of both Israel and Mesopotamia are not to be expected in a judgment oracle. Even so, traces of such cries appear in the admonition for the shepherds to cry out in verse 34 as well as in the report of those cries and wails in verse 36. The precise identity of those shepherds remains unspecified. It is significant, however, that it is *shepherds* and their *sheepfolds* that are the subject of these verses. For while the surviving *balag/eršemma* materials have little to say about shepherds and their folds, one of their predecessor compositions, the city lament LU, begins by listing the various cities, described as

---

125 Cf. v *rāšā'* in BDB. Examples appear both in the plural (e.g., Ps 3:8; 7:10; 9:18; Isa 48:22; 57:20,21; Ezek 21:34; Mal 3:21) and in the singular, understood as a collective (e.g., Ps 9:6,17; 10:2; Isa 11:4; Hab 3:12).

126 Cf. *balag*s 2:27–31; 43:a+36; *eršemma* 35.2:27–31.

sheepfolds, which have been abandoned and destroyed by the gods.[127] Similarly, the destruction of the sheepfold finds mention elsewhere in LU and well as in LSU.[128] In the context of these writings, the sheepfolds clearly stand as figures for the various cities and temples. If, as seems likely, the sheepfolds in Jeremiah's prophetic oracle represent nations or cities (and the shepherds their kings)[129] the idea expressed is quite similar to both the city laments as well as to the frequent lists of destroyed cities and temples which appear in the *balag/eršemma* compositions.

Yet another potential point of correspondence between the present verses and the *balag/eršemma* materials appears in verse 38 and the MT's reference to *hayyônāh*. The validity of this connection, of course, depends on whether or not verse 38 was original to the poem. Holladay, for one, judges the verse to be a later insertion, arguing that verses 36–37 conclude the poem while verse 38 represents an adaptation of the diction of Jeremiah 4:7. But while 4:7 is, in Holladay's view, original to Jeremiah, the differences between that verse and Jeremiah 25:38 lead him to the opposite conclusion in regard to the latter verse. Holladay believes it significant, for example, that "lion" in 25:38 is *kĕpîr* and functions in a simile while in 4:7 the noun is *'aryēh* used as a metaphor; "thicket" in 25:38 is *sukkâh* but *sĕbōk* in 4:7.

In spite of these observations, however, several factors weigh against Holladay's conclusion that the present verse is simply a later adaptation of 4:7. First, as Holladay himself admits, the relationship of 4:7 to 4:5–8 is elusive.[130] Not only is it difficult to discern from the context if the speaker is Yahweh or the prophet, the metaphor of the lion in 4:7 is not self-evidently a reference to either an invading northern nation or to Yahweh. Nor should much be made of the difference between *kĕpîr* and *'aryēh*, since both terms appear in Jeremiah as metaphors and similes to signify, variously, foreign nations, Yahweh, or Judeans.[131] In context, Jeremiah 4:7 *'aryēh* can easily be understood as referring to Yahweh rather than to the "evil

[127] LU 1–37; cf. *ANET*[3], pp. 455–456.

[128] LU 391–2; LSU 6.

[129] On shepherds as a figurative expression of kings, see Jer 10:21; 22:22; 23:1–4; Ps 78:70–72; Isa 44:28; Ezek 34:1–10.

[130] Holladay, *Jeremiah 1*, p. 146.

[131] Cf. *kĕpîr* in Jer 2:15; 51:38 (foreign nation); *'aryēh* in Jer 5:6 (foreign nation); 49:19// 50:44 (Yahweh); 2:30; 12:8 (Judean citizenry).

from the north" mentioned in verse 3, especially since the rather rare *sĕbbōk* ("thicket") from which the lion emerges also appears in Psalm 74:5 as a reference to some feature of the Temple (*bisă̆bok-ʿēṣ*) destroyed by the invading enemies. If this is the case, the distinction made by Holladay between these two verses lessens considerably.

In any event, it is clear that the simile of Jeremiah 25:38 does refer to the activity of Yahweh who leaves his *sukkô* (covert). *Sukkāh*, likewise a rare word, occurs once as a reference to the place of the wicked,[132] while twice it refers explicitly to the Temple.[133] If, therefore, the reference to "his fold" in verse 30 refers to Judah or Jerusalem with its Temple, as indeed seems to be the case, verse 38 can be understood as the end of an *inclusio* begun at verse 30 where Yahweh "roars" from his place. The *inclusio* finds confirmation in the verb of verse 30, *sā̓āg* ("roar"), which explicitly connotes the roar of the lion of verse 38,[134] as well as in the poetic structure which Holladay has partially illuminated.

With respect to that structure, Holladay proposes a chiasmus centered around verse 33 whereby that tetracolon is bracketed by the five-cola verses of 30–31 and 36–37. But in fact, verses 30–31 are a pair of five cola verses which find only partial correspondence in the five cola of verses 36–37. Rather than the five cola of verses 36–37, one might expect a second five cola verse where verse 38 appears which would correspond to verse 30. As just noted, there is a correspondence between verses 30 and 38 relative to their content and the simile of the lion. Verse 38 as it appears in the MT, however, has suffered corruption. Verse 38b provides particular difficulty and, evidently, posed a problem for the Greek translators as well. In the MT one finds *mippĕnê ḥărôn hayyônāh*, literally "from/before the wrath of the dove." Some Hebrew manuscripts, the Greek and the Targum read *ḥrb* for the MT's *ḥărôn*, a circumstance which suggests that the MT's *ḥărôn*, has either been corrupted from an original *ḥarbô* or that they had a different *Vorlage*. That the latter is the case is suggested by (1) the corroboration of the Greek and the Targum,

---

132 Ps 10:9.

133 E.g., Ps 76:3; 27:5.

134 On *šā̓ag* in connection with lions, see Judg 15:5; Amos 3:4,8; Ps 104:21; cf. *šĕ̓āgā* in Zech 11:3; Job 4:10; Ezek 19:7. While the verb and the related noun also frequently find use in describing the activity of the invaders and foes (e.g., Jer 2:15; Ps 22:14; 74:4; cf. Isa 5:29), the poetic structure of the present passage suggests that is not the sense here.

(2) the difficulty of explaining how *ḥarbô* could have become *ḥărôn*, (3) the division in the Greek tradition over the following word as the Septuagint reads *tēs megalas* while Aquila, Theodotion, followed by the Vulgate have *tēs peristeras*, (4) the Greek omission of the final colon of the MT verse. Nevertheless, evidence for a different Vorlage behind the Greek text does not legitimate dismissal of the MT text, especially in the Book of Jeremiah. Holladay, for example, offers a suggestion to the effect that a corrected *ḥarbô* for the present *ḥărôn* allows the possibility for one to construe *hayyônāh* as a feminine participle of *ynh*, "oppress." Even so, he admits, the definite article remains a problem and, consequently, he judges the Greek reading preferable.[135]

The fact that this verse has obviously suffered in the transmission process, coupled with both the incoherence of 38b and the expectation of a five-cola verse all raise the possibility that the difficulty in the MT has come about as a result of a missing colon. Noteworthy in this connection is the fact that Jeremiah 4:7, which does parallel 25:8 in a number of aspects (albeit without the latter's textual problems), also appears as a five-cola verse. While it is impossible given the present text's disrepair to reconstruct the Hebrew verse, if one assumes that *hayyônâh* is original to the text and the text is original to the poem, a number of intriguing possibilities emerge. Of the occurrences of this noun in the Hebrew Bible, the majority appear in ritual texts where two pigeons or two turtle doves (*tôrîm*) serve as sacrificial substitutes for an offering of a sheep.[136] No significant distinction seems to be made between the two species of birds in these texts. The latter observation applies as well to the appearance of *yônâh* and *tôr* in the Song of Songs where both terms appear as zoomorphic similes intended to depict the beauty or tender cooing of the beloved.[137] *Yônâh* also appears several times in Genesis 8:8–12 as the creature whose behavior signaled the abatement of the chaos waters in the flood story. Beyond these references, however, the characteristics of the dove which emerge in the poetic texts are the moan-like noises issued by the birds and their shared

---

[135] Holladay, *Jeremiah 1*, p. 678, n. 38a, wonders if the definite article might not be an early pseudocorrection.

[136] Cf. Lev 1:14; 5:7,11; 12:8; 14:22,30; 15:14,29; Num 6:10. For further details, see G. Johannes Botterweck, "yônâ," *TDOT*, VI, 39.

[137] Song 2:12 (*tôr*); 1:15; 2:14; 4:1; 5:2, 12; 6:9 (*yônâh*).

penchant for inhabiting remote or desolated places. Evidently, the vulnerable pigeon or turtledove, whose cooing suggested moaning to a number of biblical poets and whose normal habitat included remote or destroyed areas, provided an apt metaphor for the effect of invasion and destruction on human beings. With the lone exception of the present verse, the image finds employment in contexts which, strikingly, have to do with a catastrophe. The disaster is, moreover, normally one of national consequences such as the invasion and the destruction of the city and its Temple as the following examples illustrate:

Moaning

Like a swallow or a crane I clamor, I moan like a dove.
My eyes are weary with looking upward.
O Lord, I am oppressed; be my security! Isaiah 38:14

He calls his officers; they stumble as they come forward;
 they hasten to the wall, and the mantelet is set up.
The river gates are opened, the palace trembles.
It is decreed that the city be exiled,
 its slave women led away,
 moaning like doves and beating their breasts. Nahum 2:5–7

We all growl like bears;
 like doves we moan mournfully.
We wait for justice, but there is none;
 for salvation, but it is far from us. Isaiah 59:11

Abandonment or Inhabitation of Remote Quarters

And I say, "O that I had wings like a dove!
 I would fly away and be at rest;
truly, I would flee far away;
 I would lodge in the wilderness.
I would hurry to find a shelter for myself
 from the raging wind and tempest." Psalm 55:6–8

Leave the towns, and live on the rock, O inhabitants of Moab!
Be like the dove that nests on the sides of the mouth of a gorge.
 Jeremiah 48:28

They shall go after the LORD, who roars like a lion;
 when he roars, his children shall come trembling from the west.
They shall come trembling like birds from Egypt,
 and like doves from the land of Assyria;

and I will return them to their homes, says the LORD.
  Hosea 11:10–11[138]

Who are these that fly like a cloud,
  and like doves to their windows? Isaiah 60:8

If any survivors escape, they shall be found on the mountains like
  doves of the valleys, all of them moaning over their iniquity.
  Ezekiel 7:16

The Lord gives the command;
  great is the company of those who bore the tidings:
  "The kings of the armies, they flee, they flee!"
The women at home divide the spoil,
  though they stay among the sheepfolds—
the wings of a dove covered with silver,
  its pinions with green gold. Psalm 68:12–14

Of these, three passages are particularly intriguing. Psalm 55, an individual lament, includes a simile whereby the poet wishes for the wings of a dove in order that he might flee to the wilderness. That from which the psalmist would flee appears in verse 4: the assault of the enemy, likened by the poet in verse 9 to a *mērûaḥ sᶜār missāᶜar* (raging wind from a tempest). As noted previously,[139] the *sᶜr* can denote the activity of the enemies or God's own violent action taken against either God's enemies (Ps 83:15–17) or Jerusalem and its inhabitants (Isa 29:6). This, in turn, may be a reflex of the Mesopotamian "Storm of Enlil" tradition, ubiquitous in that culture's lamentations where the effect of the deity's storm upon the dove finds frequent reference (see below).

Likewise, Psalm 68:12–14, and the reference to the dove found there, is provocative. This psalm is "widely admitted as textually and exegetically the most difficult and obscure of all the psalms,"[140] these verses not excepted. The significance of a "dove covered with silver, its pinions with green gold" remains elusive as does that creature's relationship with women who remain at home among the sheepfolds but nevertheless participate in the spoils of victory.[141]

---

[138] Cf. Hosea 7:11.

[139] Cf. Chapter 4, "The Agents of Destruction."

[140] Dahood, *Psalms II: 51–100*, p. 133.

[141] Cf. Judges 5:16 where the clans of Reuben are upbraided for tarrying among the sheepfolds, searching their hearts, rather than joining the battle with Deborah and Barak.

If verses 13–14 and 14b are to be understood as a continuous thought,[142] it may be that the women are, collectively, the dove; the latter's adorning silver and gold include the spoil gotten in the wake of kings routed by Yahweh's command. Here then, as elsewhere in the poetic texts, the dove would be understood as a metaphor for the people, as it appears to be in Psalm 74:19 where the psalmist urges God not to deliver the "soul of your dove" to the wild beasts.[143] The other interpretive difficulties presented by these verses aside, however, it should be noted that the reference to the dove and sheepfolds occurs in a context that includes Yahweh's commanding word and the rout of kings. The collusion of precisely these concepts in the poem which is Jeremiah 25:30–38 hardly seems accidental.

Finally, there is the reference to doves in Isaiah 60:8. The message of Isaiah 60, rooted in a reworking of themes long familiar

---

[142] That a discernable relationship exists between verses 13 and 14 is far from assured. Cf. the seminal contribution by W.F. Albright, "A Catalogue of Early Hebrew Lyric Poems," *HUCA* 23 (1950), 1–38, wherein he claims that Psalm 68 represents a list of thirty separate hymns, cited by their opening incipits, dating from the Solomonic period. Albright believes that vv. 13–14a and 14b represent seperate incipits. Nevertheless Albright's thesis is often vigorously challenged as are the particulars of his assessment of this psalm. Artur Weiser, for example, believes the psalm is a "partial liturgical score" stemming from the festival cult [*The Psalms*, 481f.], while Dahood, *Psalms II: 51–100*, p. 133, sees in the poem the genre of "triumphal hymn." A.A. Anderson, *The Book of Psalms*, vol. 1, pp. 481–82, understands the poem to be a "song of procession." Kraus, *Psalms 60–150*, pp. 51–6 and John Gray, "A Cantata of the Autumn Festival: Psalm LXVIII," *JSS* 22 (1977), 2–26, each divide the psalm into twelve distinct units with some variation between them while S. Mowinckel, *Der Achtundsechzigste Psalm* (Oslo: J. Dybwad, 1953), pp. 22–68, finds nine distinct units in the poem.

[143] Mowinckel, *Der Achtundsechzigste Psalm*, pp. 38–39. Although Mowinckel is correct in identifying the dove as a stereotypical image of the people, a reference to a dove in the obscure lines of *balag*, 15:69–70 remains intriguing. There Enlil is enjoined to arise from various parts of the temple precints including the place

where the small, good lambs . . .
from the "Dais," where the dove nests,

One wonders if, as "Dais" here refers to some aspect of the temple, so the "soul of your dove" in Psalm 74:19, a textually disputed phrase, might not refer to some aspect of the temple's architecture. That this may be the case finds some confirmation by the reference in verse 5 to another architectural aspect of the temple, the "wooden trellis" (cf. above). In any case, the coordination of the sheepfold, or at least the place "where the small, good lambs . . ." with the dove in the *balag* provides another instance where the particular language of the Mesopotamian laments corresponds to what one finds in the Hebrew communal laments and related poetry.

from the Royal Zion tradition,[144] represents Trito-Isaiah's[145] attempt to resuscitate the flagging hopes of the returned exiles in the face of oppressive historical circumstances. The prophet holds before his auditors a vision of Jerusalem as a light in the world's darkness by which the earth shall be illumined and toward which both the people of God and the nations of the world shall converge. The universal character of the prophet's vision is seen particularly in verses 4–7, 9, 10–14, and 16: even foreign nations will travel to the city of God, bringing their wealth, glory and offerings to the Temple. Those who will stream toward Jerusalem include peoples whose lands are found south of Palestine (Midian/Ephah, Sheba, Kedar and Nebaioth, vv. 6–7), as well as representatives from the coastland regions and far away Tarshish (v. 9). Between the mention of these various peoples, however, appears the bi-cola question of verse 8: "Who are these that fly like a cloud, and like the doves to their windows?" While this verse presents no particular textual or translational difficulties, the conceptual link between these ones "like doves" and either the sacrificial animals mentioned in verse 7 or the exiles returning on the ships of Tarshish in verse 9 remains elusive, as does the meaning of the verse as a whole. Perhaps for this reason, commentators generally refrain from treating this verse. When Isaiah 60:8 finds mention at all in the secondary literature, the two similes are often understood as poetic depictions of the ships of Tarshish mentioned in the following verse.[146] This solution is neither particularly convincing nor satisfying, however, and in its

---

[144] On the Royal Zion tradition, see R.E. Clements, *God and Temple* (Philadelphia: Fortress, 1965), pp. 40–78; J.J.M. Roberts, "Zion in the Theology of the Davidic-Solomonic Empire," in *Studies in the Period of David and Solomon and Other Essays: Papers Read at the International Symposium for Biblical Studies, Tokyo, 5–7, December 1979,* ed. by Tomoo Ishida (Winona Lake: Eisenbrauns, 1982), pp. 93–108; Ben C. Ollenburger, *Zion the City of the Great King: A Theological Symbol of the Jerusalem Cult,* JSOTSup, Vol. 41 (Sheffield: JSOT Press, 1987).

[145] On the critical questions involved in the historical location of Trito-Isaiah, see, conveniently, Christopher R. Seitz, "Isaiah, Book of (Third Isaiah)," *ABD,* Vol. 3, pp. 501–507 and the bibliography cited there. Scholars are generally agreed that the material in Isaiah 56–66 comes from some time after that of chapters 40–55 but differ with regard to the question of how far removed these prophecies may be from Second Isaiah.

[146] E.g., G. von Rad, Gerhard *Old Testament Theology* (2 vols.; New York: Harper & Row, 1962–65), vol. 2, p. 295; Westermann, *Isaiah 40–66,* p. 359.

wake one may well ask anew with the prophet, who are these ones like a dove? Further, what does this verse signify?

The origin and significance of the image is illuminated by the Mesopotamian *balag*s and, specifically, in the reference to a dove found in *balag* 50. Following a description of the devastating storm of Enlil (b+139–154) and the defilement of both the sanctuary and the goddesses' image in the sanctuary by the enemy (b+155–162), the goddess describes herself as a frightened dove who must abandon both her temple and city:

> Like a frightened dove, I spend the day (huddled) against the
> rafters.
> Like a flying bat, I disappear among the crevices.
> It causes me to fly about in my house like a bird.
> It causes me to fly about my city like a bird.
> In my house it screeches right behind me.
> As for me, the lady, in my city it screeches right behind me.
> How I pour out in my house, "You are no longer my house!"
> How I pour out in my city, "You are no longer my city!"
> How I pour out in my cella, "You are no longer my cella!"
> "I can no longer enter it!" I utter. Its wealth has been consumed.
> "I can no longer . . . !" I utter, Its laughter has dried up.
>   (b+166–176)[147]

Later in this same composition, however, the simile is abandoned; now the goddess seemingly describes the fate of a real creature that inhabits the temple's window:

> The window where I focus attention has been destroyed. Its dove
> flies away.
> The dove of the window has abandoned her nest. Where can she
> fly to?
> The bird has abandoned its built nest. Where can she fly to?
> Its men have abandoned the cella which was founded there.
>   Where can they go to? (b+258–261)

In the *balag*s the destruction of the temple spells the end of the normal resting place for the dove: the creature is forced to abandon its nesting place in the window of the temple. This fact doubtless accounts for several references in the *balag*s expressing the idea that the dove "hovers about" as a consequence of the temple's destruction. In other words, the dove, like the goddess, is homeless and

---

[147] Cf. *balag* 11:1–2, a+28–29.

wandering: "Its crenelated wall has been destroyed. Its dove hovers about."[148]

That Israel was familiar with the concept of nesting birds finding safe haven in the temple is well illustrated by Psalm 84:4, albeit the passage uses different words to describe the winged creatures:

> Even the sparrow (*ṣippôr*) finds a home,
> and the swallow (*dĕrôr*) a nest for herself,
> where she may lay her young,
> at your altars, O Lord of hosts,
> my King and my God.

Moreover, Psalm 55:6–8 clearly demonstrates the fact that Israel was quite familiar with the lament motif of the fleeing dove:

> And I say, "O that I had wings like a dove!
>   I would fly away and be at rest;
> truly, I would flee far away;
>   I would lodge in the wilderness.
> I would hurry to find a shelter for myself
>   from the raging wind and tempest." Psalm 55:6–8

Once again it is worthwhile noting that there is a linkage between the dove imagery in this Psalm and the devastating storm, a feature shared generally by the *balag*s and specifically *balag* 50. Furthermore, the doves of Isaiah 60:8 and the motif imagery of the Mesopotamian *balag* are also consistent with the second-person feminine singular address present throughout Trito-Isaiah's poem. God speaks directly to the city, here as elsewhere (e.g., Lam 1; 2:14–19) personified as woman. As discussed above, the city as a personified woman appears to be another Israelite reflex of the Mesopotamian lament tradition.

Of course the Mesopotamian laments, as laments, never undertake a description of the restoration of the temple or its precincts. Indeed it has already been shown that the original cultic *raison d'être* of these compositions was to avert any wrath of the deity which may have been accidentally incurred on those occasions when temples were renovated. Consequently, one would not expect a de-

---

[148] UTU-gin₇ è-ta *aḫû* (*balag* 33), 143. Cf. é tùr-gin₇ nigin-na-àm (*balag* 3), 19; mu-tin nu-nuz dím-ma (*balag* 10), a+12 for identical statements.

scription of the restoration of the goddess' city or of her temple. The hope of restoration of both Jerusalem and especially its Temple is, however, precisely that which Trito-Isaiah means to instill in his auditors. As a part of this proclamation, the prophet appears to have reversed an image quite familiar to his listeners through their exposure to the *balag* compositions: even as the dove once abandoned the temple, the dove will be seen flying to the window of God's "glorious house" (v. 7) on the coming day of Jerusalem's exaltation. Thus, this verse strongly suggests Israel's familiarity with this aspect of the Mesopotamian lament tradition, here transformed by the prophet into a message of restoration hope.

In sum, all of the references to the dove or turtle dove in the poetic texts, apart from the Song of Songs, appear in contexts of conflict, catastrophe, and often of national need. In at least one instance the dove is further associated with the sheepfold. Moreover, of those texts that can be dated with a relatively high degree of probability, the majority of the references are to be found in pre-exilic texts. Isaiah 60:8 provides a happy exception in that the connections between the Mesopotamian laments and Isaiah are difficult to dispute. The prominence of dove imagery in precisely those contexts relating to conflict and catastrophe can, therefore, be construed as further evidence of the originality of Jeremiah 25:38 with its reference to *hayyônâh* to the rest of the poem in which it appears. This possibility is further strengthened by the fact that a reference to a *yônâh* in this passage might also be anticipated should the poem as a whole be judged, as is here being suggested, as another example of a pre-exilic biblical text which betrays its familiarity with the Mesopotamian communal lament tradition. Thus, while the text's corrupted condition resists any clear determination of the exact meaning of *hayyônâh* in Jeremiah 25:38, the burden of other references to *yônâh* and *tôr* in the poetic materials suffices to indicate that, whatever the text may have said prior to the scribal errors that have crept into the MT, the reference to a dove, with its prefixed definite article, is likely original to the Hebrew *Vorlage* of this text. Moreover, even should one follow some commentators in judging the entirety of verse 38 as a secondary addition, there is sufficient similarity between the content of those verses that precede it and the Mesopotamian laments to assert that the prophet was familiar with the latter, and that that familiarity antedated 587 BCE.

SUMMARY

The evidence adduced from Jeremiah has implications for the broader question of the relationship between the Israelite communal laments and their contemporary *balag/eršemma* compositions of Mesopotamia. As shown above, the laments of both traditions share many of the same themes, motifs, and images, including the concepts of divine abandonment, the assignation of divine responsibility for the destruction of the temple and its environs, lists, an apparent ahistorical location of the events described in the compositions, and reference to the various agents of destruction. Particularly striking is the absence of penitential material in the Israelite compositions, a feature which again is shared by the *balag*s and *eršemma*s.

Nevertheless, while the communal lamentations of Israel and those of Mesopotamia do appear to share a good many common characteristics, aspects of Israel's tradition stand in contrast to the Mesopotamian compositions. The presence of unique accents and features have led some to argue for the originality of Israel's writings, concluding that the points of correspondence between the two cultures' communal lamentations represent no more than a common stock of themes and images that might be anticipated given the broad cultural and geographic milieu in which both cultures were located. This solution, however, does not adequately explain the volume of corresponding features between these lamentations. Moreover, when the Hebrew compositions do manifest unique or distinctive characteristics, these can readily be understood as Israel's own adaptations and amplification of concepts important to Israel's faith in Yahweh. Original features in the communal laments do not therefore vitiate the claim of a literary relationship between the respective writings.

Nor does a simple comparison of the respective lamentations exhaust all of the available evidence. In addition to similar thematic features, the Hebrew psalms seem to have shared certain formal characteristics with the Mesopotamian compositions, including the possibility that several of these psalms had original colophons that included a notation of their cultic use, evidently as laments, and that again bore similarities to the colophons attached to the *balag*s and *eršemma*s. In addition, and as discussed above, a number of features present in Psalm 74, a psalm whose composition, like Psalm 79, is generally located in the exilic period, appear to be problematic for that time frame. That fact, plus those features that the psalm does manifest and that are consistent with an awareness of the Meso-potamian lamentations, points once more to the probability that the latter materials were both known and influential in the composition of the Hebrew communal laments.

The likelihood of Israel's familiarity with the Mesopotamian lamentations is further strengthened by the evidence adduced from the preexilic prophetic material, including Ezekiel's reference to the Tammuz cult and, especially, by the prophetic utterances of Jeremiah. In the latter prophet, several hallmark Sumero-Akka-dian motifs—divine abandonment, the weeping deity, and God's destructive storm—were known and included in Israel's lament tradition. The texts discussed above, moreover, seem likely to have originated from a time prior to the exile, a circumstance that not only calls into question the dating of the Israelite lamentations, but has implications relative to their cultic use as well.

CHAPTER 6

THE SOURCES OF COMMUNAL LAMENTS IN THE PSALMS: CONCLUSIONS

The comparison of the Sumero-Akkadian *balag/eršemma* lamentations and the communal laments points toward the strong possibility of a specifically literary connection between the two collections. The evidence remains circumstantial, and at present the question of Israel's *specific* borrowing cannot be demonstrated with absolute certainty. Even if new parallels to the Psalter's communal lamentations were discovered, one suspects that the correspondence would be inexact since the comparative principles of creative adoption and creative adaptation, amply witnessed by the cuneiform tradition, suggest that the Hebrew laments would bear the impress of Israel's understanding of God as well as testimony of Israel's cultural and geographic location. Nevertheless, and in the absence of an Akkadian version of a Hebrew communal lament, the concatenation of thematic features, structural elements, and the evidence drawn from prophetic texts all point toward the conclusion that Israel was familiar with Mesopotamia's literature of communal lament.

This conclusion has several implications for our understanding of the Hebrew psalms as well as for related inquiries.

IMPLICATIONS FOR RELATED STUDIES

The connection between *balag/eršemma* materials and these psalms contributes to the evidence that the Book of Lamentations does in fact have more than an accidental affinity with aspects of the communal laments of Mesopotamia. If these psalms manifest the literary influence of *balag/eršemma* materials, it is not unreasonable to suppose that Lamentations—a book demonstrating pronounced similarities with the *balag/eršemma*—has been similarly influenced. That, of course, is the burden of Gwaltney's argument.[1] The present work supports Gwaltney's case, in spite of the challenges recently leveled against it by Dobbs-Allsopp.

Dobbs-Allsopp rejects what he perceives as the unidirectional approach of Gwaltney since that posture, in his view, ignores the possibility of polygenesis for a given genre, underestimates the difficulties in establishing literary dependence between two cultures' writings, and, even assuming the fact of some time of literary influence, represents a too simplistic view.[2] Rather than positing literary influence, Dobbs-Allsopp explains the similarities between Mesopotamian laments and the Book of Lamentations as a consequence of a native city lament genre within Israel which was only generically related to the Mesopotamian genre. His arguments for his own position are as follows.

First, he maintains that literary dependence cannot account for the fairly widespread occurrence of the genre in the Hebrew Bible since "one would have to make the improbable supposition that several different writers (i.e., poets and prophets) had access to and chose to borrow from one or more of the Mesopotamian laments over a period of at least two hundred years."[3] However, the relative improbability of such a suggestion has been shown to be lessened by a long history of cultural contact during which time Israel might easily have been introduced to the Mesopotamian lament tradition, a tradition which included the preservation and continuous use of the *balag/eršemma* laments. In addition, the use of these materials in the cultic worship of Israel prior to 587 BCE would doubtless explain the prophets' familiarity with various aspects of that tradition and their employment of the tradition in their prophetic declarations.

Second, Dobbs-Allsopp holds that a native city lament genre better explains a variety of phenomena which are unique to the Israelite genre. Specifically, he cites the motifs of the divine warrior,

---

[1] See above, Chapter 3.

[2] Dobbs-Allsopp, *Weep, O Daughter of Zion*, pp. 5–8.

[3] *Ibid.*, p. 157.

the Day of Yahweh, sin as a breach of covenant, the presence of the *qînāh* meter, Semitic and West Semitic divine epithets for the personified cities, the taunt of the passers-by, and the Sodom and Gomorrah motif. Of these he states, "Concepts like these are integral to the genre and indicate that at least at some point prior to the eighth century, the city-lament genre was internalized in the Israelite literary tradition."[4]

Dobbs-Allsopp's research does, of course, reveal the relative antiquity of this genre. If Dobbs-Allsopp is correct to conclude that at some point prior to the eighth century the city-lament genre became internalized in the Israelite literary tradition, however, that conclusion has a double significance for the present study. First, Dobbs-Allsopp's investigation makes it clear that 587 BCE need not serve as the *terminus post quem* for the composition of similar laments in the Psalter since the (native) city-lament genre was internalized long before that time. The foregoing study tends to support the antiquity of the lament tradition, if not its native Israelite origin. In particular, the evidence adduced above relative to Psalms 74 and 79, two psalms that are generally assumed to have found their specific inspiration in the destruction of Jerusalem by Babylon in 587 BCE, indicates instead that the composition of these two psalms actually antedated that destruction. Rather these psalms, like the rest in the small collection of communal laments in the Psalter, appear to be a part of a much older lament tradition, one which the present writer maintains reflects explicit influences from the Sumero-Akkadian writings. Minimally, of course, this means that the question of dating these two psalms, as well as other communal laments in the psalter, is reopened.

Further, if Dobbs-Allsopp is correct in claiming that Israelite literary tradition internalized the lament genre prior to the eighth century, it does not then follow that the traditions were native to Israel or merely generically related to the Mesopotamian genre as he maintains. The fact that traditions may have been internalized is irrelevant to the question of literary influence, as are the appearance of some features unique to the Hebrew compositions. As was indicated above in the discussion of the 'creative adoption principle,'[5] literary borrowing frequently included redactional activities

---

[4] *Ibid.*, p. 158.
[5] See Chapter 2.

whereby material was either added or deleted in order that a given text might better accommodate a local culture, that culture's ideology, and its religious beliefs. Evidence for the literary influence of Mesopotamia on Israel not only tolerates some differences in the respective laments but expects them.

IMPLICATIONS FOR FORM CRITICAL ANALYSIS OF THE COMMUNAL LAMENTS

Chapter 3 above included an outline of the origin and evolution of the *balag/eršemma* compositions as well as an account of the changing role these public lamentations had in the cultic life of Mesopotamia.[6] The history of the genre reveals that the *balags'* original purpose, to assuage the deity's inadvertent anger on those occasions when the temple was razed for purposes of restoration, came to be expanded. The laments, formally coupled by the first millennium with specific *eršemmas*, began to appear routinely in the cultic calendars of the *gala* priesthood where they seem to have been understood as efficacious for averting divinely generated disaster in general.[7] In other words, by the first millennium, rituals involving texts of communal lament *and* praise were firmly fixed in both the literature and public worship of Mesopotamia.

Both the content and the cultic use of the *balag/eršemma* lamentations become extremely interesting if, as the evidence reflects, the Hebrew psalms benefit from an affinity to these materials and perhaps were directly influenced by them. As we have seen in Chapter 4, form critical analysis of these psalms, and particularly the analysis of Claus Westermann, fails to isolate even a single remaining example of a "pure" communal lament among the Hebrew compositions. Westermann views the communal laments still remaining in the Psalter as "mixed" remnants of the original "pure" form; they manifest expansionary elements such as introductory praise, expressions of confidence or the certainty of a hearing, and a concluding petition or praise of God.[8] To the contrary, however, the middle expansionary elements identified by Westermann—expressions of confidence and especially the certainty of a hearing—have

---

[6] See Chapter 3, "Ritual Use."

[7] Cohen, *Balag-compositions*, p. 15; *idem, SH,* p. 49.

[8] Westermann, *Praise and Lament*, p. 52.

been shown to be absent from the psalms in question. Moreover, the remaining additional features—introductory praise and concluding petitions or praise to God—are normal features of the *balag/eršemma* lamentations. That observation, coupled with the structure and poetic integrity of the Hebrew laments, at the minimum calls into question the judgment that the communal lament psalms repre- sent the final stages of an evolutionary process whereby a "pure" form of the lament, no longer present in the Psalter, has given way to mixed types. To the contrary, Westermann's remaining expan- sionary features—introductory praise and a concluding petition or praise of the deity—are what one might expect if the Hebrew com- positions were modeled on the communal laments of Mesopotamia.

A comparison of the respective communal lament traditions likewise casts doubt on another aspect of form critical analysis of the Hebrew psalms, namely the *Sitz im Leben* of these materials within Israel's cult. Long ago H. Gunkel proposed that these psalms were used on occasions of public calamity (or threat of calamity) and in connection with expiatory rituals designed to persuade Yahweh to act on behalf of the community.[9] Gunkel himself observed that not all of the communal laments included explicitly penitential ele- ments; some, like Psalm 44, were understood by him to be con- fessions of innocence.[10] Nevertheless, even for Gunkel the central concern of these psalms appeared to be expiation for sin. Nor was Gunkel alone. As M. Haar has noted, Gunkel was followed in this interpretation by a company of scholars sufficiently large that

> it is accurate to say, that the majority of scholars who have worked on the community lament psalms believe that these psalms were used during public cultic festival days of fasting, during which the main issue was confession and repentance of sin.[11]

As discussed in Chapter 4, M. Haar successfully demonstrates that the primary concern of communal laments is not the forgive- ness of sins, but rather the fidelity of Yahweh to God's people.[12]

---

[9] Gunkel and Begrich, *Einleitung in die Psalmen*, pp. 117–119; Gunkel, "The Poetry of the Psalms: Its Literary History and Its Application to the Dating of the Psalms," p. 126.

[10] Gunkel, *The Psalms*, p. 14.

[11] Haar, "The God-Israel Relationship," p. 12. Cf. Chapter 4, n. 137, for a list of scholars considered representative by Haar.

[12] *Ibid.*, pp. 93–95.

Haar breaks the connection made by Gunkel and others which links public disaster or the threat of disaster with penitential rites for the forgiveness of sin. But since, in Haar's view, Yahweh's fidelity was *the* theological center of these laments and, further, since the divine faithfulness would have become an issue "whenever the nation was threatened or had undergone a terrible hardship,"[13] Haar understands these psalms to function in the cult in the same manner as would the similar corporate prayers for help, i.e., to persuade God to act to save God's people. Thus, on the one hand, Haar divorces the life setting of these psalms from any penitential rites that were precipitated by public disaster. On the other hand, Haar has at least this much in common with the Psalms scholars he criticizes: he too believes that the cultic *Sitz im Leben* of these communal laments has to do with a historical threat to the people of God. Again, one wonders that historical disasters could have been frequent enough to account for the preservation of these psalms at all. Add to that wonder the ahistorical character of these laments, especially Psalms 74 and 79, and the clues that their composition actually antedated the historical calamity of 587 BCE, and a different sort of picture of the *Sitz im Leben* of these poems begins to emerge. S. Mowinckel, who seems to have been incorrect in his stress of the relationship of these psalms to penitential rites, surely came closer to the facts when he suggested that these psalms were "originally intended perhaps for the purpose of averting the disaster or protecting against it."[14] That understanding, of course, describes precisely the use to which the *balag/eršemma* laments were put by Israel's contemporaries. In Mowinckel's view this quasi-magical understanding "in Yahwism became a token of penitence and 'self-humiliation' before Yahweh in order to temper his wrath and rouse his compassion."[15] And yet there is nothing in the communal laments themselves to suggest that any such development took place in Yahwism. On the contrary, given the similarities between the Hebrew communal lament psalms and the *balag/eršemma* texts, it seems at least as likely that the Hebrew compositions were recited under similar circumstances and for similar reasons as their Mesopotamian counterparts.

---

[13] *Ibid.*, p. 93.
[14] Mowinckel, *The Psalms,* vol. 1, p. 193.
[15] *Ibid.*

What might those circumstances have been? Again, the *balag/ eršemma* texts were used in their original cultic setting on those occasions when ruined temples were demolished prior to their renovation; from the Old Babylonian period on, these same texts came to be included routinely in cultic calendars evidently as a means to pacify the gods over unknowingly committed offenses totally unrelated to the demolition of temple buildings. The Hebrew psalms give no reason to suppose that the motives undergirding their use in Yahwism were substantially different. Moreover, while detailing the contours of Israel's cultic life during the monarchical period or afterwards is notoriously difficult, the Bible offers ample testimony of occasions when adoption and adaptation of the *balag/eršemma* texts would have been appropriate. The Temple was frequently the object of plunder before its destruction in 587 BCE,[16] and the Bible offers ample testimony of occasions when the Temple was renovated.[17] Cultic mourning and fasts were demonstrably a part of Israel's worship in the exilic and post-exilic period. Jeremiah 41:5, for example, records a procession of eighty mourners from Shechem, Shiloh, and Samaria who brought grain offerings and incense to the "Temple of the Lord" after the Temple fell. Noteworthy too is the fact that cultic mourning and fasts were included in the liturgical calendar during this period. Zechariah 7:3–5 speaks of such rituals as having occurred during the fifth and seventh month "these seventy years," and Zechariah 8:19 records additional fasts in the fourth and tenth month. Ezra 3:12–13 mentions weeping in connection with Zerubbabel's rebuilding of the Temple and Joel 2:15–17 appears to record a public fast and lamentation such as might have been enacted even prior to the destruction of the Temple.

Is it plausible that public lamentation such as these passages describe would have originated only in the exilic period? Dobbs-Allsopp's study of the city lament genre demonstrates that Israel was quite familiar with the features of Mesopotamian public lamen-

---

16 E.g., 1 Kgs 14:25–26 (Shishak of Egypt plunders the Temple); 15:18ff. (Asa pillages the Temple to bribe Ben Hadad); 2 Kgs 14:11–14 (sack of Jerusalem and Temple by Jehoash of Israel); 2 Kgs 16:8 (Temple pillaged for tribute to Tiglath Pileser III); 2 Kgs 18:15 (Hezekiah pillages Temple for tribute).

17 E.g., 2 Kgs 12 (major renovation of the Temple under Jehoash); 2 Kgs 16:10ff. (renovation, replacement of bronze altar); 2 Kgs 18:4 (Hezekiah breaks and removes bronze serpents in context of Temple renovation); 2 Kgs 21:4–5,7 (Manasseh's "renovation" of the Temple); 2 Kgs 22 (renovation of Temple under Josiah).

tation at least as early as the eighth century, albeit he denies the influence of the contemporaneous tradition. The present study has shown that even those psalms that are putatively dependent upon the events of 587 BCE for their inspiration antedate the Babylonian invasion and were likely used in public worship before that time. This investigation has also uncovered evidence that these laments manifest characteristics common to the Mesopotamian *balag/eršemma* compositions to a sufficient degree that it remains difficult to explain their origin as simply a reflex of common human experience or a Semitic *Weltanschauung*. As that is the case, it is perhaps not too far fetched to suppose that the cultic employment of these psalms found its motivation in the same religious impulses that moved the use of the *balag/eršemma* lamentations of the *gala* priesthood, namely, to avert disaster or protect against it.

Evidence for this last suggestion can tentatively be adduced from Joel 2:15–17. Arvid S. Kapelrud.[18] has noted the unusual concatenation of words and terms appearing in verse 17 that are likewise met in Psalm 79: *nḥlh*, *ḥrph*, and *lmh ymrw bᶜmym ʾyh ʾlhyhm* appear also in Psalm 79:1, 4, and 10, respectively. In addition, the verb *qnʾ* of verse 18 (*wayqannēʾ yhwh lěʾarṣô*) appears in a nominal form in Psalm 79:5 (*qinʾātekā*). Kapelrud remarks:

> It is not easy to determine how the connexion in the present case is to be interpreted, whether there is a direct dependence on one of the parts, or whether both are dependent on a certain cultic ritual from which they derived their ideas and terms. It is undoubtedly of significance that the agreement occurs in a definite sphere of ideas: that, pertaining to Yahweh's "property," the nation which is put to shame and thereby becomes an object of derision for other nations, but which is then restored by Yahweh "being zealous" for it. Undoubtedly, this theme appertains to the psalms of mourning and prayer, and was perhaps succeeded by a cultic oracle, promising Yahweh's "zeal" and aid in distress so that other nations had no longer occasion to triumph.[19]

Although unstated, one suspects that Kapelrud's difficulty in sorting out the connection between these two passages stems from the assumption that Psalm 79 owed its inspiration to the Babylonian in-

---

[18] Arvid S. Kapelrud, *Joel Studies* (Uppsala: Uppsala Universitets Arsskrift, 1948), p. 89.

[19] *Ibid.*, pp. 89–90.

vasion and therefore had as its compositional date some time in the exilic period or thereafter. This, in turn, would damage Kapelrud's thesis relative to the historical setting of the Book of Joel, judged by him to have been around 600 BCE, "possibly already to King Jehoiakim's time (609–598), but probably rather to King Zedekiah's reign (598–587)."[20] Had Kapelrud suspected a preexilic use of Psalm 79, he quite likely would have marshaled the traces of the psalm in Joel's prophecy as further evidence for his larger thesis.

As it is, the context of Joel 2:15–17 remains suggestive. Kapelrud views the Book of Joel as a single liturgy and, specifically, a ritual of repentance at the Temple.[21] The parts of this liturgy include an initial psalm of lamentation (1:2–2:18) followed by a divine oracle of salvation (2:19–4:21). Kapelrud further divides Joel 1:2–2:18 into a community lament (1:2–12), a description of distress (2:1–11), and two sections summoning the people to repentance (1:13–20, 2:12–18).[22] Whether Kapelrud's thesis can be maintained in its entirety remains as a matter of debate, especially given the larger question of whether or not chapters 1–2 and 3–4 originate from the same historical setting.[23] Nevertheless, it hardly seems coincidental that a number of motifs and features familiar to the *balag/eršemma* lamentations do emerge in the first two chapters of the book. One encounters, for example, a description of the ruin of the countryside (1:2–12); an appearance of an army, the approach of which signals divinely wrought eschatological disaster rather than an actual historical crisis (2:1–11); references to fire (2:3) and earthquake (2:10); the "voice" of the deity associated with the invading host (2:11); the cessation of cultic offerings (1:9,13) coupled with the mourning of priests (1:9,13;

---

20 *Ibid.*, p. 191.

21 For the following, see Kapelrud, *Joel Studies*, pp. 3–9.

22 Hans Walter Wolff, *Joel and Amos*, edit. by Waldemar Janzen, S. Dean McBride, Jr., and Charles A. Muenchow (Philadelphia: Fortress, 1977), p. 9, likewise describes the book as a message "articulated in the form of a great 'lamentation liturgy.'" Wolff, however, sees the unity in the whole book resting less on any liturgical structure and more on the symmetry of literary parallelism present throughout the book's four chapters. Cf. pp. 6–8, 10–11.

23 Theodore Hiebert, "Joel, Book of," *ABD*, Vol. 3, pp. 878–879, conveniently summarizes the issues involved in the debate regarding the unity of Joel. Basically, as Hiebert explains the problem, "the issue of Joel's unity has a direct bearing on the question of date, since a two-stage development of the book, which appears likely, would involve two different historical settings for the two parts of the collection" (p. 878).

2:17); and a call to public lamentation that, most strikingly, lacks any reference to sin or guilt.[24] These features,[25] coupled with the terminological links to Psalm 79 in 2:17 and that verse's specific association with a call to lament, suggest not only that the first two chapters are to be understood as a single lament liturgy, but also that the composer of the liturgy was quite familiar with the Mesopotamian lament tradition.

Unfortunately, the historical setting for Joel 2:15–17, like the rest of the book, remains a matter of no small uncertainty. Hans Walter Wolff argues powerfully for a historical location in the early fourth century.[26] and reports a growing consensus for this position.[27] The

---

[24] *Pace* Wolff, *Joel and Amos*, p. 52, who, fully aware of the fact that Joel lacks any reference at all to sin or repentance, nevertheless argues that the call to return (*šûb*) in 2:12 in fact signals repentance. Even were one to grant his point, it must be conceded that any emphasis on the theme of guilt in Joel is, at best, muted.

[25] It is tempting to add the presence of the weeping city, Israel's adapted version of the Mesopotamian weeping goddess motif, to the foregoing list. Joel 1:19, cast in the first-person, *can* be understood to represent the prophet's own cry (so Wolff, *Joel and Amos*, p. 35), although elsewhere in this chapter the first person singular suffixes of verses 1:6 and 7, so reminiscent of the sort of divine speech encountered in the *balag/eršemma* laments as well as elsewhere in the Hebrew Bible (e.g., Jer 10:19–20; cf. Wolff, *Joel and Amos*, p. 29), suggest that the speaker behind verse 12 may be the personified city. Supporting this, perhaps, is Joel 1:8 and the second-person singular imperative found there. The text is suspect: MT's imperative *ʾĕlî* lacks a corresponding vocative and is in any event a *hapax legomenon*. This verse, in fact, represents the only time *ʾlh* appears in this form or with the meaning of "lament." Cf. Ludwig Koehler and Walter Baumgartner, *HALOT*, p. 51. The LXX has *thrēneson pros me*, presupposing a longer text than the MT. However the MT, if revocalized, can be understood to represent *pros me < ʾēlay*. Wolff, *Joel and Amos*, p. 18, resolves the sundry difficulties by assuming that verses 8 and 9 were misplaced early in the tradition. He reconstructs the passage's order, reading 9b, 8, 9a, and 10. Wolff further proposes that the verb in verse 8 is a mutilated remainder of a second exhortation of which the LXX had a bit more of the original. However, he concludes, "Such a proposal must remain tentative, especially since the simile in v 8 leads us rather to expect a feminine singular addressee" (p. 18).

[26] Wolff, *Joel and Amos*, pp. 4–5. Evidence for this position includes (1) the assumption of the destruction of Jerusalem and the dispersion of its citizens (3:1–2), (2) the assumption of the 515 BCE restoration of the Temple (1:9,13,14), (3) references in 2:7 and 9 to the reconstruction of the city walls, presumably those rebuild by Nehemiah about 440 BCE, and (4) mention of Sidon (3:4), a city destroyed in 343 BCE. Moreover, the lack of references to any king in favor of frequent references to priests and a positive view of cultic ritual are said to favor a post-exilic historical setting.

[27] *Ibid.*, p. 6. This judgment is verified by Hiebert, "Joel," *ABD*, Vol. 3, pp. 878–879, who conveniently summarizes the various difficulties involved in dating Joel. Other

issue of the book's historical setting seems insoluble at this point. If it could be definitely determined that at least the first two chapters of the book originated from a time prior to 587 BCE, Joel could be added to the list of prophetic texts confirming the thesis of this study. At the minimum, however, the evidence from Joel points toward the sort of cultic activity and occasion wherein the communal laments of the Psalter might have been employed as an ongoing part of the cultic calendar of the Temple. And whatever the precise relationship of the text of Joel to that public lament, it comes as no surprise that traces of the older Mesopotamian lamentations would be found there.

CONCLUSION

Given the opportunities for contact between the neighboring Israelite and Mesopotamian cultures, it seems reasonable to suppose that the ritual calendar of Israel, like those calendars of the residents of Mesopotamia for the nearly one thousand years prior to the biblical period, were marked by the use of ritual communal lament. Were aspects of Israel's lament tradition specifically influenced by those of Mesopotamia? An examination of the similarities and differences between the communal lamentations of the respective cultures again and again points to an affirmative answer to that question. Indeed, at this juncture what appears to be less likely and less reasonable is the supposition that Israel could simply have composed communal laments that corresponded in so many ways with the *balag/eršemma* compositions apart from any contact or influence by them.

---

significant proposals offered include the above-mentioned position of Kapelrud as well as G. Amon, "Die Abfassungszeit des Buches Joel" (Ph.D. dissertation, Würzburg, 1942) and Miloš Bič, *Das Buch Joel* (Berlin: Evangelische-Verlagsanstalt, 1960), who argue for a date near the end of the ninth century in the time of King Joash; Josef Schmalohr, *Das Buch des Propheten Joel, übersetzt und erklärt*, ATA, Vol. 7/4 (Müster i. W., 1922) who would locate Joel in the time of Amos and Hosea; G.W. Ahlström, *Joel and the Temple Cult of Jerusalem* (Leiden: E.J. Brill, 1971), who believes that the book was composed in the late sixth century.

SELECTED BIBLIOGRAPHY

Ackerman, Susan. *Under Every Green Tree: Popular Religion in Sixth-Century Judah.* HSM, no. 46. Atlanta: Scholars Press, 1992.

Adams, Robert McC. "Contexts of Civilizational Collapse: A Mesopotamian View." In *The Collapse of Ancient States and Civilizations,* edited by Norman Yoffee and George L. Cowgill, 20–43. Tucson: University of Arizona, 1988.

Albrektson, Bertil. *History and the Gods: An Essay on the Idea of Historical Events as Divine Manifestations in the Ancient Near East and in Israel.* Coniectanea Biblica; Old Testament Series, vol. 1. Lund: C.W.K. Gleerup, 1967.

Albright, W. F. *Archaeology and the Religion of Israel.* 2d ed. Baltimore: Johns Hopkins, 1946.

———. "A Catalogue of Early Hebrew Lyric Poems." *HUCA* 23 (1950): 1–38.

———. "The Psalms of Habakkuk." In *Studies in Old Testament Prophecy,* edited by H. H. Rowley, 1–18. Edinburgh: T. & T. Clark, 1950.

———. *Archaeology, Historical Analogy, and Early Biblical Tradition.* Baton Rouge: Louisiana State University, 1966.

Anderson, A. A. *The Book of Psalms.* Edited by R. E. Clements and M. Black. New Century Bible. London: Oliphants, 1972.

Anderson, Bernhard W. "Introduction: Mythopoeic and Theological Dimensions of Biblical Creation Faith." In *Creation in the Old Testament,* 1–24. IRT, no. 6. Philadelphia: Fortress, 1984.

———. *Out of the Depths: The Psalms Speak for Us Today.* Philadelphia: Westminster, 1983.

———. *Understanding the Old Testament.* 4th ed. Englewood Cliffs, NJ: Prentice-Hall, 1986.

Auffret, Pierre. "Essai sur la structure littéraire du Psaume LXXIV." *VT* 33 (1983): 129–48.

———. "'Pourquoi dors-tu, Seigneur?' Etude structurelle du Psaume 44." *JANES* 21 (1992): 13–33.

Barr, James. *Comparative Philology of the Text of the Old Testament.* Winona Lake, IN: Eisenbrauns, 1987.

———. *Old and New in Interpretation: A Study of the Two Testaments.* 2nd ed. London: SCM, 1982.

———. "Revelation through History in the Old Testament and in Modern Theology." *Int* 17 (1963): 193–205.

Barton, John. "Form Criticism (OT)." In *ABD,* edited by David Noel Freedman, et. al., vol. 2., 838–41. New York: Doubleday, 1992.

———. *Reading the Old Testament: Method in Biblical Study.* Philadelphia: Westminster, 1984.

Beckman, Gary. "Mesopotamians and Mesopotamian Learning at Hattuša." *JCS* 35 (1983): 97–114.

Ben-Amos, D. "Analytical Categories and Ethnic Genres." In *Folklore Genres,* edited by D. Ben-Amos, 215–42. Austin: University of Texas, 1976.

Berlin, Adele. *Poetics and Interpretation of Biblical Narrative.* Winona Lake, IN: Eisenbrauns, 1994.

Bernhardt, Karl Heinz. *Das Problem der altorientalischen Königsideologie im Alten Testament, unter besonderer Berücksichtigung der Geschichte der Psalmenexegese dargestellt und kritisch gewürdigt.* VTSup, no. 8. Leiden: E. J. Brill, 1961.

Biddle, Mark E. "The Figure of Lady Jerusalem: Identification, Deification and Personification of Cities in the Ancient Near East." In *The Biblical Canon in Comparative Perspective: Scripture in Context IV,* edited by K. Lawson Younger, Jr., William W. Hallo, and Bernard F. Batto, 173–94. ANETS, vol. 11. Lewiston: Edwin Mellon, 1991.

Birkeland, H. *The Evildoers in the Book of Psalms.* Oslo: J. Dybwad, 1955.

———. *Die Feinde des Individuums in der israelitischen Psalmenliteratur.* Oslo: Grondahl, 1933.

Black, J. A. "The New Year Ceremonies in Ancient Babylon: 'Taking Bel by the Hand' and a Cultic Picnic." *Religion* 11 (1981): 39–59.

———. "Sumerian Balag Compositions." *BO* 44 (1987): 32–79.

———. "A-še-er Gi₆-ta, a Balag of Inana." *ASJ* 7 (1985): 11–87.

Bloch, Marc. "Two Strategies of Comparison." In *Comparative Perspectives: Theories and Methods,* edited by A. Etzioni and F. L. Dubow. Boston: Little Brown, 1970.

Block, Daniel Isaac. *The Gods of the Nations: Studies in Ancient Near Eastern National Theology.* Jackson, Miss.: Evangelical Theological Society, 1988.

Böhl, F. M. Th. de Liagre. *De Psalmen: tekst en uitleg.* Nijkerk: G.F. Callenbach, 1969.

———. "Hymnisches und Rhythmisches in den Amarnabriefen aus Kanaan." *Theologisches Lituraturblatt, Leipzig* 35 (1914): cols. 337ff.

Botterweck, G. Johannes. "Yônâ III. OT." In *Theological Dictionary of the Old Testament,* 37–40. VI. Grand Rapids: William B. Eerdmans, 1990.

Bourguet, Daniel. *Métaphores de Jérémie.* Études Bibliques, NS 9. Paris: J. Gabalda, 1987.

Bright, John. *Jeremiah: A New Translation with Introduction and Commentary.* AB, vol. 21. Garden City: Doubleday, 1965.

Broyles, Craig C. *The Conflict of Faith and Experience in the Psalms: A Form-Critical and Theological Study.* JSOTSup, no. 52. Sheffield: JSOT, 1988.

Bunnens, Guy. "Emar on the Euphrates in the 13th Century B.C.: Some Thoughts about Newly Published Cuneiform Texts." *AbrN* 27 (1989): 23–36.

Callaway, Mary. *Sing, O Barren One: A Study in Comparative Midrash.* SBL-Diss, no. 91. Atlanta: Scholars, 1986.

Caquot, A. "Purification et expiation selon le psaume LI." *RHR* 169 (1966): 133–54.

Carroll, Robert P. *Jeremiah.* Old Testament Library. Philadelphia: Westminster, 1986.

Castellino, R. G. *Le Lamentazione Individuali e gli Inni in Babilonia e in Israele.* Torino: Societe Editrice Internazionale, 1940.

Civil, Miguel. "The 10th Tablet of úru àm-ma-ir-ra-bi." *Aula Orientalis* 1 (1983): 45–54.

———. "Enlil, The Merchant: Notes on CT 15 10" *JCS* 28 (1976): 72–81.

———. "The Texts from Meskene-Emar." *Aula Orientalis* 7 (1989): 5–25.

Clements, R. E. *God and Temple.* Philadelphia: Fortress, 1965.

Clifford, Richard J. "The Hebrew Scriptures and the Theology of Creation." *TS* 46 (1985): 507–23.

Cogan, Mordechai. *Imperialism and Religion: Assyria, Judah, and Israel in the Eighth and Seventh Centuries B.C.E.* Missoula: Scholars Press, 1974.

Cohen, Harold R. (Chaim). *Biblical Hapax Legomena in the Light of Akkadian and Ugaritic.* SBLDS, no. 37. Missoula: Scholars Press, 1978.

Cohen, Mark E. *The Canonical Lamentations of Ancient Mesopotamia.* 2 vols. Potomac: Capital Decisions Limited, 1988.

———. *The Cultic Calendars of the Ancient Near East.* Bethesda, MD: CDL, 1993.

———. *Balag-compositions: Sumerian Lamentation Liturgies of the Second and First Millennium B.C.* MANE, vol. 1, fascicle 1. Malibu: Undena, 1974.

———. *Sumerian Hymnology: The Eršemma.* HUCA Supplement, no. 2. Cincinnati: Hebrew Union College-Jewish Institute of Religion, 1981.

Cooper, Jerrold S. *The Curse of Agade.* Johns Hopkins Near Eastern Studies. Baltimore: Johns Hopkins University, 1983.

———. "Gilgamesh Dreams of Enkidu: The Evolution and Dilution of Narrative." In *Essays on the Ancient Near East in Memory of J.J. Finkelstein,* edited by M. de Jong Ellis, 39–44. Memoirs of the Connecticut Academy of Arts and Sciences. Hamden, Conn.: Archon Books, 1977.

———. "Symmetry and Repetition in Akkadian Narrative." *JAOS* 97 (1977): 508–12.

Craigie, Peter C. " Ugarit and the Bible: Progress and Regress in 50 Years of Literary Study." In *Ugarit in Retrospect: Fifty Years of Ugarit and Ugaritic,* edited by G. D. Young, 99–111. Winona Lake, IN: Eisenbrauns, 1981.

Croft, S. J. L. *The Identity of the Individual in the Psalms.* Sheffield: JSOT, 1987.

Cross, Frank Moore. *Canaanite Myth and Hebrew Epic: Essays in the History of the Religion of Israel.* Cambridge, Mass.: Harvard University, 1973.

Cumming, Charles Gordon. *The Assyrian and Hebrew Hymns of Praise.* Columbia University Oriental Studies, vol. 12. New York: Columbia University, 1934.

Dahood, Mitchell. *Psalms I: 1–50.* AB, vol. 16. Garden City: Doubleday, 1966.

———. *Psalms II: 51–100.* AB, vol. 17. Garden City: Doubleday, 1968.

———. *Psalms III: 101–150.* AB, vol. 18. Garden City: Doubleday, 1970.

Dalglish, E. R. *Psalm Fifty-One in the Light of Ancient Near Eastern Patternism.* Leiden: E.J. Brill, 1962.

Day, J. *Psalms.* OTG. Sheffield: Sheffield Academic, 1992.

Day, Peggy L. "The Personification of Cities as Female in the Hebrew Bible: The Thesis of Aloysius Fitzgerald, F.S.C." In *Social Location and Biblical Interpretation in Global Perspective.* Vol. 2 of *Reading from This Place: Social Location and Biblical Interpretation,* edited by Fernando F. Segovia and Mary Ann Tolbert, 283–302. Minneapolis: Fortress, 1995.

Delitzsch, Friedrich. *Babel und Bibel: ein Vortrag.* Leipzig: J.C. Hinrichs, 1902.

Demsky, Aaron. "The Education of Canaanite Scribes in Mesopotamian Cuneiform Tradition." In *Bar-Ilan Studies in Assyriology Dedicated to Pinhas Artzi,* edited by Jacob Klein and Aaron Skaist, 157–70. Bar-Ilan Studies in Near Eastern Languages and Culture. Ramat Gan: Bar-Ilan University, 1990.

Dobbs-Allsopp, F. W. "The Syntagma of *bat* Followed by a Geographical Name in the Hebrew Bible: A Reconsideration of Its Meaning and Grammar." *CBQ* 57 (1995): 451–71.

———. *Weep, O Daughter of Zion: A Study of the City-Lament Genre in the Hebrew Bible*. Rome: Editrice Pontificio Istituto Biblico, 1993.

Dohmen, C. "kābēd." In *Theological Dictionary of the Old Testament*, edited by G. Johannes Botterweck, Heinz-Josef Fabry, and Helmer Ringrenn, 13–17. VII. Grand Rapids: William B. Eerdmans, 1994.

Dossin, G. "Un rituel du culte d'Istar." *RA* 35 (1938): 1–13.

Driver, G. R. "The Psalms in the Light of Babylonian Research." In *The Psalmists*, edited by D. C. Simpson, 109–76. London: Oxford University, 1926.

Durlesser, James A. "The Book of Lamentations and the Mesopotamian Laments: Experiential or Literary Ties." In *Eastern Great Lakes Biblical Society Proceedings*, edited by Phillip Sigal, 69–84. Westerville: EGLBS Proceedings, 1983.

Eaton, J. H. *Kingship and the Psalms*. 2nd Ed. Sheffield: JSOT, 1986.

Edzard, Dietz Otto. *Die Zweite Zwischenzeit Babyloniens*. Wiesbaden: O. Harrassowitz, 1957.

Eissfeldt, O. *The Old Testament: An Introduction*. Translated by P. Ackroyd. New York: Harper & Row, 1965.

Emerton, J. A. "Leviathan and Ltn: The Vocalization of the Ugaritic Word for Dragon." *VT* 32 (1982): 327–31.

Engelken, Karen. *Frauen im alten Israel: Eine begriffsgeschichtliche und sozialrechtliche Studie zur Stellung der Frau im Alten Testament*. Stuttgart: W. Kohlhammer, 1990.

Fabry, Heinz-Josef. "lēb." In *Theological Dictionary of the Old Testament*, edited by G. Johannes Botterweck, Heinz-Josef Fabry, and Helmer Ringrenn, 399–437. VII. Grand Rapids: William B. Eerdmans, 1994.

Falkenstein, A. "Fluch über Agade." *ZA* 57 (1965): 43–124.

———. "Sumerische religiöse Texte." *ZA* 49 (1950): 80–150.

Falkenstein, A., and W. von Soden. *Sumerische und akkadische Hymnen und Gebete*. Die Bibliothek der alten Welt. Zürich: Artemis-Verlag, 1953.

Farber, Gertrud. "me (ĝarza, *parṣu*)."In *Reallexikon der Assyriologie und Vorderasiatischen Archaologie*, vol. 7, 610–13. Berlin: W. de Gruyter, 1990.

Ferris, Paul Wayne, Jr. *The Genre of Communal Lament in the Bible and the Ancient Near East*. SBLDS, no. 127. Atlanta: Scholars Press, 1992.

Finet, André. "Allusions et réminiscences comme source d'information sur la diffusion de la littérature." In *Keilschriftliche Literaturen. Ausgewählte*

Vorträge der XXXII. Rencontre Assyriologique International, Münster, 8.–12.7.1985, 13–17. Berlin: Dietrich Reimer, 1986.

Fitzgerald, Aloysius. "BTWLT and BT as Titles for Capital Cities." *CBQ* 37 (1975): 167–83.

———. "The Mythological Background for the Presentation of Jerusalem as a Queen and False Worship as Adultery in the Old Testament." *CBQ* 34 (1972): 403–16.

Foster, Benjamin R. *Before the Muses: An Anthology of Akkadian Literature.* 2 vols. Bethesda, MD: CDL, 1993.

Fretheim, Terence E. *Exodus.* Louisville: John Knox, 1991.

———. "The Reclamation of Creation: Redemption and Law in Exodus." *Int* 45 (1991): 354–65.

Frymer-Kensky, Tikva. *In the Wake of the Goddesses: Women, Culture, and the Biblical Transformation of Pagan Myth.* New York: Free Press, 1992.

Gadd, C. J. "The Second Lamentation for Ur." In *Hebrew and Semitic Studies Presented to Godfrey Rolles Driver,* edited by D. W. Thomas and W. D. McHardy, 59–71. Oxford: Oxford University, 1963.

Galpin, F. W. *The Music of the Sumerians and Their Immediate Successors, the Babylonians and Assyrians.* Cambridge: University Press, 1937.

Gelston, A. "A Note on Psalm 74:8." *VT* 34 (1984): 82–87.

Gibson, J. C. L. *Canaanite Myths and Legends.* Edinburgh: T. & T. Clark, 1977.

Gilkey, L. "Cosmology and the Travail of Biblical Language." *JR* 41 (1961): 194–205.

Gomi, T. "On the Critical Economic Situation at Ur Early in the Reign of Ibbisin." *JCS* 36 (1984): 211–42.

Gordis, Robert. "On Methodology in Biblical Exegesis." *JQR* 61 (1970): 93–118.

Gottwald, Norman. "Biblical Theology or Biblical Sociology? On Affirming and Denying the 'Uniqueness' of Israel." *Radical Religion* 2 (1975): 42–57.

———. *The Hebrew Bible—A Socio-Literary Introduction.* Philadelphia: Fortress, 1985.

Gray, John. "A Cantata of the Autumn Festival: Psalm LXVIII." *JSS* 22 (1977): 2–26.

Grayson, A. K. *Babylonian Historical-Literary Texts.* Toronto: University of Toronto, 1975.

Green, M. W. *Eridu in Sumerian Literature.* Ph.D. Dissertation, University of Chicago. 1975.

———. "The Eridu Lament." *JCS* 30 (1978): 127–67.

———. "The Uruk Lament." *JAOS* 104 (1984): 253–79.

Gressmann, Hugo. "The Development of Hebrew Psalmody." In *The Psalmists*, edited by D. C. Simpson, 1–22. London: Oxford University, 1926.

Gunkel, Hermann. *Ausgewählte Psalmen*. 4th ed. Göttingen: Vandenhoeck und Ruprecht, 1917.

———. "The Influence of Babylonian Mythology upon the Biblical Creation Story." Translated by Charles A. Muenchow. In *Creation in the Old Testament*, edited by Bernhard W. Anderson, 25–52. IRT, no. 6. Philadelphia: Fortress, 1984.

———. "The Poetry of the Psalms: Its Literary History and Its Application to the Dating of the Psalms" In *Old Testament Essays: Papers Read before the Society for Old Testament Study at Its Eighteenth Meeting, Held at Keble College, Oxford, September 27th to 30th, 1927*, edited by D. C. Simpson, 118–42. London: Charles Griffin, 1927.

———. "Psalmen." In *Die Religion in Geschichte und Gegenwart*, edited by Hermann Gunkel and O. Scheel. 1st ed., cols. 1927–49. Tübingen: J.C.B. Mohr, 1913.

———. "Psalmen." In *Die Religion in Geschichte und Gegenwart*, edited by Hermann Gunkel and O. Scheel. 2d ed., cols. 1609–27. Tübingen: J.C.B. Mohr, 1930.

———. *The Psalms: A Form Critical Introduction*. Translated by Thomas M. Horner. Philadelphia: Fortress, 1967.

Gunkel, Hermann and Joachim Begrich. *Einleitung in die Psalmen: Die Gattungen der religiösen Lyrik Israels*. Göttingen: Vandenhoeck und Ruprecht, 1933.

Gütterbock, H. G. "The Composition of Hittite Prayers to the Sun." *JAOS* 78 (1958): 237–45.

Gwaltney, W. C. "The Biblical Book of Lamentations in the Context of Near Eastern Lament Literature." In *More Essays on the Comparative Method: Scripture in Context II*, edited by W. W. Hallo, J. C. Moyer, and L. G. Perdue, 191–211. Winona Lake, IN: Eisenbrauns, 1983.

Haar, Murray Joseph. *The God-Israel Relationship in the Community Lament Psalms*. Ph.D. Dissertation. Richmond: Union Theological Seminary, 1985.

Hallo, William W. "Biblical History in Its Near Eastern Setting: The Contextual Approach." In *Scripture in Context: Essays on the Comparative Method*, edited by Carl D. Evans, William W. Hallo, and John B. White, 1–26. Pittsburgh: Pickwick, 1980.

———. "Compare and Contrast: The Contextual Approach to Biblical Literature." In *The Bible in the Light of Cuneiform Literature: Scripture in Context III,* edited by William W. Hallo, Bruce William Jones, and Gerald L. Mattingly, 1–30. ANETS, vol. 8. Lewiston, NY: Edwin Mellen, 1990.

———. "The Concept of Canonicity in Cuneiform and Biblical Literature: A Comparative Appraisal." In *The Biblical Canon in Comparative Perspective: Scripture in Context IV,* edited by K. Lawson Younger, Jr., William W. Hallo, and Bernard F. Batto, 1–19. ANETS, vol. 11. Lewiston, NY: Edwin Mellon, 1991.

———. "The Cultic Setting of Sumerian Poetry." In *Actes de la XVIIe Rencontre Assyriologique Internationale,* 116–34. Ham-sur-Heure: Universite Libre de Bruxelles, 1970.

———. "The Expansion of Cuneiform Literature." *PAAJR* 50 (1980): 307–22.

———. "Individual Prayer in Sumerian: The Continuity of a Tradition." *JAOS* 88 (1968): 71–89.

———. "Lamentations and Prayers in Sumer and Akkad." In *Civilizations of the Ancient Near East,* edited by J. M. Sasson, vol. 3, 1871–81. New York: Scribners, 1995.

———. "Letters, Prayers, and Letter Prayers." In *Proceedings of the Seventh World Congress of Jewish Studies Held at the Hebrew University of Jerusalem, 7–14 August 1977 Under the Auspices of the Israel Academy of Sciences and Humanities,* World Congress of Jewish Studies, 17–27. Jerusalem: World Union of Jewish Studies; Magnes, 1981.

———. "New Moons and Sabbaths: A Case-Study in the Contrastive Approach." *HUCA* 48 (1977): 1–18.

———. "New Viewpoints on Cuneiform Literature." *IEJ* 12 (1962): 13–26.

———. *Origins: The Ancient Near Eastern Background of Some Modern Western Institutions.* Edited by B. Halpern and M.H.E. Weippert. Studies in the History and Culture of the Ancient Near East, vol. 6. Leiden: E.J. Brill, 1996.

———. "Problems in Sumerian Hermeneutics." *Perspectives in Jewish Learning* 5 (1973): 1–12.

———. "The Royal Correspondence of Larsa: I. A Sumerian Prototype for the Prayer of Hezekiah?" In *Cuneiform Studies in Honor of Samuel Noah Kramer.* AOAT, vol. 25. Neukirchen-Vluyn: Neukirchener, 1976.

———. "A Sumerian Amphictiony." *JCS* 14 (1960): 88–114.

———. "Sumerian Literature: Background to the Bible." *BR* 4 (1988): 28–38.

———. "Toward a History of Sumerian Literature." In *Sumerological Studies in Honor of Thorkild Jacobsen on His Seventieth Birthday, June 7, 1974,*

181–203. Assyriological Studies, vol. 20. Chicago: University of Chicago, 1975.

Hartmann, H. *Die Musik der sumerischen Kultur.* Ph.D. Dissertation, Johann Wolfgang Goethe Universität. 1960.

Hayes, John H., ed. *Old Testament Form Criticism.* San Antonio: Trinity University, 1974.

Hengel, Martin. *The Charismatic Leader and His Followers.* Translated by James Grieg. New York: Crossroad Publishing, 1981.

Hillers, Delbert R. *Lamentations.* AB, vol. 7a. Garden City: Doubleday, 1972.

Hirsch, E. D., Jr. *Validity in Interpretation.* New Haven: Yale University, 1967.

Holladay, William L. *Jeremiah 1: A Commentary on the Book of the Prophet Jeremiah, Chapters 1–25.* Hermeneia. Philadelphia: Fortress, 1986.

———. *Jeremiah: A Fresh Reading.* New York: Pilgrim, 1990.

Hoskisson, Paul Y. "Emar as an Empirical Model of the Transmission of Canon." In *The Biblical Canon in Comparative Perspective: Scripture in Context IV,* edited by K. Lawson Younger, Jr., William W. Hallo, and Bernard F. Batto, 21–32. ANETS, vol. 11. Lewiston, NY: Edwin Mellon, 1991.

Hunger, Hermann. *Babylonische und assyrische Kolophone.* AOAT, no. 2. Kevelaer: Butzon und Bercker, 1968.

Hyatt, J. P. *Exodus.* Grand Rapids: Wm. B. Eerdmans, 1971.

Jacobsen, Thorkild. *The Harps That Once . . . : Sumerian Poetry in Translation.* New Haven and London: Yale University, 1987.

———. *The Intellectual Adventure of Ancient Man.* Edited by Henri Frankfort. Chicago. University of Chicago, 1946.

———. "The Reign of Ibbi-Suen." *JCS* 7 (1953): 36–47.

———. "Review of Lamentation over the Destruction of Ur by Samuel N. Kramer." *AJSL* 58 (1941): 219–24.

———. *Toward the Image of Tammuz and other Essays on Mesopotamian History and Culture.* Edited by William L. Moran. HSS, vol. 21. Cambridge, MA: Harvard University, 1970.

———. *The Treasures of Darkness: A History of Mesopotamian Religion.* New Haven: Yale University, 1976.

Jeremias, Alfred. *Das Alte Testament im Lichte des alten Orients.* 3rd ed. Leipzig: J.C. Hinrichs, 1916.

Jirku, Anton. "Kana'anäische Psalmenfragmente in der vorisraelitischen Zeit Palästinas und Syriens." *JBL* 52 (1933): 108–20.

Johnson, A. R. "The Psalms." In *The Old Testament and Modern Study,* edited by H. H. Rowley, 162–209. Oxford: Clarendon, 1951.

Kaiser, Barbara Bakke. "Poet as Female Impersonator: The Image of Daughter Zion as Speaker in Biblical Poems of Suffering." *JR* 67 (1987): 164–82.

Kaiser, O. *Introduction to the Old Testament.* Minneapolis: Augsburg, 1975.

Kapelrud, Arvid S. *Joel Studies.* Uppsala: Uppsala Universitets Arsskrift, 1948.

Keel, Othmar. *The Symbolism of the Biblical World: Ancient Near Eastern Iconography and the Book of Psalms.* Translated by Timothy J. Hallett. New York: Crossroad, 1987.

King, L. W., ed. *Annals of the Kings of Assyria.* London:British Museum, 1902.

Knierim, R. "Old Testament Form Criticism Reconsidered" *Int* 27 (1973): 435–68.

———. "Cosmos and History in Israel's Theology." *HBT* 3 (1981): 59–123.

Koch, Klaus. *The Growth of the Biblical Tradition: The Form Critical Method.* Translated by S. M. Cupitt. 2d ed. New York: Charles Scribner's Sons, 1969.

———. *Was ist Formgeschichte?* 2nd ed. Neue Wege der Bibelexegese. Neukirchen-Vluyn: Neukirchener Verlag, 1967.

Koehler, Ludwig, and Walter Baumgartner. *The Hebrew and Aramaic Lexicon of the Old Testament.* Translated by M. E. J. Richardson. 3 vols. Leiden: E.J. Brill, 1994.

———. *Lexicon in Veteris Testamenti Libros.* Leiden: E.J. Brill, 1985.

Kramer, S. N. "BM 98396: A Sumerian Proto-type of the Mater-Dolorosa." *ErIsr* 16 (1982): 141–46.

———. "CT XLII: A Review Article." *JCS* 18 (1964): 35–48.

———. "Lamentation over the Destruction of Sumer and Ur." In *Ancient Near Eastern Texts Relating to the Old Testament,* edited by James B. Pritchard. 3d ed., 611–19. Princeton: Princeton University, 1969.

———. "Lamentation over the Destruction of Ur." In *Ancient Near Eastern Texts Relating to the Old Testament,* edited by James B. Pritchard. 3d ed., 455–63. Princeton: Princeton University, 1969.

———. *Lamentation over the Destruction of Ur.* Assyriological Studies, no. 12. Chicago: University of Chicago, 1940.

———. "Lamentation over the Destruction of Nippur: A Preliminary Report." *ErIsr* 9 (1969): 90–93.

———. "Lisin, the Weeping Goddess: A New Sumerian Lament." In *ZIKIR ŠUMIN: Assyriological Studies Presented to F.R. Kraus on the Occasion of His Seventieth Birthday,* edited by G. van Driel, Th. J. H. Krispijn, M. Stol, and K. R. Veenhof, 133–44. Leiden: E.J. Brill, 1982.

———. *Sumerian Literary Texts from Nippur in the Museum of the Ancient Orient at Istanbul.* AASOR, vol. 23. New Haven: American Schools of Oriental Research, 1943–44.

———. "Sumerian Literature: A General Survey." In *The Bible and the Ancient Near East: Essays in Honor of William Foxwell Albright,* edited by G. Ernest Wright, 249–66. 2d ed. Winona Lake, IN: Eisenbrauns, 1979.

———. "Sumerian Literature and the Bible." In *AnBib,* vol. 12, 185–204. Studia Biblical et Orientalia, vol. 3. Rome: Pontificio Istituto Biblico, 1959.

———. "The Weeping Goddess: Sumerian Prototypes of the Mater Dolorosa." *BA* 46 (1983): 69–80.

———. "Mythology of Sumer and Akkad." In *Mythologies of the Ancient World,* edited by Samuel Noah Kramer, 93–137. Garden City: Doubleday, 1961.

———. *The Sumerians: Their History, Culture, and Character.* Chicago: University of Chicago, 1963.

Kraus, Hans-Joachim. *Psalms 1–59.* Translated by Hilton C. Oswald. Minneapolis: Augsburg, 1988.

———. *Psalms 60–150.* Translated by Hilton C. Oswald. Minneapolis: Augsburg, 1989.

———. *Theology of the Psalms.* Translated by Keith Crim. Minneapolis: Augsburg, 1986.

Krecher, Joachim. *Sumerische Kultlyrik.* Wiesbaden: Otto Harrassowitz, 1966.

Kutscher, Raphael. *Oh Angry Sea (a-ab-ba hu-luh-ha): The History of a Sumerian Congregational Lament.* Yale Near Eastern Researches, no. 6. New Haven: Yale University, 1975.

Labat, René. "Le rayonnement de la langue et de l'écriture akkadiennes au deuxième millénaire avant notre ère." *Syria* (1964): 1–27.

Lambert, M. "La littérature sumérienne à propos d'ouvrages récents." *RA* 56 (1962): 81–90, 214.

Lambert, W. G. "Ancestors, Authors, and Canonicity." *JCS* 11 (1957): 1–14.

———. "Great Battle of the Mesopotamian Religious Year: The Conflict in the Akitu House (A Summary)." *Iraq* 25 (1963): 189–90.

———. "Myth and Ritual as Conceived by the Babylonians." *JSS* 13 (1968): 104–12.

Lanaham, William F. "The Speaking Voice in the Book of Lamentations." *JBL* 93 (1974): 41–49.

Landsberger, Benno. *The Conceptual Autonomy of the Babylonian World.* Translated by T. Jacobsen, B. Foster, and H. von Siebenthal. MANE, vol. 1, fascicle 4. Malibu, CA: Undena, 1976.

Langdon, S. *Babylonian Liturgies.* Paris: Paul Geuthner, 1913.

———. "Calendars of Liturgies and Prayers: I. The Assur Calendar." *AJSL* 42 (1926): 110–27.

———, ed. *Oxford Editions of Cuneiform Texts.* Oxford: Oxford University, 1923.

Leslie, E. A. *The Psalms: Translated and Interpreted in the Light of Hebrew Life and Worship.* New York: Abingdon Cokesbury, 1949.

Lewy, Julius. "The Old West Semitic Sun-god Hammu." *HUCA* 18 (1943–4): 436–43.

Lipinski, E. *La liturgie pénitentielle dans la Bible.* Lectio Divina, no. 52. Paris: Editions Du Cerf, 1969.

Longman, Tremper, III. *Fictional Akkadian Autobiography: A Generic and Comparative Study.* Winona Lake, IN: Eisenbrauns, 1991.

Machinist, P. "Literature as Politics: The Tukulti-Ninurta Epic and the Bible." *CBQ* 38 (1976): 455–82.

Martinez, Robert M. "Epidemic Disease, Ecology, and Culture in the Ancient Near East." In *The Bible in the Light of Cuneiform Literature: Scripture in Context III,* edited by William W. Hallo, Bruce William Jones, and Gerald L. Mattingly, 413–57. ANETS, vol. 8. Lewiston, NY: Edwin Mellen, 1990.

Matthews, Victor H. "Holy Spirit." In *ABD,* edited by David Noel Freedman, et. al., 260–280. Vol. 3. New York: Doubleday, 1992.

Mays, James Luther. *Psalms.* Interpretation. Louisville: John Knox, 1994.

McDaniel, Thomas F. "The Alleged Sumerian Influence Upon Lamentations." *VT* 18 (1968): 198–209.

McKenzie, John L. *Second Isaiah: Introduction, Translation, and Notes.* AB, vol. 20. Garden City: Doubleday, 1968.

McKnight, Edgar V. *What Is Form Criticism?* Edited by Dan O. Via, Jr. Philadelphia: Fortress, 1969.

Michalowski, Piotr. "On the Early History of the Eršaḫunga Prayer." *JCS* 39 (1987): 37–48.

———. *The Lamentation Over the Destruction of Sumer and Ur.* Mesopotamian Civilizations, no. 1. Winona Lake, IN: Eisenbrauns, 1989.

Miller, Patrick D. "Eridu, Dunnu, and Babel: A Study in Comparative Mythology." *HAR* 9 (1985): 227–51.

———. *Interpreting the Psalms.* Philadelphia: Fortress, 1986.

———. "Review of *The Conflict of Faith and Experience in the Psalms: A Form-Critical and Theological Study* by Craig C. Broyles." *CBQ* 53 (1991): 459–60.

———. "The Absence of the Goddess in Israelite Religion." *HAR* 10 (1986): 239–48.

———. *They Cried to the Lord: The Form and Theology of Biblical Prayer.* Minneapolis: Fortress, 1994.

Miller, Patrick D., Jr. and J.J.M. Roberts. *Hand of the Lord: A Reassessment of the "Ark Narrative" of I Samuel.* Baltimore: Johns Hopkins University Press, 1977.

Mowinckel, S. *Der Achtundsechzigste Psalm.* Oslo: J. Dybwad, 1953.

———. *The Psalms in Israel's Worship.* Translated by D. R. Ap-Thomas. 2 vols. Oxford: Basil Blackwell, 1962.

Muilenberg, James. "Form Criticism and Beyond." *JBL* 88 (1969): 1–18.

Neve, L. "Realized Eschatology in Ps 51." *ExpT* 80 (1968): 264–68.

Oates, Joan. *Babylon.* London: Thames and Hudson, 1986.

Ollenburger, Ben C. *Zion the City of the Great King: A Theological Symbol of the Jerusalem Cult.* JSOTSup, no. 41. Sheffield: JSOT, 1987.

Oppenheim, A. Leo. *Ancient Mesopotamia: Portrait of a Dead Civilization.* Chicago: University of Chicago, 1964.

Owens, Pamela Jean. "Personification and Suffering in Lamentations 3." *Austin Seminary Bulletin, Faculty Edition* 150 (1990): 75–90.

Pallis, Svend Aage. *The Babylonian Akîtu Festival.* København: Bianco Lunos Bogtrykkeri, 1926.

Pardee, Dennis. "Review of *Scripture in Context: Essays on the Comparative Method.*" *JNES* 44 (1985): 221–222.

Patton, J. H. *Canaanite Parallels in the Book of Psalms.* Baltimore: Johns Hopkins, 1944.

Pritchard, James B. *The Ancient Near East in Pictures Relating to the Old Testament.* 2d ed. Princeton: Princeton University, 1969.

Rad, Gerhard von. *Old Testament Theology.* 2 vols. Translated by D. M. G. Stalker. New York: Harper & Row, 1962.

———. "The Theological Problem of the Old Testament Doctrine of Creation." In *The Problem of the Hexateuch and Other Essays,* translated by E. W. T. Dicken, 131–43. New York: McGraw-Hill, 1966.

Ringgren, Helmer. "The Impact of the Ancient Near East on Israelite Tradition." In *Tradition and Theology in the Old Testament,* edited by Douglas A. Knight, 31–46. Philadelphia: Fortress, 1977.

Roberts, J. J. M. "The Davidic Origin of the Zion Tradition." *JBL* (1973): 329–44.

———. "Divine Freedom and Cultic Manipulation in Israel and Mesopotamia." In *Unity and Diversity: Essays in the History, Literature, and Religion of the Ancient Near East,* edited by Hans Goedicke and J. J. M. Roberts, 181–90. Baltimore: Johns Hopkins University, 1975.

———. *The Earliest Semitic Pantheon: A Study of the Semitic Deities Attested in Mesopotamia Before Ur III.* Baltimore: Johns Hopkins University, 1972.

———. "The Motif of the Weeping God in Jeremiah and Its Background in the Lament Tradition of the Ancient Near East." *Old Testament Essays* 5 (1992): 361–74.

———. "Nebuchadnezzar I's Elamite Crisis in Theological Perspective." In *Essays on the Ancient Near East in Memory of Jacob Joel Finkelstein,* edited by Maria de Jong Ellis. Memoirs of the Connecticut Academy of Arts and Sciences, vol. 19, 183–87. Hamden: Archon Books, 1977.

———. "Of Signs, Prophets, and Time Limits: A Note on Psalm 74:9." *CBQ* 39 (1977): 474–81.

———. "Zion in the Theology of the Davidic-Solomonic Empire." In *Studies in the Period of David and Solomon and Other Essays: Papers Read at the International Symposium for Biblical Studies, Tokyo, 5–7, December 1979,* 93–108, edited by Tomoo Ishida. Winona Lake, IN: Eisenbrauns, 1982.

Rochberg-Halton, Francesca. "Canonicity in Cuneiform Texts." *JCS* 30 (1984): 127–44.

Sabourin, Leopold. *The Psalms: Their Origin and Meaning.* New York: Alba House, 1974.

Sachs, A. "Ritual to Be Followed by the Kalu-Priest When Covering the Temple Kettle-Drum." In *Ancient Near Eastern Texts Relating to the Old Testament,* by James B. Pritchard. 3d ed., 334–38. Princeton: Princeton University, 1969.

Saggs, H. W. F. *The Encounter with the Divine in Mesopotamia and Israel.* London: Athlone, 1978.

———. *The Greatness that was Babylon: A Survey of the Ancient Civilization of the Tigris-Euphrates Valley.* New York: New American Library, 1962.

Sandmel, Samuel. "Parallelomania." *JBL* 81 (1962): 1–13.

Schmid, H. H. "Creation, Righteousness and Salvation: 'Creation Theology' as the Broad Horizon of Biblical Theology." In *Creation in the Old Testament,* edited by B. W. Anderson, 102–17. Philadelphia: Fortress, 1984.

Schmitt, J. J. "The Motherhood of God and Zion as Mother." *RB* 92 (1985): 557–69.

————. "The Virgin of Israel: Referent and Use of the Phrase in Amos and Jeremiah." *CBQ* 53 (1991): 365–87.

Seux, Marie-Joseph. *Hymnes et prières aux dieux de Babylonie et d'Assyrie.* Littératures anciennes du Proche-Orient, no. 8. Paris: Les Éditions du Cerf, 1976.

Smith, Mark S. "Jeremiah IX 9—A Divine Lament." *VT* 37 (1987): 97–99.

Smith, Morton. "On the Differences between the Culture of Israel and the Major Cultures of the Ancient Near East." *JANES* 5 (1973): 389–95.

————. "The Present State of Old Testament Studies." *JBL* 88 (1969): 19–35.

Soden, W. von. "Gibt es ein Zeugnis, daß die Babylonier an Marduks Wiederauferstehung glauben?" *ZA* 55 (1952–5): 130–66.

Steck, O. H. "Zion als Gelände und Gestalt: Überlegungen zur Wahrnehmung Jerusalems als Stadt und Frau im Alten Testament." *ZThK* 86 (1989): 261–81.

Steinkeller, Piotr. "The Administration and Economic Organization of the Ur III State: The Core and the Periphery." In *The Organization of Power: Aspects of Bureaucracy in the Ancient Near East,* edited by M. Gibson and R. D. Biggs, 19–41. Chicago: Oriental Institute of the University of Chicago, 1987.

Stummer, Friedrich. *Sumerisch-akkadische Parallelen zum Aufbau alttestamentlicher Psalmen.* Studien zur Geschichte und Kultur des Altertums, vol. 11, no. 1 & 2. Paderborn: Ferdinand Schoringh, 1922.

Tadmor, Hayim. "A Lexical Text from Hazor." *IEJ* 27 (1977): 98–102.

Talmon, Shemaryahu. "The 'Comparative Method' in Biblical Interpretation—Principles and Problems." In *Congress Volume: Göttingen 1977,* 320–56. VTSup, no. 29. Leiden: E.J. Brill, 1978.

Tate, Marvin E. *Psalms 51–100.* WBC. Waco, TX: Word Books, 1990.

Thureau-Dangin, F. *Rituels accadiens.* Paris: E. Leroux, 1921.

Tigay, Jeffrey H. "On Evaluating Claims of Literary Borrowing." In *The Tablet and the Scroll: Near Eastern Studies in Honor of William W. Hallo,* edited by Mark E. Cohen, Daniel C. Snell, and David B. Weisberg, 250–55. Bethesda, MD: CDL, 1993.

————. *The Evolution of the Gilgamesh Epic.* Philadelphia: University of Pennsylvania, 1982.

————, "The Evolution of the Pentateuchal Narratives in the Light of the Evolution of the Gilgamesh Epic." In *Empirical Models for Biblical Criticism,* edited by Jeffrey H. Tigay, 21–52. Philadelphia: University of Pennsylvania, 1985.

————. "On Some Aspects of Prayer in the Bible." *AJS Review* 1 (1976): 363–79.

Toorn, Karel van der. "The Babylonian New Year Festival: New Insights from the Cuneiform Texts and Their Bearing on Old Testament Study." *VTSup* 43 (1991): 331–44.

Treves, Marco. *The Dates of the Psalms: History and Poetry in Ancient Israel.* Pisa: Giardini, 1988.

Tucker, Gene M. *Form Criticism of the Old Testament.* Philadelphia: Fortress, 1971.

Vancil, Jack W. "Sheep, Shepherd." In *ABD,* edited by David Noel Freedman, et. al. Vol. 5, 1187–90. New York: Doubleday, 1992.

Vanstiphout, H. L. J. "The Death of an Era: The Great Mortality in the Sumerian City Laments." In *Death in Mesopotamia: Papers Read at the XXVIᵉ Rencontre Assyriologique Internationale,* edited by B. Alster, 83–89. Copenhagen: Akademisk Forlag, 1980.

———. "Some Thoughts on Genre in Mesopotamian Literature." In *Keilschriftliche Literaturen. Ausgewählte Vorträge der XXXII. Rencontre Assyriologique Internationale. Münster, 8.–12.7.1985,* edited by K. Hecker and W. Sommerfeld, 1–11. Berliner Beiträge zum Vorderen Orient, no. 6. Berlin: Dietrich Reimer, 1986.

Vogelzang, Marianna E. "Kill Anzu! On a Point of Literary Evolution." In *Keilschriftliche Literaturen. Ausgewählte Vorträge der XXXII. Rencontre Assyriologique International, Münster, 8.–12.7.1985,* edited by K. Hecker and W. Sommerfeld, 61–70. Berliner Beiträge zum Vorderen Orient, no. 6. Berlin: Dietrich Reimer, 1986.

Volk, Konrad. *Die Balag-Komposition úru àm-ma-ir-ra-bi. Rekonstruktion und Bearbeitung der Tafeln 18 (19'ff.), 19, 20, und 21 der späten, kanonischen Version.* Stuttgart: Franz Steiner Verlag Wiesbaden GMBH, 1989.

Wakeman, Mary K. "Sacred Marriage." *JSOT* 22 (1982): 21–31.

Waltke, Bruce K. "Superscripts, Postscripts, or Both." *JBL* 110 (1991): 583–96.

Weiser, Artur. *The Psalms: A Commentary.* Translated by Herbert Hartwell. Philadelphia: Westminster, 1962.

Weiss, Meir. *The Bible From Within: The Method of Total Interpretation.* Jerusalem: Magnes, 1984.

———. "Die Methode der 'Total-Interpretation'" *VTSup* 22 (1972): 88–112.

———. "Wege der neuen Dichtungswissenschaft in ihrer Anwendung auf die Psalmenforschung." *Bib* 42 (1961): 255–302.

Westermann, Claus. *Creation.* Translated by John J. Scullion. Philadelphia: Fortress, 1974.

———. "Geist im Alten Testament." *EvT* 41 (1981): 223–30.

———. *Isaiah 40–66.* Translated by David M. G. Stalker. Philadelphia: Westminster, 1969.

———. *Lamentations: Issues and Interpretation.* Translated by Charles Muenchow. Minneapolis: Fortress, 1994.

———. *The Living Psalms.* Translated by J. R. Porter. Grand Rapids: William B. Eerdmans, 1989.

———. *Praise and Lament in the Psalms.* Translated by Keith R. Crim and Richard N. Soulen. Atlanta: John Knox, 1981.

———. *The Praise of God in the Psalms.* Translated by Keith R. Crim. Richmond: John Knox, 1965.

———. *The Psalms: Structure, Content and Message.* Translated by Ralph D. Gehrke. Minneapolis: Augsburg Publishing House, 1980.

Widengren, Geo. *The Accadian and Hebrew Psalms of Lamentations as Religious Documents.* Stockholm: Bokförlags Aktiebolaget Thule, 1937.

Wilcke, C. "Formale Gesichtspunkte in der sumerischen Literatur." In *Assyriological Studies,* vol. 20, 205–316. Chicago: University of Chicago, 1975.

———. "Die Emar-Version von 'Dattelpalme und Tamariske'—ein Rekonstruktionsversuch." *ZA* 79 (1989): 161–90.

Willesen, Folker. "The Cultic Situation of Psalm LXXIV." *VT* 11 (1952): 289–306.

Wilson, Gerald H. *The Editing of the Hebrew Psalter.* SBLDS, no. 76. Chico, CA: Scholars Press, 1985.

Wolff, Hans Walter. *Anthropology of the Old Testament.* Translated by Margaret Kohl. Philadelphia: Fortress, 1974.

———. *Joel and Amos.* Translated by Waldemar Janzen, S. Dean McBride, Jr., and Charles A. Muenchow. Hermeneia. Philadelphia: Fortress, 1977.

Wright, G. Ernest. *The Old Testament against Its Environment.* SBT, vol. 2. London: SCM, 1950.

Wright, R. B. "Psalms of Solomon." In *The Old Testament Pseudepigrapha: Expansions of the "Old Testament" and Legends, Wisdom and Philosophical Literature, Prayers, Psalms, and Odes, Fragments of Lost Judeo-Hellenistic Works,* edited by James H. Charlesworth, vol. 2, 639–70. Garden City: Doubleday, 1985.

Yoffee, Norman. "The Collapse of Ancient Mesopotamian States and Civilization." In *The Collapse of Ancient States and Civilizations,* edited by Norman Yoffee and George L. Cowgill, 44–68. Tucson: University of Arizona, 1988.